Fresco of the Priest-King from a wall of the Palace of Minos at Knossos. The conventionalized irises (probably Xiphiums) in this relief, painted nearly 4,000 years ago, are the oldest pictured irises yet discovered.

THE
IRIS BOOK

by Molly Price

Photographs by the author
Drawings by Allianora Rosse

(except as noted)

SECOND REVISED EDITION

DOVER PUBLICATIONS, INC.
NEW YORK

Published in Canada by General Publishing Company, Ltd., 30 Lesmill Road, Don Mills, Toronto, Ontario.
Published in the United Kingdom by Constable and Company, Ltd., 10 Orange Street, London WC 2.

This Dover edition, first published in 1973, is an unabridged and corrected republication of the text as originally published by the D. Van Nostrand Company, Inc., in 1966. This edition also contains a new Preface by the author.
A four-page section of color photographs has been omitted from this reprint edition.

International Standard Book Number: 0-486-21522-9
Library of Congress Catalog Card Number: 72-93767

Manufactured in the United States of America
Dover Publications, Inc.
180 Varick Street
New York, N.Y. 10014

TO BEE AND TO FRED

who started me off

AND TO JOHN

who sustains me

In Gratitude

The generosity and helpfulness of many people are reflected in this book. My deep appreciation goes especially to Carol Woodward, for continuing and patient advice and encouragement; to Dr. L. F. Randolph, who took time from a busy schedule to answer all my questions promptly, and to check for accuracy the chapter on hybridizing; to W. Percy King, president of the British Iris Society, for his kindness in providing historical source material; to Dr. Lee W. Lenz, for sending me reprints of his published work on the Pacific Coast irises and for answering questions; to Dr. Harold W. Rickett who checked and made additions to the Glossary; to Allianora Rosse, for her careful and beautiful drawings; and to my editor, Helen Van Pelt Wilson, for her ability and willingness to turn mountains into molehills.

Grateful acknowledgment is made to *The New York Times, Flower Grower, The Home Garden Magazine,* for their permission to use material from articles originally published by them; to the British Iris Society for permission to quote from its annual publication, *The Iris Year Book;* and to the American Iris Society for permission to quote from its quarterly *Bulletins* and from *Garden Irises.*

It is not possible to mention by name all who have helped to make this book possible, but I want to thank all those who answered my questionnaire and to express my appreciation to my good friends Fred and Marcia Cassebeer, Harry Kuesel, Dr. William McGarvey, Mary Redford, Edwin Rundlett and Bee Warburton. And especially to my husband who spent long hours reading and typing chapters, and cheerfully endured playing second fiddle to a book.

Preface
to the Dover Edition

Since the first edition of *The Iris Book* was published, serious hybridizers have produced many admirable and exciting new varieties in every iris group. Irises do grow lovelier every year, it seems. Current bearded favorites, starting with the April-blooming 'Sun Sparkle', include the May-blooming standard dwarfs 'Cotton Blossom', yellow 'Laced Lemonade' and the rich red 'Cherry Garden'; intermediates 'Lemon Flurry', light blue 'June Prom', and 'Butterscotch Frills'; and border bearded 'Brownie Scout' and pale pink 'Lace Valentine'.

The annual Judges' Choice list has proved to be a reliable gardener's guide for future selections. Top tall bearded vote-getters on the 1972 list include one most unusual plicata — the frilly, fringy 'Kilt Lilt' in gold and apricot with falls heavily stippled dark red; two very different pinks, 'Elizabeth Stuart' and 'Pink Sleigh'; tall, coppery-red 'Post Time'; true-brown 'Dutch Chocolate'; 'Cream Taffeta' — the best cream-colored variety I've seen lately; and black-bearded "black" 'Night Owl'.

Tall bearded iris varieties keep on winning the Dykes Medal (top iris award) with one notable exception: in 1971, the British Iris Society bestowed this honor on the Siberian variety, 'Cambridge'.

All the American Dykes winners in the following list are widely available and moderately priced. White 'Winter Olympics', the striking plicata 'Stepping Out', and lavender-blue 'Skywatch' headed the 1965 Judges' Choice list (see Appendix E).

DYKES MEDAL WINNERS
1966-1972

England		North America
Ancient Egypt	1966	Rippling Waters
Blue Eyed Brunette	1967	Winter Olympics
	1968	Stepping Out
Golden Forest	1969	
Constance West	1970	Skywatch
Cambridge	1971	Debby Rairdon
Shepherd's Delight	1972	Babbling Brook

Siberian irises have been worked over by expert hybridizers for some years, now—and the results are stirring, to say the least. From 'White Swirl', the Cassebeer triumph described in Chapter 8, have come a number of more recent triumphs. Dr. Wm. Mc-Garvey has used it to produce three Morgan Award winners, all in varying shades of blue: 'Dewful', in 1970; 'Ego', '71; and 'Super Ego', '72. His new 'Wing on Wings' is the first white descendant of 'White Swirl'.

Dr. Currier McEwen has introduced descendants of 'White Swirl', too, but his important achievement has been to obtain—by the use of colchicine—the first tetraploid Siberians. First varieties to be introduced, in 1970, were 'Orville Fay' and 'Fourfold White' both second generation tetraploids with six-inch horizontal flowers. These new-under-the-sun Siberians will probably be expensive for a number of years.

Another highly rated new Siberian, also from 'White Swirl', is the medium blue 'Swank', bred in California by Ben Hager. Incidentally, Mr. Hager's recent spuria introduction, the lovely yellow 'Archie Owen', should become very popular. And his blue-violet 'Port of Call' won the highest spuria award in 1972. (McCown's 'Highline Lavender' won this honor in '71.)

Originations from first one and then another breeder of Japanese iris varieties have won the Payne Award recently: Maddocks' 'Leave Me Sighing'—a pink double; Rich's dark violet 'Star at Midnight'; Worley's orchid-pink double 'Worley Pink'; and Hazzard's large white single 'Numazu'.

In preparing this reprint edition, I have taken the opportunity to correct a few typographical errors and to update Appendices B and F.

The Genus Iris is a wonderful genus to get tangled into your heart. Have fun.

New City, New York   Molly Price
November, 1972

Preface
to the First Edition

Writing this book has been a difficult chore and a delight. It is not finished, for the story of irises is a never-ending one; it is not even quite up to date, since a book cannot be written and published in a day.

A complete presentation of all the irises and their close relatives that could be grown in some region of the United States would fill several volumes and require much more information and gardening experience than I possess. I am an amateur gardener, writing for amateur gardeners. I have tried to present a balanced and accurate, if limited, picture of the Genus Iris, in a form simple enough for beginning gardeners to enjoy, yet detailed enough to interest experienced gardeners.

My double purpose has been to provide material for gardeners who merely want to accent a foundation planting with a few well-chosen clumps of one kind of iris, or to feature several kinds in a border or a shady garden, plus detailed information for those gardeners who have fallen under the spell of irises and elect to plant whole iris borders or to try their hand at breeding their own varieties.

If I seem overly optimistic in recommending certain irises, it is because I have learned to disregard those cautious authorities who recommend only sure-fire species and varieties. But then, I especially enjoy growing the species behind horticultural varieties.

As I succumbed to the lure of irises, my garden became progressively lopsided—and increasingly satisfying. There are so many sorts of irises, more than any one woman can care for. I partially solved the problem by growing a few kinds for a few years, then discarding them and trying others. I say "partially," because some irises are impossible to discard; they are too delightful.

When, some thirteen years ago, we built our present house in a small woods clearing ringed with dogwood trees, I welcomed the opportunity to start my gardening anew with plants I had not grown before. My paper plans did not work out very well in a terrain of rocks and roots, and I learned—gradually—to take the path of least resistance. The first time my shovel hit a buried boulder in the middle of a staked-out border, I spent hours with a railroad spike and sledge-hammer in an exhausting and unsuccessful attempt to crack the thing into removable pieces. Now I simply plant a ground cover over such a spot. The resulting landscaping effect is haphazard, to say the least, but the plants are there and we would not change our woods for the most fertile and boulder-free field in Rockland County.

The fact that irises of many sorts grow and bloom for me among the rocks, and with fewer hours of sun than most of them would like, is proof of their vigor and adaptability.

In addition to irises, my book includes perennials that bloom at the same time and are compatible with irises in culture and habit. While an all-iris garden is possible, like most gardeners, I prefer a combination with other flowers.

Because interest in the dwarf species and their hybrids is on the increase, I have allotted generous space to descriptions of small bulbous, bearded, and beardless irises that are charming in the perennial garden and for choice corners.

The discussion of beardless irises is separated into two chapters on the basis of origin. I have grouped those native to the United States, to present a clear picture of the largely unexploited wealth that our native irises offer. There must be gardens in which many native irises are featured, but I have yet to see one.

Advice given on culture, diseases, and pests is based primarily on my own experience and observations here in New York state. Gardeners who live in regions with different cultural and disease problems can consult local authorities.

The book is not all on a practical level. Because I like to bring irises into the house, I have given my own amateur ideas on arranging the different types. Books on flower arrangement seldom mention irises, though many types are ideal for cutting, and most types are moderately satisfactory.

The use of some technical terms is essential for clarity and accuracy. Such terms are defined either in the text or in the glossary.

Instead of the newer and more desirable term *cultivar*, I have elected to use the ambiguous but familiar word *variety* to designate a cultivated plant that has been given an identifying common name. All varietal names are enclosed in single quotes except in lists and captions.

My authority for the use of *irises* as the plural for *iris* is Webster's *New International Dictionary, Unabridged, 1953.*

Even if I had wished to avoid the use of Latin botanical names, I could not do so: many iris species have no common or folk names, and in any case these are no more useful for identification than a nickname is. The binomial (two-name) system of plant names was begun early in the eighteenth century, and standardized in 1753 by Linneaeus in his *Species Plantarum.* The first name is always that of the genus; the second is known as the specific epithet. It may, but need not, be descriptive. *Iris pumila,* for example, tells us that the plant belongs to the genus *Iris,* and that it is dwarf. When the epithet commemorates a person, as *Iris wilsonii* (pronounced wil-son-ee-eye), the genitive or possessive case is used. Epithets are never capitalized. The plural of *genus* is *genera;* the plural of *species* is *species.*

MOLLY PRICE

New City, New York
September, 1965

Contents

IN GRATITUDE — vi

PREFACE TO THE DOVER EDITION — vii

PREFACE TO THE FIRST EDITION — ix

ILLUSTRATIONS — xvii

1 THE WORLD OF IRISES — 1

FLOWER FORMS • HOW THE GENUS IS DIVIDED

2 IN THE GARDEN PICTURE — 8

IN THE PERENNIAL BORDER • ATTRACTIVE COMPANIONS • BACKGROUNDS FOR THE ALL-IRIS BORDER • COLOR PLANNING • NATURALIZED PLANTINGS • FOR ROCK GARDENS • FOR SHADY PLACES • BESIDE POOLS AND BROOKS • SOME PLEASING COMBINATIONS

3 TALL BEARDED, BORDER, AND REBLOOMING IRISES — 23

THEIR HISTORY • CHARACTERISTICS OF A SUPERIOR VARIETY • VARIETIES FOR GENERAL USE *(Pinks and Violets—Blue and Black—White, Cream, Light and Deep Yellow—Red)* • BORDER BEARDED IRISES • REBLOOMING IRISES

4 PATTERNS AND COLORS OF TALL BEARDED IRISES — 32

THE SELFS *(White—Cream—Light to Dark Yellow—Buff to Brown and Red—Pink, Apricot and Orange—Light,*

Medium and Dark Blue—Violet, Orchid and Black) •
PLICATAS • BICOLORS • BITONES • BLENDS • THE BEARD
EMERGES

5 CULTURE OF TALL BEARDED IRISES   46

CYCLE OF GROWTH AND INCREASE • FEEDING • LIME • SOIL
• PLANTING AND TRANSPLANTING • MULCHING

6 THE SMALLER BEARDED IRISES   58

MINIATURE DWARF BEARDED IRISES *(Miniature Dwarf
Hybrids)* • MEDIAN IRISES *(Standard Dwarfs—Intermediates—Miniature Tall Beardeds)*

7 ARIL IRISES AND THEIR HYBRIDS   74

REGELIAS *(Regelia Hybrids—Regeliocyclus Hybrids—
Regeliabreds)* • PSEUDOREGELIAS   THE ONCOCYCLUS
IRISES *(Oncobreds)* • CULTURE

8 THE EURASIAN BEARDLESS IRISES   83

PARDANTHOPSIS AND FOETIDISSIMA • THE APOGONS
*(Siberian Irises—Japanese Irises—Culture of Japanese
Irises—Spurias—Minor Miniature Apogons)* • CRESTED
IRISES

9 NATIVE AMERICAN BEARDLESS IRISES   101

CRESTED IRISES • APOGONS *(The Louisiana Irises—The
Pacific Coast Irises—The Longipetalae)*

10 BULBOUS IRISES   114

SUBGENUS XIPHIUM *(The Reticulatas—The Xiphiums)* •
SUBGENUS SCORPIRIS: JUNO IRISES • SUBGENUS NEPAL-
ENSIS: IRIS DECORA

11 PROGRESSION OF BLOOM   125

PEAK BLOOM DATES FOR TALL BEARDEDS • THE IRIS
PAGEANT IN SOUTHERN NEW YORK • A FEW OTHER
REGIONS

12 DISEASES AND PESTS   130

FUNGUS DISEASES • BACTERIAL DISEASES • OTHER DIS-
EASES • INSECT PESTS • MINOR PESTS • COMMENTS

13 HYBRIDIZING IRISES FOR FUN   141

REPRODUCTIVE STRUCTURE OF THE IRIS FLOWER • CHOOS-
ING PARENTS • MECHANICS OF CROSS-POLLINATION •
FERTILIZATION   THE LIFE CYCLE • HARVESTING AND
PLANTING SEEDS • TRANSPLANTING • WHAT WILL THE
SEEDLINGS LOOK LIKE • SELECTING SEEDLINGS • CROSSES
BETWEEN SPECIES

14 PEOPLE BEHIND THE PLANTS   158

SCIENTISTS • HYBRIDIZERS *(Jean Stevens—Paul Cook—
Orville Fay — David Hall — Tell Muhlestein — Robert
Schreiner)*

15 SHOWS AND ARRANGEMENTS   164

EXHIBITING *(Choosing Entries—Preparing or Grooming
Stalks — Transporting Irises to the Show — Show
Schedules)* RULES AND REGULATIONS OF AIS SPONSORED
SHOWS • IRIS FLOWERS INDOORS *(Cutting—Containers—
Miniature Arrangements—Foliage—With Other Flowers)*

APPENDIX   174

A   AVAILABLE SPECIES
B   SOURCES OF PLANTS AND SEEDS
C   IRIS AWARDS
D   AWARDS OF THE AMERICAN
     IRIS SOCIETY, 1965

E   JUDGES' CHOICE, 1965
F   IRIS SOCIETIES

GLOSSARY   189

LIST OF REFERENCES   192

INDEX   193

List of Illustrations

PHOTOGRAPHS

Frontispiece		FRESCO OF PRIEST-KING WITH IRISES—*Mansell Collection*	
	1	IRISES IN A PERENNIAL BORDER—*Genereux*	9
	2	IRISES IN FOUNDATION PLANTING—*Caldwell*	14
	3	ALL-IRIS GARDEN	16
	4	FAIR LUZON	34
	5	MY ALANA	34
	6	HENRY SHAW	35
	7	FIFTH AVENUE	35
Trans-planting			
	8	CLUMP READY FOR DIVISION	55
	9	GROSS DIVISIONS	55
	10	FOR MAXIMUM INCREASE	55
	11	PLANTING	55
	12	CHERRY SPOT	60
	13	ANGEL EYES	60
	14	*Iris pumila* WITH DAFFODILS IN GARDEN	62
	15	STALKS OF FOUR TYPES OF SMALLER BEARDED IRISES	64
	16	MOONSPINNER	66
	17	*Iris mellita* VANDEE	66
	18	PEEWEE	66
	19	DERRING DO	68
	20	*Iris korolkowii violacea*	68
	21	*Iris graminea*	88
	22	*Iris pseudacorus*	88
	23	SUNNY DAY—*Spuria Iris Society*	93
	24	*Iris gracilipes*	99
	25	*Iris tectorum alba*	99
	26	*Iris cristata—Grossman*	102
	27	CAJAN JOYEUSE	105
	28	SIBERIAN IRISES	105
	29	*Iris innominata—Grossman*	109
	30	AMIGUITA—*Downward*	111
	31	*Iris reticulata*	116
	32	*Iris danfordiae*	116
	33	*Iris magnifica*	116

xvii

*Iris
Borer*
	34	LARVA	137
	35	PUPA	137
	36	MOTH	137
	37	COMMON LEAF SPOT	137

*Arrange-
ments*
	38	FOR MARCH	168
	39	FOR JUNE	169
	40	FOR MAY	169

DRAWINGS

Fig. 1	FLOWER FORMS	3
Fig. 2	TYPES OF ROOTSTOCKS AND BULBS	4
Fig. 3	SEED PODS	5
Fig. 4	PLAN FOR MIXED BORDER FEATURING IRISES	18
Fig. 5	PLAN FOR IRIS AND PEONY BORDER—*Paul E. Kennedy*	20
Fig. 6	IRIS RHIZOME IN SPRING AND FALL	48
Fig. 7	TALL BEARDED IRIS FLOWER PARTIALLY DISSECTED	142

1

The World of Irises

In myth, legend, and religion, in heraldry, tapestries, and the robes of kings, in magic, medicine, and botany, irises have appeared since the dawn of recorded history.

Four thousand years ago in Crete, the iris was the flower of prince and priest. To the ancient Greeks, it was the personification of the goddess Iris, and was planted on the tombs of women. Much later, wandering Mohammedans carried the white-flowered iris 'Albicans' everywhere, and planted it on their soldiers' graves.

Many Biblical "lilies" may be irises, even Solomon's famous "lilies of the field." The "lilies" mentioned in Ecclesiasticus 50:8:

> And as the flowers of roses in the spring of the year,
> as lilies by the river of waters

were *Iris pseudacorus* in the belief of one authority, Dr. Harold Moldenke.

Ancient flowers that are native to many countries are likely to figure in man's history, and irises grow throughout the north temperate zone. They are found from Alaska and Kamchatka on the north to Hong Kong and Arabia on the south, and from Japan right around the world to China. Yet after several years of ardent gardening and considerable horticultural reading, I knew less about their numerous species than did the Flemish Charles de l'Ecluse (Carolus Clusius), writing in the sixteenth century, who described nine species so perfectly that they are easily recognizable today.

I passed by the world of irises until my curiosity was aroused one February night when I opened a new catalogue of unusual seeds and plants. *Iris arenaria* was the first name in a two-page list of iris species: "A rare and difficult little iris," the catalogue admitted,

1

"from Europe and Asia," with "little clumps of narrow grasslike leaves about four inches high . . . and four-inch stems with two or three yellow flowers in May."

I bought this Balkan iris, and added it to the several varieties of tall beardeds and Siberians and two nameless April-blooming dwarfs in my garden. Difficult or not, it flourished, and I was encouraged to try other strange and beautiful irises.

The wild American species first snared my imagination when I spied a little purple iris—looking for all the world like a miniature Japanese variety—in a color slide of birds on the Gaspe peninsula shown at an Audubon Society lecture. The photographer couldn't identify it. Eventually I learned it was *Iris setosa*, which grows now in my garden.

Then, through the writings of Dr. John K. Small of the New York Botanical Garden, I was diverted to that glamorous group of our native irises called the Louisianas. These too, including the famous Abbeville reds, grew for me.

As the iris world opened bit by bit, I became familiar with the flower structure, learned to recognize the different types and got their classification sorted out in my mind. Knowing something about the many iris species, their background and origins, adds enormously to my enjoyment of the various flowers when they bloom in my garden.

FLOWER FORMS

Iris flowers vary greatly in color and in shape; in size, they vary from the inch-wide flowers of the little *Iris gracilipes* to the ten-inch flowers of some Japanese varieties. In general structure, all are the same: each flower has six segments in two sets of three. The three upper or inner segments are petals and are called *standards*—whether they are vertical or horizontal, arch inward or downward. The three lower or outer segments are sepals and are called *falls*. The expanded outer portion of the fall is the blade; the narrow inner part is the claw. Falls and standards unite at their base to form the *perianth tube*.

Between standards and falls are three flat, colored bands which arch over the stamens. These *style-branches* or *style-arms* terminate in two decorative *crests*. In some species, the falls are so overlapped by style-branches that only the round blade is visible.

The standards, usually about the same length as the falls, may be narrow, as in the Siberian irises, or very broad. Among the

FIGURE 1 FLOWER FORMS. A—Tall bearded. B—Reticulata *Iris danfordiae* with large style-crests; minute standards are not shown. C—Regelia *Iris korolkowii*. D—Juno *Iris magnifica* with large erect style crests and small standards which swirl below the falls. E—Siberian iris. F—Single form of Japanese iris with large falls and small standards. G—Spuria iris. H—Crested *Iris tectorum* showing extremely narrow hafts of the standards and flat form. I—Louisiana iris.

oncocyclus irises, they often are far larger than the falls. In the
Juno irises, the tiny standards may hang *below* the falls; in the
bulbous *Iris danfordiae*, they are minute.

A complete run-down of the botanical classification of the genus
Iris would only bore or bewilder the average gardener. Yet some
of it is essential if we are to understand the culture required by
each group. Catalogues are sometimes rather casual in listings and
inaccurate in description and classification. It behooves the gardener to know what he is ordering.

HOW THE GENUS IS DIVIDED

The genus is composed of 200 or more species which are separated
into two major groups, rhizomatous and bulbous. Rhizomes are
creeping or underground stems, with roots growing from the nodes.
Bulbs are underground stems flattened to mere knobs with roots
growing from below. Above, a number of fleshy scalelike leaves
surround and protect the bud.

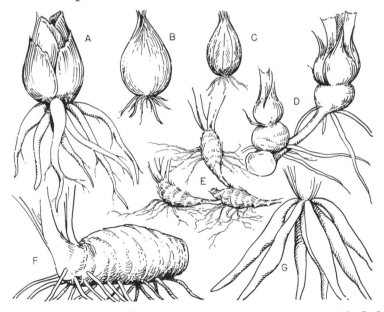

FIGURE 2   TYPES OF ROOTSTOCKS AND BULBS. A—Juno, with fleshy,
persistent roots. B and C—Dutch and reticulata iris bulbs with new roots
beginning to grow after resting stage. D—Regelia *Iris stolonifera* showing new rhizome growing from underground stolon. E—Slender rhizomes
of *Iris cristata*. F—Fleshy rhizome of tall bearded iris with roots emerging from underneath. G—Fleshy roots of Nepalensis *Iris decora*.

The genus is formally divided into four large groups or subgenera. All rhizomatous irises are included in the subgenus Iris, largest of the four, and most important horticulturally. In this subgenus are the bearded, beardless, and crested irises, most often grown in gardens. The rhizomes of bearded irises are large and fleshy; those of crested irises are slender. Beardless irises generally have small fibrous rhizomes. The characteristics of bulbous irises vary so greatly that they are separated into two subgenera: Xiphium and Scorpiris. Almost all bulbous iris flowers are beardless with narrow segments. The important differences for classification are found in the rootstocks.

In the Xiphium subgenus, the bulbs are rootless during the resting stage. All are smooth except those of the Reticulata irises, which are distinguished by a netted or reticulated covering. In the Scorpiris subgenus, they are characterized by thick fleshy roots that persist through the resting stage.

The last, and least, subgenus is Nepalensis which contains only one species, a botanical curiosity with a unique rootstock consisting of several fleshy roots attached to a growing point.

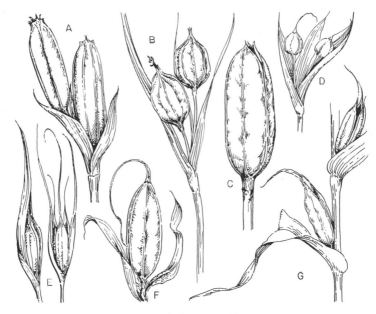

FIGURE 3   SEED PODS. A—Siberian. B—Spuria *Iris graminea.* C—Tall bearded. D—Crested *Iris cristata.* E—*Iris reticulata.* F—*Iris pumila* showing entire stem. G—Juno iris showing almost stemless pods in leaf axils.

This abbreviated outline of the genus, including only those divisions of interest to the gardener, is based on the botanical classification by Dr. G. H. M. Lawrence and Dr. L. F. Randolph as presented in the American Iris Society (A. I. S.) publication *The Genus Iris*. I have included the subgenus Nepalensis for the record, and have placed it first because it belongs neither to the bulbous nor the rhizomatous group.

GENUS IRIS

   I. Subgenus Nepalensis
      Iris decora

Bulbous Group
   II. Subgenus Xiphium
      Dutch, Spanish, English, Reticulata
  III. Subgenus Scorpiris
      Juno

Rhizomatous Group
  IV. Subgenus Iris
     A. Bearded
        Eupogon
        Aril
          Oncocyclus, Regelia, Pseudoregelia
     B. Beardless Irises
        Iris dichotoma
        Iris foetidissima
        Apogon
          Siberian, Pacific Coast, Spuria, Louisiana,
          Longipetala, Laevigata
     C. Evansia or Crested

The Eupogon—meaning true bearded—irises are further divided into the following six horticultural groups that group together species and cultivated varieties according to height and blooming season:

Miniature Dwarf
Standard Dwarf
Miniature Tall

Intermediate
Border
Standard Tall Bearded

You will notice that a few species names are included. These species are extreme individualists, so different in certain characteristics from other irises as to demand a section or sub-section of their own.

2

In the Garden Picture

The effectiveness of a garden depends on the ability of the gardener to compose groups of plants that harmonize with each other, with the type of house and with the spirit and natural conditions of the land. There is more to designing a garden than spading up a rectangular plot somewhere in the yard and filling it with plants—even iris plants. But whatever else a garden is—and it can be many things—it should, above all, be an expression of the gardener's own taste and creativity.

Some iris fanciers are interested in growing other plants only as frame or foil for the beauty of the iris flower; others, believing the Iris needs no enhancement, fill their yards with rows of the tall bearded—or, for variety's sake, add a few dwarf-bearded, some spurias, Siberians, and maybe an occasional Japanese variety.

Some iris-lovers don't object to the long barren periods that occur in a one-flower garden before and after the tall bearded bloom; others are concerned with plans for pre- and post-iris bloom. One school maintains that the one-flower garden is not even a garden, only a collection. I am of the opinion that whatever kind of gardener you are—landscaper, collector, rock-gardener, or whatever—that is the kind of gardener you should be.

IN THE PERENNIAL BORDER

The diversity of form among the species and groups of irises suitable for gardens is so great that an imaginative gardener could design a series of beautiful and unusual iris-dominated gardens without the use of a single rhizome of the popular tall bearded hybrid. However, the tall beardeds of vibrant color are the stars of early

8

1 IRISES IN A PERENNIAL BORDER

In a Massachusetts garden, grape vines on trellis form background for brilliant perennial border of tall bearded iris, lupins, budding peonies, columbine, pyrethrum, and blue flax, edged with sea thrift (*Armeria maritima*).

June. These offer almost unlimited opportunity for what William
Cowper described as,

> . . . a grateful mixture of well matched
> And sorted hues (each giving each relief,
> And by contrasted beauty shining more) . . .

Irises are important in the perennial border, whether your
approach is experimental or conventional, and there is an iris suitable for every area of the design. The very tall varieties of bearded
irises, of the beardless spurias, and of Japanese and Siberian varieties make a fine background for shorter perennials. Less tall varieties of all these may form large middle-ground masses in the garden
picture. Groups of bulbous Dutch and English types belong toward
the front of the middle area, and the standard dwarf bearded and
some species, such as *Iris tectorum* and *I. aphylla,* can serve as
accents in the foreground. Miniature dwarf beardeds and the tiny
spreading *I. cristata* are effective as irregular drifts rather than as
ribbon edges.

Years ago I decided to assign the major roles in my garden to
irises, day-lilies, and daffodils. Other assorted perennials assume
minor roles. Irises are given the preferred locations, the bulbs are
mainly naturalized, and day-lilies are planted where irises are least
happy. In one border I more or less abide by the rules I recommend to you: Do not use too many kinds of plants—let one kind
have prominence and take care that plants harmonize in color,
in form and in habit of growth.

But because I am basically an experimenter, most of my garden
is a horticultural bouillabaisse of these and all the other perennials
I happen to be trying out. In fact, my garden areas range all the
way from mostly irises to mostly not irises and in settings that
vary widely—the perennial border the rock garden, the shady
garden, and a hillside where daffodils are naturalized.

In the perennial border the very tall bearded irises, the beardless
spurias, Japanese, and Siberian varieties make a fine background
for shorter perennials. Less tall varieties of all these may form
the middle-ground masses. Groups of bulbous Dutch and English
types belong toward the front of the middle area, and the standard
dwarf beardeds and some species, such as *Iris tectorum* and *I.
aphylla,* can serve as accents in the foreground. Miniature dwarf
beardeds and the tiny spreading *I. cristata* are effective as irregular
drifts rather than as ribbon edgings.

In one large, raised, predominantly tall bearded border adjacent to the house I planted, for early bloom, a forsythia, which I keep pruned fairly flat (can't say it's really espaliered) against the wall. Beneath it I "drifted" a selection of early bulbs. First to come are the winter-blooming *Iris reticulata* and snowdrops, then a few large white-and-yellow daffodils and blue hyacinths with the tiny blue-striped *Puschkinia libonatica,* followed by the fragrant *Narcissus jonquilla simplex.* All have finished by the time the mass of iris leaves in the front of them has grown tall enough to hide their post-bloom untidiness. The bed is edged irregularly with two varieties of perennial candytuft, one blooming earlier than the other, accented by a clump of five blue parrot tulips, another of a violet Darwin, three bulbs of the yellow parrot tulip and some miniature daffodil species. While they are flowering, all the young iris leaves, lovely in their own right, are growing greener and spikier every day.

One year new varieties of standard dwarf bearded iris in the forefront of the bed took over very smoothly from the daffodils and led right into the beautiful oncobred iris. These, with the frilly yellow tall bearded 'Limelight', are the earliest of my big irises. Blooming with them are the candytufts and one lemon-lily at the corner of the house.

ATTRACTIVE COMPANIONS

For companionable bloom at iris time, bleeding hearts *(Dicentra spectabilis)* and the Siberian bugloss *(Brunnera macrophylla)* are most faithful. The bugloss, unrivaled for true-blue color and the beauty of the large heart-shaped leaves, is perhaps number one on my list of iris companions. First flowers open with the tiny pumilas and blooming continues with the late talls—a notable performance. The bleedinghearts bloom almost as long. These two are indispensable as background for the 10- to 15-inch standard dwarf iris and the slightly taller, slightly later intermediates, which combine so well with Darwin and lily-flowered tulips.

The old intermediate 'Black Magic' and the late tulips seem made to go together. I cannot imagine a lovelier combination than this iris with almost any color of tulip. The new intermediate variety 'Kiss Me Kate' is also enchanting in my garden with some airy-fairy mauve species of dianthus from Japan.

At one time or another almost all late May- and early June-blooming perennials have been suggested for grouping with irises.

Peonies, Oriental poppies, and lupines are the large-flowered plants most frequently used. Lupines, though some of the bicolors are harsh, may be used successfully as background flowers, but if they are planted beside irises, I think the wide-spreading low-growing leaves shade the iris plants too much in the post-bloom period when these need to ripen their rhizomes in full sun. I plant peonies in the background, too, and prefer single-flowered varieties. Double peonies are so huge that they dominate even the largest tall bearded iris if varieties bloom at the same time. Oriental poppies, though large, are not so overpowering and the foliage has the valuable habit of dying down shortly after bloom.

On the whole, I prefer smaller, more delicate-flowered perennials as companions in the iris-dominated border. And if only a few tall beardeds are used for color and mass in a varied planting, it is wise to arrange the design so small-leaved plants will be closest to the irises. Or you may avoid this problem in a border by using Siberian or Japanese iris instead of the tall beardeds.

Dianthus, either the many species that can be grown from seed or named cultivars such as the coral-rose 'Pink Princess', are satisfying front-of-the-border companions for irises. So are the veronicas. The gray-leaved, purple *Veronica incana* and the taller gentian-blue *V. latifolia* are my favorites, but there are kinds that I have not tried. An irregular clump of *V. latifolia* spilling brilliant blue over the edge of the border is an effective contrast.

Nor can columbines be surpassed as iris companions. Though many gardeners find the mixed colors delightful, to simplify problems of color combination I grow only blue ones. In one border there came a period in which it was largely a blue-and-lavender border with a few beginning racemes of coral-bells. Last year, to improve the color balance there, I added a clear yellow and a smoky-tan tall bearded, and several *Papaver atlanticum*. This poppy has pale orange flowers on tall, thin stems.

The exotic shrubby tree peony with its beautifully cut leaves makes a fine accent among perennials. A pale pink variety with light, medium blue, and deep purple irises provides a spectacular show.

For later color, tender bulbs of slender habit, such as acidanthera and the minature gladiolus, may be planted between iris clumps. *Aster frikarti*, which blooms from June to frost, and that long-flowering and exceptionally beautiful white phlox, 'Miss Lingard', are excellent choices, too.

BACKGROUNDS FOR THE ALL-IRIS BORDER

In the all-iris border, nearly always of tall bearded varieties, care must be used to avoid a stiffly regimented effect, and background becomes highly important for both the flowering and post-bloom periods. A shrub border provides the most usual and one of the loveliest of backgrounds, especially if it can be seen from a distance or can be in a wide curve. A coniferous evergreen hedge, dark green, and black shadowed, is dramatic and formal.

When an informal border of deciduous flowering shrubs is used, the effectiveness is greatly increased if the grouping is irregular enough to provide little bays and peninsulas. For this kind of background I would choose some shrubs that would bloom either before or after the irises bloom and that had berries or colorful foliage in the fall. But I would let the irises dominate the garden in their season.

A shrub background is not the only attractive possibility. Tall bearded irises stand out satisfyingly in front of a dry stone wall that has been planted sparingly with such plants as *Veronica repens,* the maiden pink (*Dianthus deltoides*), moss phlox, and various sedums. And in the small garden, particularly, it may be desirable to display the irises against a high screening fence. In this situation, shrubs espaliered against the fence, or vines, or climbing roses provide a pleasant background.

The lucky gardener with an unlimited view may need to provide no other background. What could be lovelier than an open sweep of lake, trees, hills, and sky? And the magnificent modern tall bearded irises do not lose their grandeur in such a setting. In the F. W. Cassebeer garden at West Nyack, New York, the flowers are displayed in long, narrow, curved beds on a grassy slope that leads down towards a lake. In this superb setting, irises are silhouetted against the water and illuminated by light shining through and around them. When their season is over, the plants recede into the general greenness and the marvelous view is again dominant.

COLOR PLANNING

Reaction to color is so individual that it is next to impossible to recommend combinations. To one, red and yellow irises planted together seem brilliant and desirable; to another, the grouping appears garish, even distressing.

2 IRISES IN FOUNDATION PLANTING
Foxfire, early-blooming yellow tall bearded variety, accents evergreen
foundation planting in garden of Mrs. H. F. Allen, Memphis, Tennessee.

A scheme often recommended, and one that I don't particularly like because it seems to remove almost all originality from the design, is to plant in color sequence beginning with white, cream, pink, wine, red-brown, golden-brown, orange, etc., using blends between the pure colors.

As a general rule in a mixed planting the lighter colors should be in the background. Dark colors have less carrying power and are more effective in the mid- or foreground. Both white and deep yellow are insistent colors; the great peacemakers are the creams and the light and pale blues. Generous use of one or another of these pacifiers in one or similar varieties throughout the border simplifies the whole problem of color contrasts.

Clear bright colors are easier to deal with than the muted blends (which I fancy) or the strongly patterned plicatas that are most attractive when planted with varieties of their base or pattern color. Blue and white plicatas combine well with pure white irises or blues of the same shade as the plicata stippling. The same holds true for bicolors; plant those with white standards and colored falls against white irises or varieties of the same color as the falls. Those with yellow standards and maroon or purple falls are striking among irises of the same shade of yellow as the standards.

An effect of "close harmony" is very attractive to me. It may be obtained by combining colors that are close together on the color scale, as medium blue, blue-violet, violet, and red-violet, with lighter tints in the same tonal range—lavender, orchid, light blue, etc. This produces an over-subtle grouping (others might call it dull) that needs to be startled into life by an accenting clump of contrasting color such as pale straw-yellow, lemon, cream, or perhaps a yellow-beige or light orange blend.

Contrasting light and dark shades of one color produce a stimulating effect. Imagine a sweep of blue irises in every shade and hue —pale silvery blue, sky blue, strong medium blue and deep dark blue against white-flowering shrubs or a white wall. Or shades of violet against pale yellow roses along a fence.

NATURALIZED PLANTINGS

If you want irises for color accent in the landscape, which I am arbitrarily defining as those areas not included in garden borders or beds, you have a wide choice. Though the modern tall beardeds do not lend themselves to naturalizing, some of the old diploids— the white 'Priscilla', 'Bluet', 'Pink Ruffles', orchid 'Dream', and

3 ALL IRIS-GARDEN

Multi-colored tall bearded irises in the New York garden of F. W. Cassebeer, with a backdrop of blue lake and sweep of hills.

'Dogrose'—are rugged enough to bloom even on a rocky hillside. Old varieties of intermediates can also sturdily maintain themselves even between large stones and half-smothered with weeds. I once found plants growing on a long-abandoned farm, in dim light and acid soil under the low branches of a great hemlock tree. They no longer bloomed but when I transplanted them to my garden out of curiosity as to what manner of rhizomatous iris could exist in such an un-iris-like environment, I discovered that they were antique hybrids of *Iris variegata*.

Perhaps some of the standard dwarf beardeds can survive with minimum cultivation, too. One summer when I was ill and unable to tend my seedling patches, the one farthest from the house became so overgrown with weeds that by August the plants were no longer visible. I said a sad goodbye to that crop of seedlings, but the following spring when I raked away the deep mulch of dead weed stems, the irises were there, green and perky as could be, and with numerous increases. I am not recommending neglect as a cultural method for irises—especially bearded irises, but I am advocating the use of the sturdiest varieties for non-garden uses. The light blue *Iris pallida dalmatica* and the lemon daylily *Hemerocallis flava* were long a favorite garden combination. Intertwined masses of the two can still be seen blooming in old neglected gardens.

Several varieties of antique diploid bearded irises—unfortunately unidentified—hold a bank in my garden and bloom profusely though they have not been transplanted for ten years. These receive only morning sun and are heavily overrun with invasive but lovely sundrops. Such irises are desirable for rough landscaping on a large property. Though the flowers cannot compete with those of even the older tetraploid varieties for beauty, size, richness of color, and lasting quality, they can provide ribbons or clumps of color that are particularly satisfying in the distance. I would not use any of these in a small garden where the form of each flower is so plainly seen.

FOR ROCK GARDENS

A flame of little irises can light a rock garden from the end of February in a favorable year, until the middle of June. Even if I didn't like rock gardens, I would build one to show off these darling miniatures. First to bloom are the little narrow-petaled reticulatas in rich violets, brilliant and light blues, purple, and yellow (*Iris danfordiae*). Plant these in a sunny well-drained and, for earliest

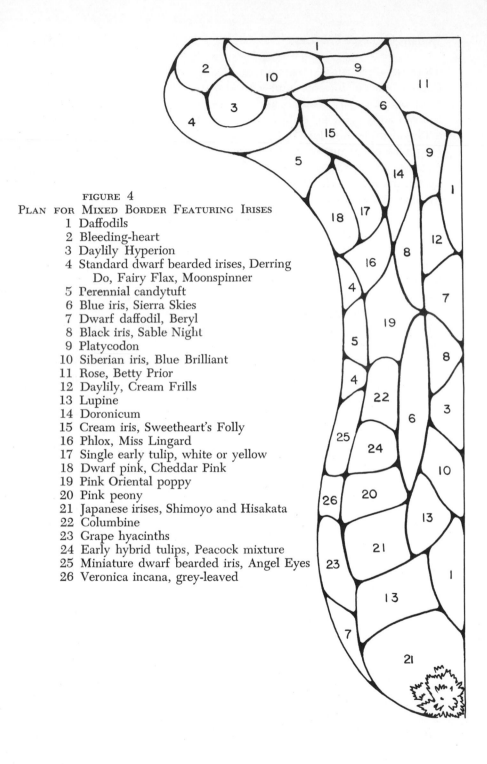

FIGURE 4
PLAN FOR MIXED BORDER FEATURING IRISES

1 Daffodils
2 Bleeding-heart
3 Daylily Hyperion
4 Standard dwarf bearded irises, Derring Do, Fairy Flax, Moonspinner
5 Perennial candytuft
6 Blue iris, Sierra Skies
7 Dwarf daffodil, Beryl
8 Black iris, Sable Night
9 Platycodon
10 Siberian iris, Blue Brilliant
11 Rose, Betty Prior
12 Daylily, Cream Frills
13 Lupine
14 Doronicum
15 Cream iris, Sweetheart's Folly
16 Phlox, Miss Lingard
17 Single early tulip, white or yellow
18 Dwarf pink, Cheddar Pink
19 Pink Oriental poppy
20 Pink peony
21 Japanese irises, Shimoyo and Hisakata
22 Columbine
23 Grape hyacinths
24 Early hybrid tulips, Peacock mixture
25 Miniature dwarf bearded iris, Angel Eyes
26 Veronica incana, grey-leaved

bloom, protected spot. A hundred or more bulbs, combined with snowdrops and accented with a few of the little early-blooming species *Tulipa kaufammiana,* will occupy only a square yard of garden space and make an unforgettable picture.

The pure pumilas, 'Blue Spot', 'April Morn', the dark 'Sulina', and pale yellow 'Carpathia' provide drifts of color around daffodils and early tulips. Blue and purple hybrid varieties combine brilliantly with the glittering golden alyssum. The maroon 'Blazon' with gold-embroidered falls, and the ruffled light blue 'Azurea'— more than a hundred years old and still charming—are good choices. Beautiful, new and more expensive varieties include 'Blue Frost' with light blue flowers of perfect form and 'Angel Eyes,' a lavish bloomer in white with the falls eyed in pure blue.

Slightly taller, 6 to 10 inch, and later hybrids, such as the purple-toned 'Black Baby' and the light yellow and white 'Gay Lassie', look well with the low pink-flowered shrub, *Daphne cneorum.*

The white and red 'Cherry Spot', a favorite of mine, makes a fine accent for clumps of lavender-blue polemonium. Some dwarf species of the curious tuberous rooted Juno iris, which bloom in April, are interesting to try in a clay pocket in the rock garden. Clumps of the May-blooming standard dwarf bearded hybrids are as effective in the larger rock garden as in the perennial border and charming as accents in even a tiny grace note of a rock garden.

All of these dwarf bearded varieties require full sun, but dwarf beardless species grow well in semi-shade.

FOR SHADY PLACES

Though no iris can bloom in deep shade, a number of beardless types either need or can endure partial shade. Apparently dainty dwarf *I. gracilipes,* the curious *I. foetidissima* and the tiny *I. verna* demand part shade. In both the midsouthern and northeastern states the dwarf crested *Iris cristata* will form wide mats in high shade, under deciduous shrubs and at the edge of plantings of broad-leaved evergreens. I have also seen colonies of *I. verna* blooming gloriously on a sunny gravelly bank in North Carolina, but it will not grow for more than two years in my garden either in sun or in shade.

Iris tectorum, the roof iris of China, prefers some shade; the spurias, Louisianas, *Iris versicolor* and the vesper iris (*I. dichotoma*) prefer full sun but are satisfactory in semishade. The Siberian irises also bloom in part shade, and three Pacific Coast natives, *Iris in-*

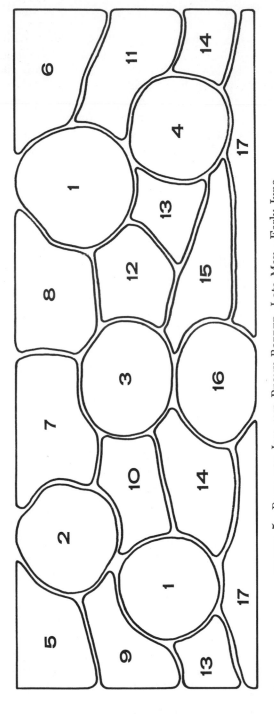

FIGURE 5 PLAN FOR IRIS AND PEONY BORDER, Late May—Early June.

PEONIES: 1, Minuet; 2, Mrs. Franklin D. Roosevelt, rose-pink double; 3, Krinkled White.
single, with gold stamens and pale pink buds; 4, Westerner, pink Japanese.

SIBERIAN IRISES: 5, White Swirl; 6, Mountain Lake, bright blue;

BEARDED IRISES: 7, Allegiance, dark blue; 8, Lula Marguerite, blue and gold blend;
9, Blue Sapphire, light blue; 10, Waxing Moon, light yellow; 11, Bravado, golden
yellow; 12, Summer Sunset, apricot; 13, Black Taffeta dark blue-purple.

EDGING PLANTS: 14, *Veronica latifolia* (*teucrium*) Crater Lake Blue; 15, *Phlox divaricata*,
lavender-blue; 16, *Iberis sempervirens* Snowflake; Dianthus Beatrix, salmon pink.

nominata, *I. tenax* and *I. douglasiana* have flowered equally well in sun and light shade in my garden.

Because I love the cool tranquility of white flowers against the green shadows of arching branches, I have planted some white Japanese and tall bearded seedlings in my shady garden where they receive only morning sun. They bloom, but not freely. While I cannot recommend such perverse gardening practices, I derive a guilty pleasure from the serene loveliness of even a few beautiful blooms in this setting.

BESIDE POOLS AND BROOKS

It is a cliche that the beauty of any garden is enhanced by water but it is true—as many cliches are. The smallest garden can include a tiny pool even if it is a washtub or kitchen sink set in the ground, or a little saucer-shaped bird bath.

Decorate your pool but avoid overplanting or it may become almost invisible by late spring. Siberian and Japanese irises with narrow, vertical graceful foliage are attractive all summer and are among the best plants for pool planting. One clump of irises, a flutter of airy maidenhair fern and, say, three primroses grouped at the far side of a little pool—and there you have it. Simple, in scale, and lovely.

A large reflecting pool can support a bigger group of either of these irises, or even the flourishing *Iris pseudacorus*. "The water Flower-de-luce, or yellow flag," as John Gerard called it, "prospereth well in moist meadows or in the borders and brinks of rivers, ponds and standing lakes. And although it be a water plant by nature yet being planted in gardens, it prospereth well" (and self-sows).

All three of these irises as well as the wild blue flag, *Iris versicolor*, may be grown in glorious profusion in sunny stretches along a brook or around the edges of a pond in combination with sweet rocket, globe flower, and rose-mallow.

In northern states, the Siberian varieties are planted high, so that their roots will not be water-logged in winter. In the south, they can endure winter wet. In the extreme north, the species *Iris kaempferi* and *I. laevigata* will probably naturalize better than the Japanese hybrids. In North Carolina, I have seen hybrid varieties of Japanese irises successfully naturalized in low, partly shaded areas along a brook.

SOME PLEASING COMBINATIONS

For Late April and Early May
Dark red dwarf irises 'Red Gem' and pink 'Promise' with dwarf
Doronicum clusii and grape hyacinths.
Flowering quince, white daffodils, blue anchusa, white grape
hyacinth and dwarf iris 'Blue Frost' or 'Cherry Spot'.

For Mid-May
Intermediate irises 'Drummer Boy', blue, and 'Cutie', white and
blue, behind white and black-red Darwin tulips and bleeding-heart.
Blue standard dwarf iris 'Tinkerbell' in the foreground.

Late May and Early June, Tall Bearded Iris Border

Sparkling Waters, light blue	Midnight Blue
Sierra Skies, medium blue	Violet Harmony
No Mohr (oncobred), cream effect	Happy Birthday, light coral
	Fair Luzon, shorter bright pink
Cool Comfort, clear yellow	

For Late June and Early July
Yellow Spurias, 'Sunny Day', and 'Lark Song' behind dark red
and pink hybrid tea roses with daylily 'Little Cherub' in foreground.
Add white and blue toned Japanese irises, as 'Ivory Glow', 'Joyous
Cavalier', 'Pinstripe', and 'Pomp and Circumstance'.

3

Tall Bearded, Border, and Reblooming Irises

The majority of gardeners, including iris specialists, regard the showy modern tall bearded varieties as the most desirable of all. Certainly there can be no doubt that they are an outstanding accomplishment of horticulture. The art, intuition, scientific knowledge and educated guesses of twentieth-century hybridizers have gone far towards perfecting this one group.

THEIR HISTORY

Bearded irises have been grown in gardens since gardens began. In Europe, at least as early as the sixteenth century, hybrids were grown from collected seed of the two native European diploid species, *Iris variegata,* the Hungarian iris, and *I. pallida*, the sweet flag.

By the beginning of the eighteenth century, collections of natural hybrids between these species were being marketed by French and Dutch nurserymen. Early in the nineteenth century, William Prince, one of America's outstanding nurserymen and owner of the "Linnean Botanic Garden of Flushing, Long Island, near New York," imported some of these hybrids. In 1823 his catalogue listed some twenty "iris or flower-de-luce" (at 25 cents each) in addition to bulbous irises and several species—both native and foreign—including dwarf *Iris pumila*.

Apparently no American in the nineteenth century became seriously interested in either growing or breeding irises, for in succeeding issues of the catalogue fewer and fewer sorts appeared. In

23

France, during this same period, irises flourished commercially. In 1822 a M. De Bure, an amateur grower in Paris, introduced to commerce the first named iris variety, Buriensis. M. Jaques, an eminent horticulturist, also raised irises from chance seed. He encouraged a M. Lemon to grow irises in his nursery in Belleville, France; in 1840, the latter introduced one hundred varieties stemming from *Iris pallida* and *I. variegata*. These men did not hybridize but relied on insect pollination to produce seed pods. There was no known reason for them to do otherwise, for the science of genetics was not yet born. Mendel was alive, but his revolutionary peas had not yet been planted. Even so, a few of the best of these chance Lemon varieties such as the white-and-blue 'Mme. Chereu' and the white 'Innocenza' were fine irises, and they are still available in the catalogues of specialists.

However, at least one iris grower was ahead of his time. In 1842 *The Gardener's Chronicle* published an unsigned article, believed to have been written by the English nurseryman John Salter, which contained this statement: "From artificial impregnation of [the irises] Germanica, Plicata, Buriensis, Swerti, Pallida, new colors have been produced."

While Lemon, later joined by Vilmorin and Millet, continued to produce irises in France, major interest shifted across the channel to England. Beginning in 1860, Barr and Sons, who established the Covent Garden in London, raised and introduced new varieties. It is not known whether they relied on bees or made crosses by hand. In 1865 Barr classified his extensive collection of varieties in six main species groups: amoena, neglecta, pallida, plicata, squalens, and variegata. The only two of his six "species" still recognized as species are *Iris variegata* and *I. pallida* which have several forms. Dr. Randolph has collected and grows in his garden in Ithaca, New York, about a dozen different hardy forms of pallida from central and northern Italy and Yugoslavia. The form *I. pallida dalmatica*, known to have been in gardens as early as 1600, and the variant called 'Princess Beatrice' are still found in many American gardens. Pallida was so named because it was thought to be a pale form of *Iris germanica*, which, though it has given its name to the whole race of tall bearded irises, has not been involved in their breeding, is not native to Germany and—at least in the form usually seen—is not a species but a hybrid and probably of natural origin.

The other species, *Iris variegata*, from the more northern European range of bearded irises, is winter-dormant and exceptionally hardy. Most of our modern yellow tall bearded irises have been developed from this species.

Toward the close of the nineteenth century, Sir Michael Foster, a noted English physician who for some years had collected iris species from far-away places via missionaries and world travelers, imported from Syria and Asia Minor several tetraploid tall bearded species. These included *Iris cypriana,* the huge *I. mesopotamica, I. trojana, I. kashmiriana,* and also the hybrid, 'Amas'. That was the end of the beginning.

Heretofore, all new iris varieties had come from collected seed. Now hand-pollinated crosses began to supersede bee-crosses. The newly discovered tetraploid species were vigorous, large-flowered, well-branched, and much taller than the old diploid species. They produced seedlings that, in comparison to diploid seedlings, were spectacular. Some of these, named and introduced early in the twentieth century, were the original modern tall bearded varieties, forerunners—and ancestors—of today's magnificent irises. Sir Michael Foster raised the pale lavender 'Caterina' from crossing *Iris cypriana* and *I. pallida.* 'Kashmir White' came from the white *I. kashmiriana* crossed with an unknown species, possibly *I. pallida.*

The two men whom Foster greatly influenced were A. J. Bliss and W. R. Dykes. During World War I, Bliss produced the variety 'Dominion', the first big iris with velvety falls; Dykes created the first completely yellow tall bearded variety, given the name 'W. R. Dykes' by his widow.

Around 1905, the United States began to enter the field of iris breeding. Bertrand Farr in Pennsylvania imported large numbers of tall bearded varieties from England and France and produced many seedlings, notably 'Juniata', 'Quaker Lady', and 'Mildred Presby'. In 1915 his seedlings received first prize at the San Francisco Exposition.

At the same time in Massachusetts, Miss Grace Sturtevant was breeding beautiful diploids from varieties that she imported. From the French 'Oriflamme', she produced the blue-and-white plicata 'True Charm', a charming little iris which still exists in several historical collections, including that at Presby Gardens in Montclair, New Jersey.

The year 1920 saw the formation of the American Iris Society, with John A. Wister of Swarthmore, Pennsylvania, as its first president. The original membership of less than two hundred has now risen to over five thousand. The British Iris Society was founded two years later.

Since then, the number of important breeders and the rate of introductions has increased rapidly. The most recent *Check-List* by the American Iris Society, 1949-1959, includes approximately

5600 new varieties of all kinds registered during that decade from all over the world. Most of the registrations are of the tall beardeds, and the majority of registrants are from the United States.

CHARACTERISTICS OF A SUPERIOR VARIETY

For the majority who specialize in irises, today's standard tall bearded varieties offer all of heaven—and small wonder. Especially in the United States during the past quarter of a century, advances in the size and substance, texture and form of the flower, and the diversity and purity of color have been phenomenal. Muddy colors and ugly haft markings have been eliminated. Standards are strongly arched or firmly domed; falls are extremely wide at the haft and proudly held, flaring in varying degrees. Petal edges are often ruffled or laced.

The English breeders are more concerned than we are with vigor of plant, strength of stem, placement of branches, and number of buds; they attach less importance to enormous flower size and prefer tailored or slightly ruffled flowers. A few new American varieties are top-branched, with the flowers crowded together at the top of the stalk, but there is evidence that American hybridizers are taking a long look at the stems, at their sturdiness, and at the branching of the plant they have brought to such perfection of flower.

During the season of tall bearded bloom, these queens of the iris world seem to me also to be the fairest of all irises, though I wander through one iris heaven after another from the beginning of March through July. The June display of tall beardeds in a specialist's garden which may contain as many as a thousand varieties (no self-respecting iris fancier grows fewer than, say, 300) is spectacular.

Iris specialists may coddle a few unusually beautiful but slightly miffy varieties if they like, but for the average gardener the iris must above all be a good garden flower, a plant suited to a mixed border. It must be sufficiently vigorous in growth and increase to survive some neglect. It must be resistant to disease and bloom freely and dependably each year on stems strong enough to stay upright in wind and rain. To prolong the season, flowers should open a few at a time rather than all at once in a brief glory; to prolong it further, there should be several buds in each socket. Individual blossoms should be rain-resistant and remain in good condition for several days. The type of branching and the placement of buds are not quite so important for garden flowers; a top-branched variety, for instance, with flowers of a good clear color (which are not crowded together so their form is lost) and with strong stems and general vigor is desirable for mass effect in gardens.

VARIETIES FOR GENERAL USE

Selecting a few varieties from the several thousand available today is not easy. The annual A.I.S. awards are helpful, though an award iris is not always a satisfactory garden variety. There has been some tendency among judges of the American Iris Society to give awards to varieties that show new and unusual features in the flower even though plants lack one or more valuable garden qualities.

These short lists include only those older and less expensive varieties (none cost more than one dollar) that I rate as satisfactory *garden* irises, either from having grown them in my own garden or having observed them in other gardens in this area.

Pinks and Violets

The two best tall beardeds for garden use today are easy to name: 'Violet Harmony', 1957 Dykes medalist, and the salmon-pink 'Happy Birthday'. Both are faultless. Other good pinks include the smaller-flowered and more intensely colored 'June Bride' and 'Helen Louise', the coral 'May Hall' and the buff-pink 'Palomino'. 'First Violet', another Dykes winner, is my second choice among violets. In the orchid-pink group, 'Crispette' and 'May Magic' are excellent.

Blue and Black

The old 'Great Lakes' (Dykes Medal 1942) is still a good blue iris, though no longer generally listed in catalogues. So are 'Chivalry' and 'Blue Rhythm' (both Dykes medalists), 'Praiseworthy', 'South Pacific' and 'Seafarer'—all in the medium-blue range; and 'Blue Sapphire' (Dykes), 'Celestial Blue' and the exquisite satiny 'Rehobeth' among light blues. My favorite light-to-medium blue is 'Sierra Skies'. The dark blue 'Midnight Blue'—a wonderful iris, indispensable in garden design—stands alone in the low-price group. Though the best inexpensive "black" tall bearded iris is 'Black Taffeta', the taller 'Black Hills' is also good; and so, still, is the old 'Sable'.

White, Cream, Light and Deep Yellow

All these are of high quality: the white 'Cliffs of Dover,' 'Tranquillity' (a tailored variety), 'White Sprite' and 'Snow Goddess'; the creamy 'Starshine,' 'Bellerive,' white-and-yellow 'Patrician,' flashy yellow-and-white 'Golden Garland,' lemon-and-white 'Butterhorn' (my favorite inexpensive yellow); the early-flowering lime-toned light yellow 'Limelight'; and the deeper yellow 'Full Reward', 'Golden Hawk', 'Golden Sunshine', 'Solid Gold', and 'Zantha'.

Red

Among inexpensive dark red irises, my choices are still 'Solid Mahogany' (a brown-red), 'Ranger', and 'Ebony Echo'. The old rosy-red 'Garden Flame' is a most desirable garden iris, vigorous and beautiful—hard to find now but worth a search.

More extensive lists are given in the next chapter.

BORDER BEARDED IRISES

Standard tall bearded irises must, by definition, be at least twenty-eight inches tall. In the past, the heights of some excellent seedlings were stretched a bit by the hybridizer in order to qualify them for registration as tall bearded. 'Black Forest', a perfectly beautiful little twenty-four-inch satiny blue-black variety, now classed as a border iris, was one of these. No one could blame the hybridizer for such a slight exaggeration, since there was no alternative classification.

That problem has now been solved by the creation of a new classification for "tall" bearded irises that are under twenty-eight inches: the border bearded irises. This group is properly classified as median bearded. They are sometimes called "bantams," a term that perfectly describes the better ones. They should have smaller flowers and more slender stems than the tall beardeds, and I myself judge new varieties eligible for A.I.S. awards on this basis. Some new border introductions have flowers that are, from a judge's point of view, too large for the height of the stem. 'Summer Sunset' and 'Blue Flute' are such varieties; they could not be called bantams. And some varieties, such as 'Tulare', have stems a little too thick for the size of the flower. From a gardener's point of view, these are minor faults—if, indeed, they can be called faults at all.

The varieties named are beautiful and vigorous, acceptable in any garden.

For the small garden these engaging flowers are a better choice than tall bearded irises, since they give the same effect in less space. However, the daintier varieties in this class should not be used to face down the tall beardeds. Each spoils the other—the borders make the talls seem gross Amazons; the talls make the smaller border varieties seem depauperate.

Fitting perfectly into the border iris class are some of the older diploid "tall" beardeds, such as 'Pink Ruffles', orchid 'Fluff', the brilliant variegata 'Gaucho', white 'Columbine', and the hybrid 'Bluet' (*I. pallida dalmatica* × *I. cengialtii*) with charming small blue flowers. The collected tetraploid 'Amas,' mentioned before, is now classed as a border iris.

Though border irises were at first accidental achievements, the present emphasis on smaller gardens has caused hybridizers to make deliberate efforts to produce smaller scaled irises in the full color range of the standard tall beardeds—and with the same advances in form and in such imponderables as charm and personality. The number of garden desirables increases annually.

Winners of the annual Knowlton award for the best border iris were 'Frenchi', 1961; 'Jungle Shadows', 1962; 'Fairy Jewels', 1963; and 'Tulare', 1964.

'Frenchi' is a rose-violet bitone with orange-tangerine beard. 'Jungle Shadows' is an exotic blend which is fascinating at close range—gray-blue-brown with a dark beard. 'Fairy Jewels' is a sparkling white, narrowly bordered and bearded in gold. 'Tulare' is admired by everyone who sees it for its beautifully formed, bright yellow, ruffled flowers accented by an orange-apricot beard. An excellent new variety is the vivid 'Robby' with rose-violet standards edged in brown, and rose-brown falls edged in violet.

Here is a list of new and old, expensive to inexpensive (starred), diploid and tetraploid varieties.

RECOMMENDED LIST OF BORDER IRISES

Bayadere, brown
Black Forest, blue-black*
Bluet, blue*
Blue Flute
Chocoleto, brown*
Echoette, white *

Fairy Jewels, white-and-gold
Frenchi, rose-violet
Glacier Bay, white-and-blue
Jungle Shadows, gray-and-brown
Lady Kay, orchid
Little Dude, blue

Little Reb, plicata
Little Sir Echo, white*
Pagoda, pink
Pinata, violet-and-buff*
Pink Ruffles, orchid-pink*
Priscilla, white *

Robby, rose-violet
Summer Sunset, apricot
Tulare, golden yellow
Yellow Dresden*
Timmie Too, deep violet

REBLOOMING IRISES

Many modern varieties of tall bearded irises rebloom in California but not in colder regions. The reverse, also, is sometimes true. Some dwarf bearded varieties and older types of intermediates, as 'Black Magic', 'Golden Bow', and 'Zua' occasionally throw up a few bloomstalks in my autumn garden. I have never paid particular attention to this phenomen other than to enjoy it when it occurred. Neither, apparently, had anyone else except Dr. Percy Brown in Massachusetts who has worked for many years to produce rebloomers.

All at once, a few years ago, keen interest in this type of breeding sprang up and an interesting little publication, *The Reblooming Iris Reporter*, edited by Edwin Rundlett of Staten Island, New York, was born in January 1962. Dr. William McGarvey of Oswego, New York, has had quick success in his aim to create reblooming varieties which will flower for exhibition on a given date, that of the New York State Fair the first week of September.

A photograph of the yellow rebloomer 'Polar Flame' created by Dr. Raymond Smith shows good branching and an acceptably shapely flower with smooth hafts. Dr. Smith has reblooming pink seedlings in his Indiana garden. Though Dr. McGarvey thinks it will be years before the average gardener will fail to be surprised at seeing irises blooming in an autumn garden, I predict that it will not be many years before, surprised or not, he finds them there.

The yellow 'Double Date', 'Polar Flame', and 'Fall Primrose' top Dr. McGarvey's list of reliable attractive rebloomers for northern New York. Red may be obtained through 'Potawatomi' and 'Summer Red.' 'Summer Whitewings' (white), 'Summer Blue', and the pink 'Beau Catcher' are all reliable and early enough in their second period of bloom to provide a good display before frost.

A problem in recommending reblooming varieties is that those that are proven rebloomers in one or more climates in the United States may not rebloom in other parts of the country. Here are some notes from a list in the January 1962 *Reblooming Iris Reporter* of varieties suggested for trial in various regions: 'Autumn Twilight' for southern New York, New Jersey, Ohio, northern Alabama, northeast Texas, Sacramento Valley. 'Fall Primrose' for southern New York, New Jersey, Ohio, northeast Texas. 'September Sparkler' for southern New York, New Jersey, northeast Texas. 'Happy Birthday', 'Snow Goddess', 'Savage', and 'Lady Mohr' are among varieties suggested for southern California where "those most in favor start in December or January and continue into May or June."

Two recent tall bearded rebloomers bred in southern New York State are 'Renaissance' (Cassebeer 1964) and 'Violet Virgo' (Rundlett 1964). 'Renaissance' produces large, well-formed, bronze-tan flowers again in August. 'Violet Virgo' is a white-ground plicata with violet standards and white falls with violet stitching. On Staten Island, it reblooms in October.

While reblooming irises give some second-season bloom, even if neglected, they respond to extra attention; a light application of fertilizer following first bloom and water during summer dry periods result in increased fall bloom.

4

Patterns and Colors
of Tall Bearded Irises

In the middle of the nineteenth century, Christina Rossetti could describe iris color and pattern in two lines:

> Blue Flags, yellow Flags, Flags all freckled,
> Which will you take? Yellow, blue, speckled?

Today, the poet would have to write a very long poem indeed to list all the patterns, colors, shades, tints, and hues that exist in modern "flags."

Classifying varieties as to pattern and color is complicated. I have followed the *1963 Color Classification of the American Iris Society*. There are five major categories of color patterns:

1. *Self*, all one color
2. *Plicata*, stitched with a second color
3. *Bicolor*, standards one color, falls another
4. *Bitone*, standards and falls two values of one color
5. *Blend*, two or more colors mixed

These over-simplified definitions are explained for each category. Out of the many hundreds available I will name a few newer varieties that are well suited to the Northeast and also give a short list of recommended varieties. Some of those described are still too expensive to recommend and some of the inexpensive recommended varieties are not described. Not all those listed are award winners; excellent garden irises are sometimes overlooked by judges.

THE SELFS

Selfs have standards and falls of the same color tone. In the complete absence of a secondary color, the flower is known as a *pure self*. Varieties with markings of another color in the heart of the flower, on the shoulders or edges of the falls or standards, or on the falls as blazes, thumb prints, or lines are classed as selfs with subordinate color markings—provided the second color covers less than half the fall surface. For example, the arilbred 'Striped Butterfly', a pale blue self with a design of darker blue veining on the falls, is classed as a pale blue self with conspicuous markings. 'Emma Cook', a new tall bearded with white as the basic color but with a narrow band of violet around the margin of the falls, is classed as a white self with tint of violet. The self-colored iris is the most popular, most varied, and most effective for the mixed or the all-iris border.

White

'Henry Shaw' and its pollen parent, 'Irish Linen', are my favorites among today's white irises. The vigorous 'Henry Shaw' bears perfect, heavily fluted, large white flowers on well-branched stalks. The older and less expensive 'Irish Linen', also has ruffled flowers of pure glistening white, bearded in pale lemon, and well placed on the stalk. The new white selfs sparkle frostily, reflecting considerable light—or they are as smooth, rich, and cool as carved white jade. There are so many fine whites today that it is difficult to list only a dozen, each as beautiful as its name.

RECOMMENDED WHITE SELFS

Celestial Snow	Immortal Hour
Christmas Angel	Irish Linen
Cliffs of Dover	My Alana
Curl'd Cloud	Poet's Dream
Helen Hayes	Snow Goddess
Henry Shaw	The Citadel

Cream

The old cream-colored 'Amandine', attractive and vigorous but lacking substance, is still popular because there are few low-priced varieties in cream or pale yellow, and these are a necessity in the

4 *Left* FAIR LUZON
Bright pink with luxuriant cerise beard and cupped standards. For middle of the border.   Hamblen.

5 *Right* MY ALANA
Tall flaring white with fluted petals and many buds.
S. Jensen.

6 *Left* HENRY SHAW
White-bearded pure white,
heavy ruffled flowers.
C. Benson. A.M., 1961.

7 *Right* FIFTH AVENUE
Lace-edged violet bitone with
amber hafts and orange beard.
Medium height.
Hamblin. Judges' Choice,
1964.

garden. 'Largesse', 'Irma Melrose' and 'Ivory Satin' stand almost alone.

Recent breeding in this color range has produced 'Cream Crest', smooth and ruffled; 'Utah Cream'; and 'Speak Softly', a waxy ivory with peach-colored beard. 'Country Cream' has ruffled, wide-petaled flowers on tall stalks. The well-branched and ruffled 'Flaring Ivory' gives a cream effect, as do 'Sweetheart's Folly', 'Patrician's Sweetheart', and other white and light yellow combinations.

RECOMMENDED CREAM SELFS

Country Cream	Paleface
Cream Crest	Sweetheart's Folly
Crinkled Ivory	Soaring Kite

Light to Dark Yellow

The green-toned and lightly ruffled 'Waxing Moon' and the yellow 'Cool Comfort' are the loveliest of the light yellows. Lacing is especially attractive on yellows, imparting a light-hearted air to the flowers. The recently introduced 'Golden Years' has white and golden flowers edged with lace.

Hybridizers, trying for green-flowered irises, have produced a number of attractive varieties in unusual tones. 'Woodland Sprite', a pale greenish yellow with a blue-tipped violet beard, was my favorite among the so-called "green" irises until I saw 'Wayward Wind'. It isn't yellow, but it isn't brown either, so it may as well stand as yellow. The many large flowers, gently waved and flaring, are a burnished greenish tan. Two new ones in the green class are 'Emerald Fountain' and 'Green Quest'. The first produces lace-edged flowers of a blended greenish yellow with a faint blue tinge in the falls, and a dull gold beard. I don't know how vigorous it is, but it is fascinating. 'Green Quest' has flaring ruffled flowers of greenish primrose; this one can take wind and hot sun.

'Golden Masterpiece' is the current favorite among golden yellows. The cream blaze on the wide flaring falls lightens the effect. Best of the new dark yellows are the lace-edged 'Bravado', 'Gold Piece', and the laced, deep gold variety 'Rainbow Gold'.

RECOMMENDED LIGHT YELLOW SELFS

Cool Comfort	Sunnydale
Golden Anniversary	Waxing Moon

RECOMMENDED DARK YELLOWS

Bravado	Gold Piece
Bright Forecast	Golden Masterpiece
Front Page	

Buff to Brown and Red

Where does yellow stop and brown begin? It's hard to tell with these chrysanthemum colors. "Butterscotch Kiss' is a beige-toned yellow with lace edges—an excellent garden iris. It grows well but it fades in hot sun, so plant where it receives light shade for the hottest part of the day. The darker lacy 'Caribou Trail', a medium golden brown, is of equal excellence and does not fade. 'Argus Pheasant' (Dykes 1952) is still one of the desirable golden browns.

Among medium browns, 'Dark Chocolate', though flowers are marked at the haft, is my favorite inexpensive variety for gardens. I don't know another brown variety so generally useful, unless it is the English 'Tarn Hows' with flowers of tobacco brown perfectly placed on a fine stalk (English Dykes Medal 1958).

A group of brown blends—described as brass, copper, and bronze —have a wonderful burnished metallic finish. This group includes 'Bronze Bell', 'Olympic Torch', and the newer 'Brazilia' and 'Doctor K'.

RECOMMENDED BUFFS TO BROWNS

Brass Accents	Carmela
Bronze Armor	Dark Chocolate
Bronze Bell	Millionaire
Butterscotch Kiss	Olympic Torch

And where does brown stop and red begin? Is 'Carnton', a blend of cardinal and copper, red? Or is it bright brown? The garden effect is brilliant red.

Red hues of high saturation and brilliance—vermilion and scarlet

—have not yet appeared. Most red irises are purple-reds or brown-reds and blue-reds, such as Venetian and crimson; or orange-reds, such as cardinal. The darker reds are beautiful beyond compare, but the flowers of some varieties fade in sun or have haft markings that detract from their beauty; many of them increase slowly, and some have inadequate branching and few buds. Gardeners who love rich velvety or satiny red flowers will continue to plant red irises and ignore their numerous faults.

'Bang' is a bold and vibrant brown-red with good branching; 'Captain Gallant', a dark red with wide falls free of haft markings and with excellent branching, won the 1963 cup for the best red iris.

Exciting to me are the varieties 'Jungle Fires' (best red, 1964) a smooth and silken hot-red blend, and 'Velvet Robe', a velvety mahogany-red, gold-bearded self. The bright chestnut-red 'Barbizon' is tall for a red iris; the brilliant light-garnet 'Ahoy', with smaller flowers on well branched stalks, is excellent for gardens.

RECOMMENDED REDS

Ahoy	Jungle Fires
Bang	Main Event
Carnton	Tall Chief
Captain Gallant	Tomeco
Garnet Royal	Velvet Robe

Pink, Apricot and Orange

To gardeners whose idea of pink irises stems from the old orchid-pink diploids such as 'Pink Opal' and 'Pink Satin', the modern tangerine-bearded pinks will be a surprise. As with other plants in which pink is bred from yellow varieties, the yellow influence is still discernible in many of these irises that produce such a dazzling garden show. Two of the tallest pink varieties—and my choice for the back of the border—are 'Spring Charm' and 'Garden Party'.

There are, as yet, comparatively few true pinks. 'June Meredith' was the first and is the most famous. 'Fairy Fable' is new with smooth ruffled flowers shading from deeper to pale pink; but the finest of all true pink irises is 'Esther Fay'—even the beard of Esther Fay is a deep true pink. 'Fair Luzon' has smaller laced flowers of deep pink with a cerise beard.

'One Desire' shows a faint blue tone but this somehow makes

it seem pinker. The new orchid-pinks are a far cry from the old diploids. 'Pretty Carol', 'Mauve Mink', 'Lovely Diana', and the very crimped and laced 'Crinkled Beauty are all beautiful as well as vigorous irises.

Rose-toned pinks include 'Mary Randall' (Dykes 1954); the new 'Rose Flame'—brilliant in a color of great carrying power; 'La Rosita'; and 'Rose Hermosa', with charming flowers of delicate rose-pink.

RECOMMENDED PINKS

Fleeta	Pink Fulfillment
Garden Party	Pretty Carol
Lynn Hall	Rose Flame
Mary Randall	Spring Charm

'Orange Parade' is the first true orange—a radiant flower and an important accomplishment. Orange and apricot hues overlap in most of these new varieties. 'Apricot Lustre' is the deepest in color, 'Chinese Coral' the clearest and most dazzling, with the most extravagant beard.

RECOMMENDED APRICOTS AND ORANGE TONES

Apricot Dancer	Magnet
Apricot Lustre	Orange Crush
Glittering Amber	Orange Frills

Light, Medium and Dark Blue

Blue bearded 'Marriott' is an appealing pale, satiny blue. 'Sparkling Waters' is bright pale blue, lighter around the lemon beard— very different from the serene, powder-blue 'Eleanor's Pride' (Dykes 1961). 'Patterdale' (English Dykes Medal 1961) is marvelously branched and vigorous with smooth, light blue flowers.

Top ranking medium blues include the late-flowering, sea-blue 'Pacific Panorama' and 'Jean Sibelius,' an unsual steel-blue of exceptionally smooth texture.

Dark blue irises give an illusion of rich depth to the garden picture. 'Allegiance' (Dykes Medal 1964) is superb—a navy-blue self with velvety falls; the new 'Blue Raven' is slightly brighter in tone but still deep blue. 'Blue Baron' displays its large, ruffled, deep blue-violet flowers with a wonderful type of branching inherited from the bearded species *Iris aphylla*.

RECOMMENDED BLUES

Allegiance	Jean Sibelius
Blue Raven	Marriott
Demetria	Pacific Panorama
Eleanor's Pride	Melissa
Fox Grapes	Sparkling Waters

Violet, Orchid and Black

From blues, the tall bearded iris colors shift to blue-violets. 'Polka Time', is a stately wide-petaled and ruffled variety with a long flowering period. The velvet-falled 'Royal Violet' and the darker-toned 'Indiglow' are also blue-violet. The blue-bearded 'Violet Hills' is true violet. Among red-violets, the huge blue-bearded 'Jersey Beauty' is my first choice.

RECCOMMENDED VIOLETS

Indiglow	Polka Time
Jersey Beauty	Violet Hills

In the orchid and lilac class, my favorites are the vibrant 'Amethyst Flame', Dykes Medal 1963, and the newer 'Lilac Festival'.

RECOMMENDED ORCHIDS AND LILACS

Alpine Rose	Hope Divine
Amethyst Flame	Lilac Festival
Dave's Orchid	Orchid Jewel

Out of the red-black 'Sable Night' (Dykes 1955) has come another superior red-black—the sooty 'Edenite', with falls curving in to form a rounder flower. The stately 'Black Swan' grows vigorously and bears its flowers on tall, erect, well-branched stems. And what flowers! Black with only a hint of red; enormous and perfectly formed, with flaring, moderately ruffled, velvet falls.

RECOMMENDED BLACKS

Black Onyx	Edenite
Black Swan	La Negriflor
Early Dusk	Licorice Stick

PLICATAS

The *plicata* pattern is said to have originated as a mutation, probably from *Iris pallida*. These are the "freckled" irises. Plicatas are white or yellow, dotted, feathered, flaked, mottled, or stippled with a second color.

Fancies are plicata patterns gone wild. 'Gene Wild', intricately netted in rose-red on cream, and its even more richly hued child, 'Ankara', are typical of the fancy plicata pattern.

The most unusual examples of a new trend in the plicata pattern are the sparingly stippled white-and-medium-blue plicatas, 'Moongate' and 'Tea Apron'. In both, the color is concentrated in the style arms and crests.

'Chinquapin' is so heavily marked in light golden brown that the effect from a distance is of a deep beige self. 'Memphis Lass' is a much ruffled variety with standards of almost solid rose and falls of stippled burgundy.

Black-and-white plicatas such as 'Dot and Dash' are highly regarded, as is 'Rococo', with fluted standards and falls, both bordered in violet-blue.

Among yellow-ground plicatas are the cream and brown 'Mocha Polka', 'Golden Spice', and the cream and brown English variety 'Benton Susan'. 'Ankara' and 'Glowing Amber' are true fancies, with yellow grounds.

RECOMMENDED PLICATAS

Azurite	Golden Spice
Caroline Jane	Mocha Polka
Chinquapin	Memphis Lass
Dot and Dash	Tahola

BICOLORS

The *bicolor* iris pattern, with standards of one color and falls of another, usually darker, color, varies from the subtle to the sensational. It includes the *amoena* and *variegata* patterns, and a scattering of varieties in other color combinations. The American Iris Society Color Classification makes a nice distinction in its definition of the term *bicolor*—those varieties in which the second color extends over more than one-half the area of the fall. (If the second color covers less than half the fall area, the variety is classed as a *self*.)

The *amoena* pattern, in the old diploids and early tetraploids such as 'Wabash', always meant white standards and purple falls. This pattern now includes falls of clear yellow, and strong medium blues as 'Miss Indiana', with beginnings in pink and greenish-brown amoenas, and reverse amoenas with colored standards and white falls. Purple amoenas are effective in gardens. Desirable varieties are 'Bright Hour ' and 'Elizabeth Noble'.

Because of unusual problems in amoena breeding very few varieties were produced until Paul Cook began to work on the problem. Mr. Cook tried an entirely different approach involving the use of a dwarf species. His methods were so successful that in 1962 his medium-blue amoena 'Whole Cloth' won the Dykes Medal. It has already been superseded by his 'Miss Indiana'.

'Baby's Bonnet', the first pink amoena, has pale salmon-pink falls; the falls of 'Pin Up Girl' are a blend of apricot and pink. Both varieties are bearded. 'Panay' has falls of an off-yellow which some consider greenish and some, brown.

Technically a reverse blue amoena is the "white" 'Arctic Skies', with standards that open pale blue but change to white, matching the falls. Other reverse amoenas are 'Wide World' and its new seedling, 'Blue Fantasy'.

RECOMMENDED AMOENAS

Bright Hour	Panay
Elizabeth Noble	Soft Answer
Flame Kiss	Miss Indiana
Gaylord	Wide World
Mystic Melody	

The bold *variegata* pattern of contrasting yellow standards and purple, red, or brown velvety falls is not popular because these irises are hard to place in a garden. Nevertheless, variegatas are as gay as the similarly patterned little Mexican marigolds.

The unusual 'Pretender' is my favorite variegata with falls almost navy blue; it perfectly accents a blue-and-yellow garden. 'Nashborough' is probably the best of the typical variegatas; and the variant, 'On Parade', has standards of a sort of golden tan and nearly red falls. The newer 'Kahili' shows more contrast with beautifully formed flowers in pale gold and red.

RECOMMENDED VARIEGATAS

Bold Contrast	On Parade
Fire Chief	Nashborough
Kahili	Pretender

BITONES

The bitones differ from bicolors in having standards and falls of two values of one color. The classic *bitone* pattern is that of the *neglecta*, with lavender or light blue standards and dark purple or blue-purple falls, as in the familiar old 'Amigo'. Current in this lovely pattern are 'Helen Collingwood', with very pale lavender-blue standards and deep violet purple falls; 'Braithwaite', an English variety with a narrow lavender edge around the dark falls; my favorite the ruffled 'Shiloh'; and the new 'Toll Gate', in which the pattern is varied by pale yellow hafts.

Bitones in pastel colors include the large and strikingly beautiful 'Melodrama', with broad full-petaled flowers, tinted pale blue-violet in the standards and deep lilac in the falls. 'Arcady' (English Dykes 1962) is a pale blue version of the reverse bitone pattern.

RECOMMENDED BITONES

Braithwaite	Shiloh
Helen Collingwood	Toll Gate
Melodrama	

BLENDS

The *blend* or *polychrome*, one of the most delightful patterns in irises, results from the mixture or infusion of two or more colors in the same parts of the flower.

When a darker color overlies or veils a lighter base color, a smoky blend results. 'Rum Jungle', introduced in 1963, with a reddish-copper base, is smoothly overlaid with a darker, almost sooty color. 'Smoke Mist' is more delicately toned with a mauve shadow veiling the apricot base color.

'Lula Marguerite' is most popular of the delicate, iridescent blends; it is a pale blue, merged and edged with pale gold. There are gay polychromes too and sultry rich types—'Jungle Bird' is a blend of rose, violet and claret; 'Hindu Wand' is a real polychrome, a mixture of yellow, buff, brown and chartreuse; 'Watermelon' is an excellent garden variety in a bright pink and greenish-lemon combination. 'Melbreak', an English variety, is rose pink and warm brown. 'Allaglow' is a bright golden-brown blend with a tiny blue blaze.

Various types of blends, from delicate to deep, are included in the recommended list.

RECOMMENDED BLENDS

Allaglow	Lula Marguerite
Brigadoon	Melbreak
Hindu Wand	Rose Garland
Holy Smoke	Smoke Mist
Jungle Bird	

THE BEARD EMERGES

Yellow beards are commonly found on all colors of tall bearded irises, though a few older dark blue and purple varieties had blue beards. The advent of the flamingo-pink irises brought tangerine beards and, to iris-breeders, so keen an interest in beard colors that the development of vari-colored beards has progressed rapidly.

First, the tangerine-colored beard was deepened into nasturtium-red, then softened to almost pure pink. Then came red-bearded white varieties; 'Frost and Flame' was the first really good one—it will be an excellent garden variety for years to come—but improvements were quickly achieved. The best that I have seen to date is 'Arctic Flame,' an even whiter flower with a larger and more brilliant beard.

'Herald Angel' is a new velvety white with greenish hafts. With a white or lemon beard it would be a pleasant iris—but it has a red beard, and it's spectacular! A light yellow iris with a self-colored beard, such as 'Waxing Moon', is cool and serene; substitute a bright orange beard, as in the popular 'Techny Chimes', and the whole flower is enhanced. 'Flame Kiss' is a yellow amoena (listed under bicolors) with a glowing tangerine beard.

After achieving red-bearded white irises, breeders sought to ornament blue varieties with red beards. The ruffled and laced 'Rippling Waters', a blend of blue and orchid, has a tangerine beard. The older 'Firenze' and 'Enchanted Violet', both red-bearded light violets, were among the first to exhibit this combination. Now breeders, casting about for new combinations, are trying for red beards on brown irises.

Blue beards in tall bearded irises are another gift from the species *Iris aphylla*. 'Blue Crest' has been heralded as a blue-bearded white. I was most disappointed to find this beard, though undeniably blue, of low brilliance. 'Woodland Sprite', a pale greenish yellow, mentioned earlier, is bearded in violet tipped with blue. 'Charmed Land' has an unusual orchid-blue beard on palest orchid flowers.

Many new black irises are noted for handsome black or bronze beards; and an odd blue blend, 'Exotic Blue', is bearded in dark blue, tipped bronze-gold. Dark beards may eventually grace white and pastel irises.

RECOMMENDED VARIETIES WITH UNUSUAL BEARDS

Blue Crest	Exotic Blue
Charmed Land	Frost and Flame
Cloud Dancer	My Happiness
Enchanted Violet	Techny Chimes

5

Culture of Tall Bearded Irises

Any gardener can grow tall bearded irises of fair quality. The plants adjust themselves to most soils, from heavy clay to almost pure sand, and they endure a higher degree of acidity than was formerly supposed. The gardener who is willing to give special attention will be rewarded with abundant bloom and magnificent flowers.

The same cultural fundamentals of good drainage, adequate moisture, fertile soil well supplied with humus, and clean cultivation that apply to other garden plants apply also to irises. However, some gardeners whose only experience in growing irises has been with the self-sufficient old diploids may need to be reminded that modern tetraploid hybrids require as much care for top performance as other desirable perennials. The old diploids can survive and produce flowers under conditions of almost total neglect; the modern hybrids may survive such conditions, but very few of them will bloom.

The "sun and good drainage" theme has been stressed so often as the basic requirement of irises that gardeners may take it *too* seriously. Some go to the trouble of constructing raised beds to increase drainage, when the drainage in their ground-level borders is perfectly adequate to prevent accumulation of moisture at the base of plants. Though the bearded iris is a sun plant, it does not relish arid conditions. In their zeal to provide perfect drainage, gardeners may create a situation in which water runs off so fast that in dry summers plants suffer severely. And they suffer hunger as well as drought since their food is held in solution in the soil water.

The same goes for sun. It is a mistaken notion that irises must receive the direct rays of the sun from the time it peeps above the horizon in the morning until it sinks at night. I have even known

46

a few gardeners to go so far as to cut down beautiful trees to provide this uninterrupted sunshine. Actually, many varieties benefit from light shade during the hottest part of the day. This is especially true of some of the red and brown varieties, and a few of the yellow ones, which fade so badly in sun that they look scorched. Given some shade, the same varieties are richly beautiful.

I am not advocating growing bearded irises in woodland—though in part of my garden I do almost that. I am torn between love for irises and love of trees, ferns, and wild flowers. Somehow, I manage to have them all.

CYCLE OF GROWTH AND INCREASE

The key to successful iris culture lies in understanding the growth cycle and thus the basic needs of these plants. Many modern varieties contain enough blood of species native to mild climates to be semi-evergreen—though in the north their life processes are slowed to a minimum during the colder weeks of winter. Active growth, however, starts in earliest spring, and is most rapid shortly before and at the time the bloom-stalks begin to emerge from the leaves. All the energy of the plant, at this stage, is concentrated on the production of leaves and flowers; no new buds appear on the rhizomes. An amazing amount of invisible work goes on within the plant during this period; flower production is an exhausting business for plants, and the iris is no exception. After flowers fade, plants take a vacation. During the resting period, which lasts a month or more, rhizomes ripen. This ripening is important because the rhizome is a food storehouse, and its prime condition is essential to the continued health, even the existence, of the plant.

The wild species produce seed during this period. Modern hybrids set few pods from insect pollination; such pods are a waste of plant energy, and should be removed if they appear. Hybridizers never use first-year plants as pod parents; the production of seed exhausts the plant to a point where it may not be able to form the normal number of new rhizomes.

As soon as plants emerge from their annual rest, new roots begin to form, and tiny new buds show on the young, vigorous mature rhizomes that will produce flowers the following year. Each rhizome produces a bloom-stalk only once, then passes the task on to one or more of the new rhizomes it has produced, and retires to function solely as a food reservoir. Ideally, the number of bloom-stalk-producing rhizomes should double each year, but such perfect

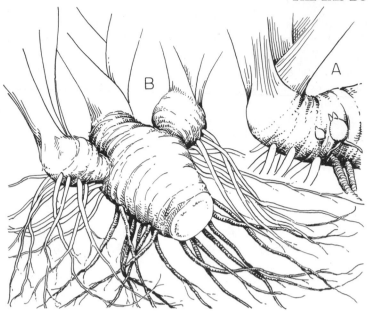

FIGURE 6   IRIS RHIZOME IN SPRING AND FALL. A—Rhizome in spring
after rhizome buds have developed. Bloom stalk will emerge from growing end of central rhizome. B—Rhizome in late summer, showing a new
rhizome bud developing in the axil of a now dead leaf. Old roots are
dark, new ones white.

performance requires perfect care plus good luck with weather.
When for any reason a *healthy* rhizome is unable to form a bloom
point at its appointed time, it keeps on growing, producing new
leaves as it lengthens. The rhythm of vegetative increase is then
upset and, instead of the usual pattern of one or two new rhizomes
branching out from the old leaf axils on each side of the rhizome,
increases may occur in leaf axils along the whole length of such
a rhizome.

These will not be stimulated to produce bloom-stalks, however,
until after the parent rhizome has finally been able to do so; the
natural order is rigidly kept. If the senior rhizome is injured or
becomes diseased, then one or two of the strongest junior rhizomes
will function in its place.

Vegetative growth continues until late fall when heavy frost
brings activity almost to a standstill. I do not know exactly when
the embryonic bloom points—invisible to the naked eye—form;
there have been many conjectures, but no one knows for certain.
I don't believe it matters, because whenever I have had time to

plant and care for them properly I have had 100 per cent bloom from first-year plants, whether the rhizomes had traveled across the continent, had come from a nursery a few miles away, or were transplanted from one spot to another in my own garden.

FEEDING

As soon as we know a plant's timetable, we can figure out when to feed it. It is useless, and may be harmful, to feed a plant during a resting stage. And encouraging growth of soft new tissue by feeding as winter approaches is likely to cause the death of any plant.

Tall bearded irises are heavy feeders and need supplementary supplies of nutrients. The time to apply these booster shots is just before the two periods of intensive production: early spring, and about four weeks after flowering. The harder plants work, the more food they need.

For spring feeding, the amount of fertilizer recommended on the bag may be used; this may come to about a half cup for one large iris clump. For mid-summer feeding, it is safer to use only half that quantity. This should be sprinkled around—but not on— the plants, and watered into the soil with a prolonged spray or a soaker hose. The area should be kept slightly moist for a week or so, to avoid producing a harmful concentration of solution.

The three major foods that plants obtain from the soil are nitrogen, phosphorus, and potassium. The percentages of these elements in commercial fertilizers are listed on the bags, always in the same order. Thus, 5-10-10 fertilizer contains 5 per cent of available nitrogen, 10 per cent phosphorus in the form of phosphoric acid, and 10 per cent potassium in the form of potash. This 5-10-10 fertilizer formula is the one best suited to irises, which need a generous supply of potash. The trace elements—magnesium, iron, manganese, zinc, copper, and boron—also necessary to the growth of green plants, are usually present in soils in sufficient quantities for irises, and need not be added. Should disease-free plants refuse to grow, lose their green color, or turn brown at the leaf tips when all the other conditions for good growth have been provided, then the need of fertilizer containing these trace elements may be indicated.

Nitrogen is present in the air, in the soil, and in all living matter. It is essential for vegetative growth (as differentiated from the production of flowers and seeds) and is found in large quantities in young tissues—new leaves, buds, and tips of shoots. It is constantly being lost from soils, and as constantly replaced—from the air via rain and snow, and within the soil from decomposition of vegetative material by the important soil fungi and bacteria. The nitrogen content of the soil is lowered under cultivation, including the gardener's tidy removal of dead leaves and plants, which in nature return themselves to the earth. In cultivated soil, it must be replaced by inorganic or organic fertilizers, or both. An important reason for loosening top soil from time to time is to let air freely enter the soil; air itself assists in the release of soil nitrogen in a form that plants can use.

Phosphorus is also present in all living cells. It is most necessary in the early stages of plant growth, and is present in large amounts in flowers and seeds. If the supply is deficient, growth stops, roots are stunted, and the maturing of the plant may be delayed. Most of the phosphorus present in the soil is in insoluble forms and it therefore cannot be utilized by growing plants, which can take in nutrients only when these are dissolved in water. The addition of a water-soluble phosphate fertilizer (usually superphosphate) helps the phosphorus already in the soil to change into more soluble forms. The acidity of soil is another important factor; increasing the pH of a very acid soil by liming increases the amount of usable phosphorus. This is highest in nearly neutral soil, in the presence of adequate nitrogen and potassium, and with adequate organic matter from manure and compost. Superphosphate is more available to a plant if it is mixed with a manure.

Potassium is the third essential fertilizing element; it too is found in all living matter. Though it is present in adequate amounts in most soils (except very sandy ones), only a small percentage is in a form (potash) that plants can use. Such plants as potatoes, bulbous plants in general, and both bulbous and rhizomatous irises require large amounts of potash, particularly during periods of rapid growth. Potassium is necessary for a number of complicated physiological functions, and it improves the rigidity of flower stalks.

Wood ashes are a valuable source, containing 4 to 6 per cent of a quick-acting, soluble form of potash. Only ashes that have been kept dry have value; potash leaches out and is lost in rain. I save wood ashes from our fireplace, storing pails of them in the basement until early spring when I dust them over the garden— especially on the bulb and iris beds.

Some forms of the three major elements make soil more acid, some make it more alkaline. The forms that leave an acid residue tend to destroy humus. The safest procedure is to vary the forms used from year to year. For instance, sulfate of ammonia, a source of nitrogen that increases soil acidity, might be used alternately with nitrate of soda that leaves soil more alkaline.

Commercial dried hen manure and sheep manure are both rich in the three essential elements. Horse manure is quickest acting, produces the most heat, and decomposes most rapidly. It should not be used in a fresh state. Gardeners who can obtain this valuable manure should compost it for at least six months before spreading it on the garden. Cow manure is both milder and slower acting. But no manure should ever be permitted to come in contact with iris rhizomes. It should be spread around the clump or along the row, *near but not on* plants.

The value of manures is not entirely in the nutrients they contain. They also contribute large amounts of partly digested vegetable matter (humus), which is of even greater importance in the culture of irises. The higher the percentage of straw and stable litter a manure contains, the better.

LIME

Few gardeners understand the function of calcium, though most of them use it; indeed, it has been used for thousands of years for the growing of crops. As a rule, it is applied in the form of finely ground limestone, though in coastal regions finely ground oyster shells may be a less expensive source. Dolomitic limestone also contains magnesium, one of the essential trace elements.

If, like me, you grew up on a farm you probably will not sprinkle lime on the soil of a growing garden or field, or add it to manure or compost, or apply it every year to the same soil. Though you may not know why you don't do this, there are sound reasons. In the first place, lime is not a fertilizer; in the second place, the effect lasts for several years. Lime should not be mixed with, or applied at the same time as, a commercial fertilizer containing nitrogen unless you don't mind wasting plant food. Lime will cause part of the nitrogen to be released in the form of gas that cannot benefit plants, since it escapes into the air. The same thing happens when it is added to the manure pile or compost heap.

In regions where the basic rock is not limestone, calcium in the soil tends to leach out gradually. The soil becomes too "sour" or acid for many plants—including bearded irises—and the availability of soil nutrients is decreased.

The scale for measuring acidity—or conversely alkalinity—of a soil is expressed in terms of pH value, which generally ranges from 4.0 (very acid) through pH 7 (neutral) to 9.0 (strongly alkaline). Most irises, except Japanese, will grow in soils varying from slightly acid (pH 6) to slightly alkaline (pH 8). You can test the acidity of your soil with a soil-testing kit or send samples to the agricultural agent in your county.

If lime is needed and a new bed is to be prepared, finely ground limestone may be dusted lightly and evenly over the surface of the unturned soil several weeks before spading. When I am re-liming an already planted bed, I sprinkle the limestone around the plants and scratch it in lightly, taking care not to miss any spots. Lime has no lateral action at all—that is, it does not spread out into adjoining soil; therefore, depositing a small heap of lime here and there in the garden is not an adequate method of liming.

Lime also helps to change phosphorus in soil into forms that plants can use. And—by a peculiar and probably entirely physical action—it makes heavy clay soils more porous and, consequently, better drained and aerated. Detailed information can be found in *Soils*, the 1957 Yearbook of Agriculture of the U. S. Department of Agriculture. Though it is primarily for growers of food crops, much of the material is useful to the amateur gardener.

SOIL

That thin layer of the earth's surface that we call soil is a constantly changing complex of solids, liquids, and gases. It contains air, particles of weathered rock, vegetation in all stages of decay, and water, in which plant nutrients are dissolved. The whole complex teems with busy micro-organisms (bacteria and fungi) that are essential to growth.

Irises endure even the two extremes of soil types—heavy clay and sand—but such soils must be modified to produce luxuriant growth and profuse flowering. Clay soils pack and bake hard in dry periods; they become waterlogged and sticky during rain. Enormous amounts of manure, compost, peat moss and sand can be incorporated into clay. It will still be clay, but with what a difference; it will be friable instead of sticky, and excess water will drain away easily. The same treatment (minus the sand) will cure quick-draining sandy soils so they will retain a proper amount of moisture and nourishment.

The ideal soil for irises is loam or clay loam. These soils contain from 20 to 30 per cent clay and up to 50 per cent sand. Soil conditions vary so widely in the United States that you have to learn to understand your own, and how to remedy defects.

When an iris bed is prepared in even moderately fertile loam, the soil should be removed to a depth of ten inches. You can safely mix into the soil at the bottom of the bed all the well-rotted manure (or Driconure, etc.) you can afford. Supplement this with 5-10-10 fertilizer at a rate of about half that given on the bag. (One hundred pounds per acre is equivalent to one pound for an area 10 by 43 feet.) As much as a three-inch layer of compost or of a good grade of peat moss may be added, and the whole mass mixed thoroughly into the bottom soil. Then replace the top soil and let the bed settle for at least a week—preferably two to three weeks—before iris rhizomes are put in place.

PLANTING AND TRANSPLANTING

When rhizomes are ordered for a new bed, it is easy to get delivery on or about a certain date, and so have the bed ready to receive them. When new varieties are added to an established garden, or when old iris clumps need transplanting, spot preparation must be made that involves moving other perennials and a general undesirable upheaval.

In this situation, many gardeners, either because they do not want to change a satisfying garden plan or because it is too hot and they want to go swimming, decide to dig up a clump that needs transplanting and reset it in the same spot, or heave out an old variety and replace it with a better one. This procedure is satisfactory provided you make allowance for two facts of iris life: that irises are heavy feeders and that they deplete a soil in which they are grown continuously.

To prevent or remedy such a condition bring in fresh soil or change your type of fertilizer, or incorporate large amounts of manure and compost or do all these things, depending on how long irises have been grown in the same place. If you do none of them, you can be sure your plants will be inferior.

The best time to divide and reset bearded irises is between the Fourth of July and Labor Day—after roots and rhizomes have begun to develop. Early transplanting, which gives plants more time to establish themselves before winter, is best except in regions so hot and dry that midsummer transplanting is hazardous. If you plan a vacation, delay transplanting until you return since irises need frequent watering for two to three weeks after they are reset.

If plants are moved quickly and carefully without permitting the new roots to dry out, irises may be transplanted up to the middle of September with a good chance of minimum bloom next year.

One summer I saw an iris field of at least a thousand plants that had been moved the previous year between late July and early October. It was a perfect demonstration of the effect of the time of transplanting on bloom. The number of bloom-stalks diminished steadily across the field. In the last section, which was planted between mid-September and early October, plants had survived and were healthy but they had produced no flowers.

After clumps are dug, wash them clean with the hose, and carefully inspect rhizomes for rot and borer damage. Make divisions with a sharp knife. Only healthy single rhizomes showing increase buds, or double rhizomes consisting of a plump older rhizome with two young rhizomes showing strong white feeder roots, should be replanted. If the iris is a prized variety, rhizomes that show soft or spongy areas may sometimes be salvaged by cutting away rotted sections. If a few healthy roots are attached, even a small section of a rhizome will grow and multiply.

If larvae of the iris borer have attacked plants, they will have tunneled into the rhizome by late summer. Extract and kill the larvae and discard damaged rhizomes or cut them back to clean tissue; it depends on the severity of the wounds. It is also a good idea to search for larvae that may already have emerged from the rhizome to pupate in the soil beneath a clump. (Chapter 12 gives detailed information on the iris borer.)

Before rhizomes are reset, cut back leaf-fans to reduce the loss of water from the plant until roots take hold again. When leaves are healthy, I cut off only the top half of the fan. If leaf spot is present, I remove all leaf portions that show evidence of this mildly debilitating disease. As a precaution against disease in general, I immerse all divisions to be reset in a pail of fungicide-antibiotic solution of Captan or Phaltan and Pfizer's Agrimycin 100—prepared as for spray—and let them soak for at least a half hour. I do the same with newly purchased rhizomes, no matter how impeccable the source. Dusting cut surfaces lightly with sulfur is also an excellent safeguard against disease.

To produce good clumps, plant three to seven sections—depending on how quick an effect is desired—of each variety so that *all leaf-fans face in the same direction.* Space them six to eight inches apart in triangular or staggered formation. If you plant them in a circle with all fans facing out, as is sometimes recommended,

8 *Above, left*
Clump of tall bearded iris, thoroughly washed with hose, ready for division.

9 *Above, right*
Gross divisions made and most vigorous rhizomes selected. Can be planted now for quick-forming clumps.

10 *Left* For maximum increase of valuable varieties, cut into single rhizome divisions as shown, leaving old, sound rhizome attached to smallest of the three young rhizomes.

11 *Above, right* Set division on mound of soil in wide shallow hole. Spread out roots as shown. In dry weather, water area around roots before filling hole with soil. Firm soil with feet. Top of rhizome should not be more than one inch below soil surface.

growth will be outward, producing a hollow-centured ring rather than a clump; if fans are planted facing inward, clumps will become confused masses that will need transplanting in a couple of years. Another method of planting is to set rhizomes, all facing in the same direction, in a curved single line either in back or in front of clumps of perennials that flower at iris time. Such an arrangement can be very effective in the garden.

Take care to plant iris divisions *firmly*—with no air pockets beneath the rhizome—and either level with the surrounding soil or on a slight mound or hill, depending on drainage. Beginning gardeners sometimes set a rhizome so carelessly that the leaf-fan may be wiggled around like a loose tooth; I have even seen clumps planted in saucerlike depressions where winter moisture is sure to collect. The old idea of planting rhizomes riding above the soil "like a duck on water" was mistaken and resulted in inferior plants with fewer increases. Rhizomes should be covered completely, but not deeply.

When planting, dig two slanting holes about two inches apart and five inches deep, leaving a shallow ridge of soil between them. Set the rhizome firmly on this saddle of soil to avoid air pockets beneath it. Spread out half the roots into each hole and cover them well. Firm the soil over them, then pull dry soil over the moist areas and around the rhizomes, covering them not more than an inch deep. In dry weather, water occasionally until new growth appears. Irises so planted should give modest bloom the next year and excellent bloom the second year.

MULCHING

Winter heaving of soil, which loosens roots, is a serious threat in regions where alternate freezing and thawing may throw iris plants completely out of the earth. Some growers refuse to winter-mulch, because it is too much trouble or because "irises are hardy plants and should go it alone." I cover all the sunny areas of my garden, where snow melts quickly, with a layer of evergreen boughs —which can be acquired cheaply the day after Christmas. And that is just about the right time to apply a mulch. Salt hay also provides excellent protection. Like evergreen boughs, it must be removed in the spring; unlike them, it can be stored and used again.

The idea of a summer mulch for irises is new. For a long time it was frowned upon, in the belief that such protection, which helps soil hold moisture, would promote rot and prevent rhizomes from maturing. Recently, iris specialists have experimented with mulches of cocoa shells, buckwheat hulls, sawdust, pine needles or peat moss, and have found them beneficial. A summer mulch should circle but not touch the rhizome or the leaf base.

Black paper or plastic, though unsuitable for the flower border, makes a satisfactory weed eliminator in a seedling bed or iris field, where it can be laid between the rows. Buckwheat hulls make the prettiest mulch I have seen. They are odorless, dark brown and look like freshly cultivated soil. Cocoa shells smell like chocolate for several weeks; I would rather smell irises.

If sawdust is used, extra fertilizer high in nitrogen should be spread over the soil first, otherwise the bacteria that work at decomposing the sawdust will draw out nitrogen from the soil—to the detriment of the garden plants. Peat moss, which tends to form a hard water-shedding crust, is the least satisfactory of mulches.

6

The Smaller Bearded Irises

When Francis Bacon wrote of "low flowers, being withal sweet and sightly," he was referring to plants such as primulas and pinks rather than irises, but the phrase perfectly describes the several new races of smaller bearded irises that are being produced, mainly in the United States and England. The breeding in these groups has resulted in such valuable garden varieties that several top-notch breeders of tall beardeds have extended their programs to include the smaller bearded hybrids.

These miniature to middle-sized irises bring colors and forms into the spring garden that have not been seen there before. Their popularity is gaining momentum rapidly as more and more garden-ers discover their charm in combination with early bulbs and perennials. The earliest start into bloom five to six weeks before the tall bearded season begins.

The small size of these irises means that they can be planted with a trowel instead of a shovel. A few rhizomes can be tucked in among other low-growing plants along the front of a small border; in the larger garden they are charming in drifts or masses. Bloom is profuse—one rhizome will produce several bloomstalks —and they come in many colors on erect little stems.

The words "dwarf" and "miniature" mean different things to different gardeners. The American Iris Society, accepting Dykes' fifteen-inch limit for dwarfs, has defined the dwarf beardeds as irises with plants *up to* fifteen inches, and has separated the dwarfs into two classes, according to height:

Miniature dwarf bearded irises are those under ten inches, with flowers two to three inches across, and leaves, usually curved or sickle-shaped, shorter than the bloom-stalks.

Standard dwarf bearded irises are from ten to fifteen inches tall, with leaves nearly as high as the bloom-stalks; the flowers are three to four inches across.

MINIATURE DWARF BEARDED IRISES

Few of the quaint miniature dwarf bearded species are suited to gardens. The smallest are the varying forms of *Iris pumila,* which in my garden cover themselves with bright bloom toward the end of April. They flower in the time of daffodils, and they are most delightful when drifted in front of daffodils clumps. Dykes described them as "extraordinarily floriferous," and he was not exaggerating.

The small nearly stemless flowers are held on long perianth tubes above the dainty three-inch leaf fans. Despite their drollness, they have a charming dignity. Some have a strong vanilla fragrance; others smell like violets. Color range: from palest to medium blue, blue-violet and black; white, cream, and chartreuse; light to deep yellow and mustard tones. A few are selfs, but in most forms the tiny falls are overlaid with a darker spot pattern.

Pumilas do not need a great deal of food but they do exhaust themselves by profuse flowering, and are supposed to be transplanted rather often. I don't transplant them at all, unless I want to create a new picture. Instead, I top-dress annually with rich soil.

The first true pumilas in this country were grown about twenty-five years ago by Robert Schreiner from seeds he had imported from Rumania. His three named clones—blue-violet 'Sulina', reddish 'Nana', and yellow 'Carpathia'—are still used extensively in breeding smaller bearded irises. Before that time, nobody had identified the dwarf species correctly, and all dwarfs were called pumilas. Even now in one important plant catalogue, an assortment of dreary ancient varieties of varying lineage, height, and bloom season are listed under the heading "Pumilas." The only certain way to obtain pumilas or pumila hybrids is to buy them from a specialist.

In the early 1940's, the astute Paul Cook obtained some of Mr. Schreiner's pumila seedlings and built up an excellent series of clones that he did not bother to introduce. He gave a rhizome of his now famous seedling #1546 to Walter Welch, who had been appointed by the president of the A. I. S. to head the newly formed Dwarf Iris Committee. That was the beginning of a new era of remarkable improvement in small irises.

Mr. Welch organized the Dwarf Iris Society about fifteen years ago, and he has developed miniature dwarf irises to their present

12   Cherry Spot.
A miniature dwarf bearded
variety with white stand-
ards and cherry-red falls,
edged white. Blooms May
1st in my garden.
    Welch. Caparne Award,
1960.

13   Angel Eyes.
White with blue "eyes" on
falls. Blooming with
johnny-jump-ups and kauf-
manniana hybrid tulips at
the end of April.
    Jones. Caparne Award,
1961.

state of garden importance. Though he now shares honors with several other hybridizers, he alone was responsible for the foundation work. In 1964, he received the Foster Memorial Plaque.

Here is a brief list of recommended forms:

April Mist, clear light blue with greenish flush at the hafts

April Morn, flax blue, blue beard

Blue Spot, light blue, with violet spot

Spring Joy, lavender with red-purple spot

Red Amethyst, dahlia purple with blue beard

Sulina, blue-violet self

Little Charmer, chartreuse with darker spot

Hanselmayer, pale lemon-yellow self

Barium Gold, orange-bearded deep bright yellow

Slightly later-blooming than pumilas, and more difficult to grow, are the various forms of the miniature *Iris mellita*. The only one that has persisted in my garden is *I. mellita* 'Vandee'. Its honey-beige little flowers are held well above the tiny sickle-shaped leaves by short stems and three-inch perianth tubes. It does well for me in a mixture of sand, loam, and calcite crystals (for poultry) at the edge of a slightly raised sunny border. And I have seen it luxuriating in six inches of pure sand in a child's abandoned sandbox.

Many gardeners when they think of dwarf irises have in mind the dull old purple and yellow chamaeirises of unknown origin which have been grown in European and North American gardens for a century or more. The six-inch, yellow-flowered true species *Iris chamaeiris,* which gets its name from the Greek word for dwarf, is a different plant, native to Italy and southern France. Though it was first described in 1837 by Antonio Bertolini, it is not often cultivated in this country.

Miniature Dwarf Hybrids

Complex breeding has produced a large selection of four- to ten-inch garden hybrids that bloom a week to ten days later than the pure pumilas and carry on to the standard dwarf bearded season. The flowers last longer than those of the pumilas, and are well formed, with flaring, sometimes ruffled, falls. They bloom in my garden at the same time as the peacock tulips and other large hybrids of *Tulipa kaufmanniana.*

To make garden planning easier I have separated my favorites into two groups according to height:

14 My own four-inch seedlings of *Iris pumila* blooming with daffodils and johny-jump-ups in late April.

Four to Six Inches

Angel Eyes, 5 inches—white with bright blue eyes on falls

Bee Wings, 5 inches—canary yellow with brown spots

Black Baby, 6 inches—black purple chamaeiris

Black Top, 5 inches—very dark violet

Blue Frost, 5 inches—pure, light, smooth blue

Cherry Spot, 6 inches—white standards, cherry-red falls

Claire, 5 inches—bright medium blue

Cup and Saucer, 5 inches— mahogany rose

Heart's Content, 5 inches—white standards and blue falls

Sky Caper, 6 inches—sky-blue self

Verigay, 6 inches—yellow standards, red-brown falls

Seven to Nine Inches

Already, 7 inches—glowing purplish red

Blue Doll, 8 inches—lavender-blue bitone

Crispy, 7 inches—dainty white

Curtsy, 9 inches—white standards, lavender falls

Fashion Lady, 8 inches—ruffled orange-yellow

Promise, 7 inches—ruffled mallow pink

Red Gem, 8 inches—velvety deep red

MEDIAN IRISES

The familiar division of bearded irises into the early-blooming dwarfs, those intermediate in height and season, and the tall beardeds was adequate as long as almost all hybridizing was confined to the tall bearded group. The smaller gardens of the 1950's, however, brought demands for smaller plants in general, and new middle-sized irises began to surge out of the seedling patches. The old classification became obsolete almost overnight. Late-blooming dwarfs, too tall for the existing dwarf class, and "tall" beardeds too small for the tall class, were registered and introduced.

The American Iris Society solved the problem by a horticultural reclassification that divided the whole range of bearded irises into six classes according to their use in gardens. The large group of median irises includes the four classes between the less-than-ten-inch miniature dwarfs, and the twenty-eight-inch-and-over tall

15 Stalks of Four Different Types of Smaller Bearded Irises,
Showing Diversity of Branching

Left to right. Brown-eyed Katie, my own fourteen-inch standard dwarf
bearded variety with two terminal flowers and two branches; Promise,
a miniature dwarf bearded with two terminal flowers and no branches;
Kochii, an intermediate hybrid with two terminal buds and three
branches; *Iris aphylla* Dark Violet, with two terminal buds and two
branches, one originating at the rhizome. The second terminal bud in
each is still hidden within the sheathing spathe.

beardeds: (1) standard dwarfs, (2) intermediates, (3) miniature tall beardeds, and (4) the border irises described in Chapter 3.

The Median Iris Society, a section of the A.I.S., was organized about ten years ago by Geddes Douglas of Tennessee, then secretary of the A.I.S., Earl Roberts of Indiana, Edwin Rundlett of New York, Bee Warburton of Massachusetts, and a number of others. In 1963, a total of 126 median iris varieties were introduced. Eight of these were bred in England, where interest in smaller irises is mounting. In addition, the same year, eighty-six new seedlings were named and registered.

Standard Dwarfs

"Une jeune fille en fleur" well describes the artless grace and charm of the ten-to-fifteen-inch standard dwarf bearded hybrids, which have a much wider appeal than the miniature group. In the brief period of their existence, these irises have already become indispensable to the May garden.

Because I breed them myself, my opinion may be thought to lack objectivity. Let me say that I was attracted to this group of irises originally because I could immediately visualize them in my garden. They were the something that had heretofore been missing from the May garden picture of bulbs and perennials.

What sparked this whole revolution in hybridizing? You could say Robert Schreiner started it when he imported those first pumila seeds. Or you could say Paul Cook started it when, in the early 1940's, he crossed one of his blue tall bearded seedlings with pumila. Or when he later suggested to Geddes Douglas in Tennessee (where the tall beardeds bloom at the same time the pumilas do in northern Indiana) that they trade pumilia and tall-bearded pollen by mail. The idea was for Mr. Douglas to use pollen from the four-inch pumilas on tall bearded irises, while Mr. Cook would pollinate the tiny pumila flowers with pollen from the Tennessee tall-beardeds to extend his line of middle-sized hybrids. Mr. Douglas, a hybridizer of tall bearded irises, was game to try it. And he must have been excited when those first seedlings bloomed. There they were; row on row of a totally new (save for Paul Cook's) kind of iris hybrid, neither miniature nor intermediate nor tall, and blooming in a period that had hitherto been barren of irises. Here were fertile hybrids (first crack out of the box), with branched stems bearing three or four shapely flowers in perfect proportion to the size of the

SMALLER BEARDED IRISES

16 *Above,* Moonspinner. Cream and white standard dwarf bearded,
blooming in my seedling patch. 17 *Below, left. Iris mellita* Vandee.
Pale yellow form of this miniature bearded species, showing peaked
standards, extruding style arms and curved leaves. Growing in gritty,
sharply drained soil. 18 *Below, right. Peewee.* A miniature tall
bearded (table) variety showing the small, white, well formed flowers
borne on slim flexuous stalks which stand well above the foliage.

plants. Now gardeners could have bearded irises in continuous bloom from daffodil to peony time.

Mr. Douglas called the new hybrids "lilliputs." Too bad it was not made official, for a more fitting name would be hard to find—and it would be easy for gardeners to distinguish between miniature dwarfs and lilliputs.

In 1951, Mr. Cook introduced four still-famous varieties from his line: 'Greenspot', 'Fairy Flax', 'Baria' and 'Brite'. Starting in 1953, Mr. Douglas introduced a dozen or so high-quality varieties from among his seedlings. The most popular of these are two quite different blues, the pure light-blue 'Small Wonder', and 'Tinkerbell', a lavender-blue with darker flush on the falls; dark blue-violet 'Little Shadow', and more brilliant 'Pagan Midget' with a conspicuous light blue beard; garnet 'Jack of Hearts'; and the bitone 'Picture Yellow'.

The annual Cook-Douglas Award, established in 1959 for the best standard dwarf, was named in honor of these two pioneer hybridizers. Mr. Cook's 'Greenspot', a white with a leaf-green spot on the horizontal falls, won the first award; Mr. Douglas's 'Tinkerbell', the second. Mr. Cook's blue 'Fairy Flax' was the 1961 winner. In 1962 Mrs. Warburton's yellow 'Brassie' won, and in 1963 it was her 'Blue Denim'. The 1964 winner was Mr. Welch's 'Lilli-White'.

The equation *superior tall bearded variety* × *pumila* = *superior* standard dwarf bearded seedling isn't always valid. The first plicata, 'Dale Dennis', was important for breeders rather than gardeners. The leaves of some otherwise attractive varieties are too large and coarse; some, like my own first introduction, 'Blue Ivory', grow slowly. A number of delicate blends should be planted where they can be seen at close range. 'Sky Torch' (Peterson '64), a changeable opalescent blend of blue and orange, is one of these. I planted it near my kitchen door, where I can step out several times a day to see its color of the moment. The flowers, like those of my own blue variety, 'Little Sapphire', have that satiny finish rare in these hybrids.

'Lilli-White', with perfectly formed, crisply textured flowers, is the most beautiful, to date, of the white standard dwarfs. Its only fault is the brevity of the bloom period. Outstanding among new whites that I have seen is 'Baby Snowflake' (Peterson '63), which blooms for two months in its native Tennessee—in my garden, not so long. The flowers are shapely and ruffled. The flowers of my own 'Moonspinner' open as a reverse amoena; the pale yellow standards form a perfect moon-globe, surrounded by horizontal, nearly circular white falls. Like 'Baby Snowflake', 'Moonspinner' is a fine performer in bloom and increase.

19 DERRING DO
Standard dwarf bearded. Dark pansy-velvet flower on ten-inch stalk. Mid-May.

Warburton.

20 IRIS KOROLKOWII VIOLACEA
A form of this regelia species from Turkestan. The long, pointed segments are veined in deep violet. The sparse beard and velvety signal patch are black. Two or three terminal flowers.

The only bright yellow variety I have seen that outshines 'Brassie' is still in the originator's seedling patch. 'Brassie' is not properly described by its name; the demure rounded flowers are a clear, true yellow, and freely produced. Both 'Brassie' and the later-blooming 'Golden Fair' are lovely with tulips of the same clear yellow, blue *Phlox divaricata,* and yellow violas or the bolder faces of pansies. Among the pale yellows are 'Lemon Flare', an excellent performer and runner-up for the 1964 Cook-Douglas Award, and the fourteen-inch smooth yellow 'Blonde Doll' (Goett '63).

The best black I've seen is the gleaming 'Shine Boy', though the blue-black 'Little Grackle' (Rundlett '64) is very dark and iridescent as the grackle. Among the dark bitones my favorite is Warburton's 'Derring-Do', with pansy-velvet falls and perfect form.

The first truly excellent plicata to appear in this group of irises is 'Circlette' (Goett '63), with a shapely white flower stitched and feathered in strongly contrasting deep blue-purple.

The important new color in standard dwarf beardeds is pink. Earl Roberts in Indiana bloomed a number of pink seedlings in 1964. I have seen them only in color slides, but they're pink as pink —and beautifully shaped. Though only one, 'Lenna M.', has been named so far, several will be available in the near future. I have already composed a special garden picture in my imagination in which 'Lenna M.' is featured in combination with taller and slightly later pink intermediates (the bloom will overlap), palest yellow and black tulips, and blue standard dwarfs.

Here are selections of both old and new varieties:

RECOMMENDED VARIETIES OF STANDARD DWARF-BEARDED IRISES

White	*Blue*	*Purple*
Baby Snowflake	Blue Denim	Dark Fairy
Dainty Delight	Little Sapphire	Pagan Midget
Moonspinner	Small Sky	*Violet bitone*
Small Cloud	Small Wonder	
White and green	Tinkerbell	Derring-Do
Green Spot	*Lavender*	*Black*
Lilli-Green	Lilaclil	Little Grackle
	Red-toned	Shine Boy
	Royal Thumbprint	
	Velvet Caper	

Cream	*Yellow and brown*	*Blends*
Baria	Brown-eyed Katie	Aqua Green
Blonde Doll	Centerpiece	Little Witch
Lemon Flare	Lilli-Var	Sky Torch
		Spring Mist
Yellow	*Brown-toned*	
		Plicatas
Brassie	Arrangement	
Coreop	Blueberry Muffins	Circlette
Golden Fair	Moonblaze	Plickadee
		Speckled Sprite

Intermediates

Intermediates are not new irises. Many gardeners are familiar with, and still grow, the ancient blue or purple "flags," though they may not know them by name. These old irises, collected from the wild and long thought to be species, are now known to be natural hybrids. "Grandmother's white flag," widely grown and even naturalized in the Southern states, is 'Albicans', not *I. albicans;* her "blue flag" is 'Germanica', not *I. germanica.* Both the fragrant blue-white 'Florentina', famed as a source of orrisroot, and the brilliant red-purple 'Kochii' are intermediate hybrids, not species.

W. J. Caparne, in England, bred intermediates more than half a century ago, but the now-popular varieties were bred later in the United States by the Sasses, Robert Schreiner, and others. The reblooming 'Autumn Queen', 'Snow Maiden', and 'Zua' of the crinkled petals are some of the well-known whites; 'Golden Bow', 'Soledad', and 'Southland' are yellow. Purples include 'Black Magic' and 'Ruby Glow'. 'Marine Wave' is deep violet-blue.

I still grow the unique 'Zua', and the accommodating, almost carefree 'Black Magic', which has no garden faults that I can see. 'Zua' is seriously flawed by the brevity of its blooming; but so far, its beauty has saved it from the discard pile. My other white and yellow old-timers met that fate several years ago; varieties with the floral characteristics of the ancient tall beardeds are hopelessly outclassed by new-style intermediates.

The increased range of colors and patterns, after only a few years breeding, has put intermediate irises back in the running as valuable garden material. Plicatas and pinks, not known before in this class, are already on the market; and there are bright coppery browns, "reds," lemon-yellows, yellow amoenas, other white-and-yellow combinations, as well as spruce new forms in the traditional blues, purples, and whites.

In 1963, Wilma Greenlee's pure white 'Cloud Fluff' won the new annual Sass Award for the best intermediate. Other high-quality whites are 'Little Angel', which blooms and blooms, and the ruffled blue-white 'Arctic Flare'.

Paul Cook's 'Kiss-Me-Kate', which won the first Sass Award (1960), can only be appreciated close up—in a doorstep garden, for instance. The delicate cream color, edged on the falls with a band of lavender-blue, has little carrying power.

Schreiners' recently introduced two sister seedlings that pair well in the garden. 'Cutie' is white with a pattern of bright blue lines; 'Drummer Boy' is light-to-medium blue, similarly patterned in dark blue, a good strong carrying color, and deepest of the blues to date. Alta Brown's 'Arctic Blue' is sky blue; her 'Arctic Ruffles' is pale blue, as is 'Blue Fragrance' (Roberts) which is large-flowered and taller (24 inches) than most intermediates. 'Moonchild', lavender-blue with reddish signal, is an older variety of oncobred breeding that I have treasured and praised in print ever since it was introduced. It won the Sass Award in 1961.

The first brilliant pink intermediate was 'Lillipinkput' (Douglas), introduced in 1960 and an immediate sensation, winning the Sass Award in 1964. It hovers around the 15-inch mark in height, though it is intermediate in breeding and bloom time. When I first saw a clump of this beauty still blooming in Presby Gardens with early tall bearded varieties, I was bowled over. It looked like a large bouquet of apricot-pink roses. What a carrying color! It should be in everybody's garden—and will be, I think, as soon as the supply can meet the heavy demand. Two new varieties, bred by Adelaide Peterson, have bloomed in my garden: peach 'Pink Reward' and 'Pink Fancy', light shell-pink with a rosy beard. Both are paler, pinker, and taller than 'Lillinpinkput'. There are even more beautiful ones in Mrs. Peterson's seedling beds. Tennessee is fast becoming the land of the pink intermediates.

The amoena pattern has now made its appearance in the intermediate class. 'Interim' (Salsman) is a yellow amoena with white standards flushed yellow and dark yellow falls. 'Frosty Lemonade' (Peterson) is a ruffled bright lemon-gold amoena. From California comes a reverse amoena, 'Indeed' (Hager '64), described as having lemon standards and wide white horizontal falls, narrowly edged in lemon. Sight-unseen it is on my want list. 'Maroon Caper' (War-burton '64) inherited the wonderful aphylla branching, with flower buds at all levels. Very good, indeed.

A few varieties in the plicata pattern are now available, all with white ground and lightly marked orchid or lavender. Unhappily, I have not seen any of them, but I'll list the two that seem to be most attractively marked. Both are Hager's, introduced in 1964: 'Doll Type' is described as having clean white domed standards edged light violet, falls same and edged with violet dots, color intensifying at the haft; bright purple style arms; blue beard. 'Chit Chat' is also bordered in orchid with purple style arms. I know that more strongly marked varieties will be coming along because I have one in my own seedling patch.

This list includes varieties in the different color classes selected for garden value.

RECOMMENDED VARIETIES OF INTERMEDIATE BEARDED IRISES

White

Arctic Flare
Astralite
Cloud Fluff
Little Angel

White marked blue

Cutie

Blue

Arctic Ruffles
Blue Fragrance
Drummer Boy
Moonchild

Lavender

First Lilac

Red-toned

Jay Kenneth
Maroon Caper
Red Orchid
Ruby Glow

Purple and violet

Black Magic
Elfin Royal
Marine Wave
Paganite

Black

Black Hawk
Dark Eden

Yellow

Barbi
Butterbit
Lilligoldput
Lime Ripples

Yellow and white

Frosty Lemonade
Interim

Pink

Lillipinkput
Pink Fancy
Pink Reward
Sweet Allegro

Brown-toned

Elfin Antique
Gypsy Flair

Miniature Tall Beardeds

In the early 1930's, when most tall bearded irises were diploids, a number of small, gracefully proportioned seedlings with small flowers on thin wiry stems appeared in the Indiana fields of the Williamsons. These were the first "table" irises, now renamed miniature tall bearded. When diploid breeding gave way to tetraploid, no further seedlings of this type appeared, and the class has remained limited. However, the original varieties have had enough admirers through the years to keep them in catalogues.

Recently attempts have been made to create new varieties in this class. A number of resourceful and dedicated breeders have been working very hard, with few successes. They have not yet hit on the proper equation—if there is one. Breeding of table irises has turned out to be a tough nut to crack. Probably breeders will eventually succeed in creating a wealth of superior new varieties. Until that day comes, I will keep my old varieties—the little all-white 'Pee Wee', white 'Daystar' with the red-gold beard, dainty yellow 'Kinglet', and blue-violet 'Tom Tit'.

Table irises are recommended to flower arrangers. I use mine in centerpieces, but their main function in my garden is to hold a slope—a job they perform admirably. And they keep on blooming freely in the midst of encroaching sedums and other ground covers, though the older varieties have not been transplanted for thirteen years.

These are the old varieties and the few new ones I have grown or seen growing:

Chewink, light blue
Dainty Dancer, yellow standards, blue-violet falls
Daystar, tiny white with orange beard
Kinglet, yellow
Little Helen, white standards, violet falls
Tid-Bit, lavender
Tom Tit, deep blue-violet
Two for Tea, orchid-pink
Warbler, yellow
Widget, white and blue plicata

7

Aril Irises and Their Hybrids

Among the wild aril species and their man-made hybrids are found some of the most exquisite of all irises, and perhaps of all flowers. The hobby gardener may find his greatest challenge in the strange arillate species that are grown in scattered gardens from Michigan and Massachusetts to Texas. They begin to bloom about a month before the tall bearded varieties, and their peak is past when the tall bearded season starts.

Aril irises differ from other bearded irises in color and shape of rhizome and in the seeds which bear a conspicuous white *aril* (collar) around one end. These variations matter little to most gardeners, but the differences in flower forms and patterns will astonish even a sophisticated flower-lover. I have heard the story of a man who, after one look at a group of arils in bloom, climbed hastily into his car and drove off. He was not in flight; he wanted to get his camera. "No one would believe me if I merely told about such flowers," he declared.

He was probably looking at oncocyclus irises, the strangest of the three groups—regelia, oncocyclus and pseudoregelia—into which the arils are divided.

REGELIAS

These species are distinguished by the narrow but prominent and often highly-colored beard that occurs on standards and falls. Botanically they are known as Hexapogons, meaning "six beards," but the name regelia is commonly accepted. The glaucous green foliage is slender and often flushed purple at the base. Stems do not branch, but bear two or even three flowers in a single terminal

74

head. Increase is by means of slender underground branches or stolons from the rhizome.

Regelia irises adapt well enough to this climate to be recommended for garden use even in our humid northeastern states. Their pointed, pagoda flowers on eighteen-inch stems are so slim and elegant that most gardeners, seeing for the first time one of these species from the steppes of Central Asia, immediately desire it for their own dooryards. In my garden I have grown four charming regelia species, *Iris hoogiana, I. korolkowii, I. stolonifera* and *I. arenaria.* The first year I lifted and stored the narrow rhizomes during their post-blooming dormant period, for I had read that they must not be exposed to summer moisture. I kept them in dry sand in our dry basement until mid-October when I replanted them in the garden among bearded irises. They need a period of low temperature before they start into growth in mid- or late winter, the time depending on temperature range, but they are able to stand New York winters when protected by a cover of evergreen boughs. The next year I was too busy to lift the rhizomes; the plants went dormant in midsummer and the rhizomes remained firm and healthy.

The regelia species *Iris hoogiana,* with narrow flowers of an intense shade of wisteria blue and an almost enameled sleekness of texture, is a native of Turkestan. The flowers of the most common form are bearded in bright orange, smoothly tailored and completely lacking in the veining so conspicuous in *I. korolkowii.* There are several named forms including Austin's 'Blue Joy' and 'Late Amethyst'.

Iris korolkowii was first collected in Turkestan about seventy-five years ago. The pointed flowers, bearded only on the falls, are strikingly veined. Some forms are lavender, intricately veined in deep purple, with a dark signal patch below the dark brown beard; most outstanding is the pink form with maroon veining on a pale pink ground, and a *blue* beard.

Flowers of *Iris stolonifera* are blended brown, flushed blue, bearded with blue, and ruffled. Selections include 'Decorated Blue Beard', a choice variety, later blooming and more free-flowering than *I. stolonifera,* and the larger flowered 'Decorated Giant' with dark velvety falls veined crimson.

Iris arenaria, a dwarf species from Hungary, has flowers that last but a day and fade in the late afternoon. Pale yellow in color, orange bearded and rather horizontal in form, the flowers are freely produced on three-inch stalks. When planting this species, I scoop out a space about three inches deep and a foot square, cover the tips of the roots with soil, and fill in around roots and rhizomes with sand. Last spring I gave a tiny nubbin of a rhizome to a friend who has a sunnier, dryer rock garden than mine. It grew amazingly, and will probably outdo my clump, which is beginning to be shaded by a flourishing pin oak.

Several arenaria hybrids such as the yellow 'Keepsake', the nearly pink 'Promise', and the reddish 'Cup and Saucer' are suitable for both border edgings and rock gardens. These are all early-blooming miniatures from *Iris arenaria* crossed with dwarf-bearded varieties.

Regelia Hybrids

In the late nineteenth and early twentieth centuries the Dutch firm of Van Tubergen produced many hybrids among those first three regelia species. Still available are 'Bronze Beauty', with lavender-veined bronze standards and dark red falls; the iridescent 'Orestes'; red-purple 'Lucia', with a conspicuous blue beard; and 'Vera' and 'Vulcanus', in shades of copper and violet.

Regeliocyclus Hybrids

The word "regeliocyclus," compounded from the names of the two major groups of aril irises, means a hybrid of regelia and oncocyclus. The British call hybrids from (oncocyclus × regelia) crosses "oncogelias," and those from the reverse cross (regelia × oncocyclus), regeliocyclus. Most hybrids listed in catalogues are the latter. In these pure aril hybrids the more exotic oncocyclus flower and the regelia vigor combine to produce fairly satisfactory garden plants.

Until recently almost all garden varieties of regeliocyclus irises were bred in the Van Tubergen nurseries. The first was 'Agatha', introduced in 1894 and still obtainable. These early hybrids resulted from crossing the regelia species *Iris korolkowii* and its cultivated varieties with various oncocyclus species. The first one I ever saw was the moody 'Andromache', veined closely in dark red on a silver ground, with a dark lustrous signal patch of velvety texture centered in each fall.

Of course I wanted to own more varieties of these fascinating flowers, and searched the catalogues. 'Camilla' was next—small and delicately formed; blue-purple standards veined darker; white falls are closely veined in reddish purple, with nearly crimson, velvety style-crests above the thick black beard. The signal is red-black. Later I grew the bronzy 'Charon', and 'Psyche', pale pink with maroon veining and a black signal. Others still listed in specialists' catalogues—include 'Isolda', 'Artemis', 'Oberon', and 'Luna'.

This breeding was interrupted by war, and it was not until after World War II that Van Tubergen began to introduce new regeliocyclus hybrids. 'Amphion', 'Ancilla', 'Bocena', 'Chione', 'Clara', 'Clotho', 'Elvira', 'Lutetia', and 'Sylphide' are mostly regeliocyclus with a dash of oncocylus blood. These varieties, introduced in the late 1950's, are even better than the early introductions. Even the newest are relatively inexpensive, and one or two clumps in a garden make all surrounding flowers seem merely palely pretty.

In the mid 1950's, the American hybridizer, Lloyd Austin, introduced the first of his excellent "Persian" series, the easy-to-grow 'Persian Bronze', bronze and lilac netted with dark brown.

More new regeliocyclus hybrids, with three-fourths oncocyclus and one-fourth regelia blood, are beginning to reach the United States from the German garden of the noted botanist and hybridizer, Dr. Peter Werckmeister. The varieties 'Aquarelle' and 'Gravure', introduced in California in 1961, are said to look like pure oncocyclus. Dr. Werckmeister finds them as easy to grow as the usual regeliocyclus, which are only half oncocyclus.

Regeliabreds

Gardeners who admire regelias but are reluctant to experiment with the species or the regeliocyclus varieties may compromise by growing some of the few available hybrids from regelias crossed with bearded irises. The wonderful blue of *Iris hoogiana* appears in the ruffled 'Blue Fairy' and in the tall 'Blue Spice', 'Hoogie Boy', and 'Rainier Valley', and these flourish among tall-bearded varieties, blooming just a few days earlier. Hybrids of *I. stolonifera,* include the yellow 'Golden Butterfly', 'Silken Dalliance', and 'Saffron Charm', the only hybrid of *Iris stolonifera* and the tall beardeds now growing in my garden. The medium-large flowers on thirty-inch stalks have an airy grace not often seen, and an intricate blue-and-yellow pattern.

REGELIA SPECIES IN CULTIVATION

I. arenaria	*I. hoogiana*
I. bloudowii	*I. korolkowii*
I. darwasica	*I. mandschurica*
I. flavissima	*I. stolonifera*

PSEUDOREGELIAS

These arils are found on the south and east slopes of the Himalayas in India, Tibet, and southwestern China. Though named and
described by W. R. Dykes, the pseudoregelias are rarely seen in
cultivation. Plants are of slender growth, according to Dykes. The
mottled purple flowers have narrow beards on the falls; rhizomes
are compact, gnarled, without stolons, and need a thorough baking
in summer; the creamy collar or aril on the seed is small.

The best known species, *Iris kamaonensis*, is occasionally seen in
gardens. A Massachusetts gardener who grows it says the purplish
pink to dark reddish-violet flowers are very attractive, and believes
several species in this group "should be prime collectors' items for
cold-climate gardens." Seeds may be purchased from G. Ghose and
Co., Townsend, Darjeeling, India.

PSEUDOREGELIA SPECIES

I. gonicarpa   *I. leptophylla*
I. hookeriana   *I. sikkimensis*
I. kamaonensis

THE ONCOCYCLUS IRISES

The term "oncocyclus" (coming from the Greek *onkos* and
kyklos) has taken on magic from the beauty of the group of irises
it designates. Numerous iris lovers find them the most beautiful of
all irises. The flowers of many oncocyclus species are huge, up to
seven inches across, globular in form with extremely wide segments, rich in color, and exotic in pattern. Flower stems are usually
short; leaves are sickle-shaped.

Most species grow rather easily in California, eastern Washington, Utah, and the Southwest. In the Northeast they are more
difficult. The celebrated silver and black mourning iris, *I. susiana*
(named apparently after Susa, the ancient capital of Persia), is
easiest. Some years ago I saw several plants blooming in a New
Jersey backyard. The grower had not known, when he received a
box of rhizomes as a gift from a friend in the Near East, that they
were supposed to be problem children.

While such results are not to be expected, *Iris susiana* can be
grown in the open in lower New York State where summer rain and

high humidity during its long dormant season—when in its native habitat it receives a thorough baking—is more harmful than our fractious winters. Species such as *I. saarii* and *I. gatesii* from their more northern range start into growth comparatively late in spring and are consequently easier to grow here. I have bloomed only *I. susiana* and *I. mariae*. When the rhizomes were delivered in September, I stored them in dry sand in our dry basement, in an effort to keep them dormant until November. By early October, green leaves were showing above the sand and I decided I might as well plant them. After freezing weather began, I poured enough sand over the leaves to cover them and resigned myself to no flowers the following year. *I. susiana* produced four bloom stalks. Little *I. mariae* bore two.

The "oncos," as they are familiarly called, are natives of Palestine, Northern Persia (Iran), Syria, Lebanon, Armenia, and Asia Minor. The most northern species, *Iris gatesii* from Kurdistan, is the largest flowered of all irises except some of the Japanese hybrids. The extremely wide standards and falls, cream with a hint of chartreuse, are veined and minutely dotted with violet; the bronze beard is broad and diffuse.

The Black Iris, *I. atropurpurea,* the species best known in Israel, is small-flowered with dark arched standards, narrow, nearly black falls; and a blacker, large velvety signal spot.

Both *Iris barnumiae* and its variety *mariae* (often given species rank) are rosy mulberry shaded brown, with black beards and large black signals.

In the late 1950's, Lloyd Austin introduced a series of pure oncocyclus hybrids including 'Judean Charmer' and 'Judean Silver'. These are said to be more vigorous and to increase more rapidly than the species.

ONCOCYCLUS SPECIES OBTAINABLE IN THE UNITED STATES

I. atrofusca	*I. lortetii*
I. atropurpurea	*I. mariae*
I. aurantica	*I. nazarena*
I. barnumiae	*I. nigricans*
I. benjaminii	*I. samariae*
I. calcaria	*I. saarii*
I. gatesii	*I. susiana*
I. haynei	

Oncobreds

Hybrids between oncocyclus species and tall-bearded irises, called oncobreds, exist in plentiful variety. They are characterized by extremely broad falls and domed standards. Flowers are of rounded form; beards are heavy and wide. There may be a small signal patch and corded or contrasting veining.

Early in this century William Mohr in California became interested in hybridizing irises. His attempts to cross tall bearded irises and oncocyclus species culminated in his famous achievement, 'William Mohr'. After many years of stubborn sterility, this oncobred iris produced the huge 'Elmohr' and the fertile 'Capitola', parent of a long line of beautiful "Mohrs," including 'Lady Mohr'. Both 'Elmohr' and 'Lady Mohr' were on the 1961 Popularity Poll of the A. I. S., and have been there every year since the early 1940's when they made their debut—that is some indication of the high quality of oncobreds or arilbreds. The term arilbred is more inclusive and preferred for that reason, since pedigrees of some of these hybrids are unavailable.

Both 'Elmohr' and 'Lady Mohr' will grow and bloom anywhere. The falls of the freely-produced flowers of 'Lady Mohr' are yellow-beige hinting of chartreuse, delicately veined in deep crimson around the brownish beard; standards are pale lavender. 'Elmohr' is a rich mulberry color.

Other handsome and inexpensive arilbreds are the early-blooming 'Heigho', blue, large, and frilled, with corded self-color veining; silvery 'Engraved', with allover blue-black engraving; deep blue 'Mary McClellan'; 'Mohr Lemonade', with ruffled lemon-cream flowers, shows its aril blood only in the wide falls and style-arms. 'No Mohr' is an excellent garden variety, well branched and long-blooming, with onco-looking creamy-beige flowers and violet signal. 'Real Gold' is darker, a golden-buff with brownish veins. 'Witch Doctor' is a big beauty, greyish lavender with a buffy-yellow glow at the heart. In 1960 it won the new C. G. White award for the best arilbred of the year.

Few of these varieties have more than one-eighth aril blood, and demand no extra care. Neither do Schreiners' delightful pair, the velvety mulberry 'Peshewar' and the violet-pattern 'Suez', both small and early-blooming, with one-fourth aril blood. However, really sharp drainage and lime added to the soil are important.

Recent winners of the annual C. G. White Award for the best arilbred, are 'Trophy', 1961; 'Striped Butterfly', 1962; and 'Mohrning

Haze', 1963. In 1964 'Real Gold' and 'Wind Shadows' tied for this award. 'Striped Butterfly', least onco-looking of the lot, has sky-blue flowers veined in darker blue belowe the yellow beard. 'Mohrning Haze' is enormous and slightly ruffled; in spite of its coloring— a quiet lavender-blue with blue beard—it stands out in the garden.

My two favorites are 'Trophy', with huge lobelia-blue flowers bearded deep blue, and 'Wind Shadows', pearl grey blended lavender, and washed golden-brown on either side of the bronze beard.

According to the dictionary, a classic is "a work of the highest class and acknowledged excellence." But it doesn't say a classic must be of any definite age—either a hundred years, or ten. 'Lady Mohr' and 'Elmohr' are arilbred classics more than twenty years old; 'Trophy' and 'Wind Shadows' are marked to become classics.

CULTURE

Recommendations from northern gardeners for growing aril irises differ widely. Some leave them in the ground the year round; others lift the rhizomes in July and store until October—in sand, vermiculite, or bare-rooted. A few grow the plants in pots, which they sink in the soil from early spring until midsummer, then store. Some gardeners winter-mulch with several inches of pure sand; others use straw; some don't mulch at all. One man reduces the mulch during subsequent winters as the plants gradually become acclimated. Some growers feed sparingly, others liberally. Likewise with lime, though dolomitic limestone, containing magnesium, is preferred by most.

The culture of oncocyclus irises is not particularly difficult, merely different from that of the bearded irises. The oncocyclus can survive annual rainfall many times greater than the four to twelve inches of their native haunts, provided there is sharp drainage. A gentle slope plus raised ridges for the plant rows will provide adequate drainage in light soils. Oncos grown in heavy, slow-draining soils need several inches of porous material under the beds.

Though complete drynes in summer is not an absolute essential, in humid regions it is wise to dig arils when leaves turn partly brown. Dry the rhizomes in shade for a few days, remove tops, dust rhizomes with a fungicide-insecticide, then store in *dry* sand until planting time in late October. When arils are left in the ground, the rhizomes should be dug every year or two and transplanted.

To keep the plants aphid-free and disease-free, and for foliar feeding, use an all-purpose combination spray from four to six times in spring during the period of leaf development and flowering. Here is a formula recommended by Mr. Austin.

> For each 2 gallons of water:
> Fungicide: Parzate (containing Zineb) ⅓ cup
> Insecticide: Isotex (containing Lindane) 4 teaspoons
> Soluble fertilizer: Miracle-Gro 2 tablespoons
> DuPont spreader-sticker ½ teaspoon

The same formula, minus fertilizer and spreader-sticker, is useful for a half-minute dip just before planting or transplanting the rhizomes.

I do not advise growing aril irises in pots because their long roots normally spread out horizontally over a considerable area. New rhizomes and new roots develop most rapidly between flowering time and mid-July, so good growing conditions during this period are important.

8

The Eurasian Beardless Irises

There is a huge and heterogeneous group of irises, growing around the world in the northern hemisphere, that produce rhizomes but do not have beards. This group is of equal rank, botanically, with the bearded iris section. The two *sections* make up the subgenus Iris. The beardless iris section, Spathula (meaning spoonshaped), is composed of four subsections, two of which contain a single species each.

Beardless irises of Eurasian origin contain a wealth of largely unexploited material for original and exceedingly charming garden designs. The dearth of beardless irises in gardens is probably due to the persistent belief that they can be grown successfully only in a bog. Nothing could be farther from the truth, at least in the Northeast, yet this misconception has kept numerous beardless beauties out of our borders. Some, it is true, require extra moisture at certain periods of the growing season, but this need is easily met and does *not* involve inundation. Others, even some species that flourish along the banks of streams, grow vigorously in the border.

PARDANTHOPSIS AND FOETIDISSIMA

Lone member of the subsection Pardanthopsis is the short-lived perennial *Iris dichotoma*, which flowers abundantly during the whole month of August. The inch-wide lavender flowers, similar in shape and color to those of the crested *I. gracilipes*, are fleeting but attractive—and new ones are produced daily on tall forked bloom stalks. This species comes easily from seed in ordinary soil and full sun.

The single species in the Foetidissima subsection, *Iris foetidissima*, is called the stinking iris because the leaves, when bruised, give off an unpleasant smell. Otherwise there is no fetid odor about plant or flower. This iris is prized by flower arrangers for the handsome seed pods that reveal many bright vermilion seeds, which adhere to the pods for a long time. The greyish flowers are unattractive. The plant will adapt to deep shade though it prefers some sun.

THE APOGONS

The name of this subsection means "without beard." This group of smooth-falled irises, one of the largest in the genus, is divided into sixteen *series*. The three Eurasian series that provide superior material for gardens are the Sibericae, the Spuriae, and the Laevigatae from which come the Japanese irises. The color range is more limited than in the bearded group; flower shapes are more open, and style-arms more evident. Leaves are long, narrow, graceful, and a darker green.

Siberian Irises

Most of the garden hybrids of Siberian irises are derived from two species of the series Sibericae: *Iris siberica* (native to Central Europe, not Siberia) and *I. sanguinea (I. orientalis)* from Manchuria. Both species are cold-hardy; both have pleasing flowers in the blue, purple, and white range; and plants of both species are attractive all summer. *Iris siberica* forms dense clumps of narrow grassy leaves from which rise slender three foot stems crowned with five or six long but not ungraceful flowers. Standards are narrow, spoon-shaped and erect. Style-arms are conspicuous and the falls hang down. In contrast, the stems of *I. sanguinea* are shorter, with showy red-purple spathes; leaves are broader ,and the May-blooming flowers are larger with wider segments. Falls are broad and rounded. A white form, 'Snow Queen', which has been cultivated for many years, was collected in Japan in 1900.

Several other species of this group, though not quite so cold-resistant as the above, grow moderately well and are attractive in gardens, where they bloom in June. Plants of some are commercially available; all of them will grow—slowly—from seed.

The variable *Iris bulleyana,* probably not a true species, has shining leaves and spreading lilac-and-purple flowers on eighteen-inch stems. (The garden variety 'Red Emperor' may be a form of *I. bulleyana.*) The black-purple, violet, or reddish flowers of *I. chrysographes*—mean "golden writing"—are inscribed with bright

yellow markings. Standards of this species—and those of *I. forrestii*
and *I. wilsonii*—are held at an angle instead of vertically. The last
two are the only yellow-flowered species in the Siberian group.
Though dainty and charming, they are rather difficult to transplant.
The one Siberian species with a solid stem is *I. clarkei*; all other
Siberians have hollow stems. Leave of *I. clarkei* are glossy, and the
blue-violet flowers are borne on two-foot stems.

These 40-chromosome species have until recently been little used
in breeding garden varieties. Walter Marx now lists unnamed
hybrids between *I. chrysographes* and *I. forrestii,* and M. E. Kitton
in England has used some in hybridizing. Once upon a time (1927)
a hybrid of *I. chrysographes,* the red-violet 'Margot Holmes', won
a Dykes Medal. This was, of course, in England where interest
in unusual species and hybrids is greater than in the United States.
It grows, though not vigorously, in my garden.

The older cultivated varieties of Siberians are familiar to many
gardeners and are highly valued for their reliability and the airy
grace of their abundant flowers. They bloom at the same time
as tall-bearded irises and form huge clumps that can go for ten
years or so without division. And they are almost entirely disease-
free. The influence of *I. siberica* is evident in both the plant and
the "classic" flower form of many of these varieties. Standards are
narrow and upright; the frequently drooping falls may also be
narrow; the thin and delicate substance of the flower permits blossoms to flutter in a breeze.

The general gardener may not yet be aware of the splendid
new hybrids that offer, in addition to these other admirable qualities, various flower forms, superior branching, and a longer season
of bloom. Some recent varieties bloom for five weeks, or even
longer in a favorable season. Varieties in new colors are in existence
and will presently be available. I have seen color prints of the
new English-bred Siberian seedlings. One was a true apricot, a
color not seen before in these irises; another was an oddly beautiful
muted shade between purple and coffee. It will be some time before
such iris colors appear in American gardens, but those enthusiasts
who prophesy that the whole iris rainbow will soon appear in
Siberians may be right.

Among new varieties already on the market, advances in flower
form are more striking than the minor variations in color. 'White
Swirl', most beautiful of all Siberians to date and a recent Morgan
Award winner, is of unique form. The horizontal falls are short,
very broad and rounded. The wide standards are even shorter. They

are held at the same angle as the style-arms, and together they create a shallow bowl which give a daffodil look. I call it the daffodil Siberian. The flowers of a number of newer Siberians show variations on this form, which I consider an improvement over the classic or standard shape preferred by some connoisseurs.

Another interesting Siberian flower form, in which both standards and falls are held on a horizontal plane, occurs in a few varieties such as the new blue-purple 'Tealwood' (Morgan Award, 1964) and the less expensive 'Blue Moon'. This type flower is most effective on a low-growing plant like 'Tealwood' (twenty-seven inches tall) where it can be seen from above.

Even semidwarfs, so welcome in the small garden, will eventually be available. A new dark and velvety-falled variety, appropriately named 'Velvet Night', is small-flowered and only twenty inches tall.

A true dwarf, not new, has recently arrived from England. 'Nana' is its name. Melrose Gardens reports it as "twelve inches tall with lush, vigorous short foliage and wide flaring white flowers that just top the leaves . . . no one seems to know exactly *what* it is, except utterly charming." I grow only one really dwarf Siberian, the twelve-inch 'Acuta', with ruffled blue-and-white flowers collected in 1813 and sometimes listed as *Iris acuta*.

Cultivation of Siberian irises is simple; they will grow anywhere, though in deep shade they bloom sparsely if at all. They *prefer* fertile well-drained soil with adequate moisture, and perform best when fed in early spring and again after flowering.

Some growers recommend moist acid soil with high humus content, but Siberians do flourish in heavy clay soil and, to my own knowledge, are at least tolerant of lime. One year a number of volunteer Siberian seedlings appeared in my aril iris seedling bed, which I keep well limed, and they grew luxuriantly there.

When a clump of Siberian irises becomes so big that transplanting is necessary, the chore can be done at your convenience. Either early spring or early fall is satisfactory. The clump should be separated into divisions of five or more fans; there will be plenty to share with neighbors. Siberians were originally meadow plants; they have dense fibrous roots growing from tiny—almost minute—rhizomes. Make the planting holes large enough to spread out the roots, and firm the soil well around them.

Pests and diseases are hardly a problem. Borers seldom attack them (those tiny rhizomes can't offer much nourishment), and the only disease I have even heard about is a botrytis-like fungus which is said to attack the plants on occasion and can be easily controlled with a fungicide dust or spray.

Recommended Siberian varieties include standard as well as newer forms:

White

Snow Crest
Tunkhannock
White Swirl

Blue

Blue Brilliant, rich blue
Blue Cape, medium blue, English
Blue Moon, medium blue
Cool Spring, light blue
Gatineau, light blue
Mountain Lake, medium blue
Silver Tip, medium violet-blue, light style-arms
Placid Waters, medium blue

Deep blue, purple, violet

Caesar's Brother, deep purple
Congo Drums, deep blue-violet
Ellesmere, vivid royal-blue, English
Tealwood, blue-purple
Tropic Night, deep purple-blue
Tycoon, deep blue-violet
Violet Flare, medium violet

Red

Eric the Red, reddish magenta
Helen Astor, pinkish purple
Royal Ensign, red and blue bi-color

Japanese Irises

Among the five species belonging to the series Laevigatae, two are the ancestors of the Japanese garden irises, and two are American natives. The fifth species, *Iris pseudacorus*, of ancient origin, is found in Asia Minor, North Africa, and all over Europe, and has naturalized itself along streams in the United States. It prospers in my garden without ever being watered. I keep the clump to manageable size by yanking out a number of the large tough rhizomes each summer immediately after its flowering. The three-foot plant bears many flowers, decorative in the garden and charming in arrangements. (So are the seed pods.) The wide, round falls of clear yellow are delicately marked with brown in the center.

The two American species in this series, *Iris versicolor* and *I. virginica* are discussed under American Irises.

The magnificent, hardy Japanese irises, still so little known to American gardeners, are the only important garden hybrids derived from species belonging to the series *Laevigatae*. The name, which

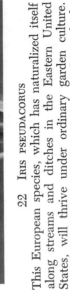

22 IRIS PSEUDACORUS

This European species, which has naturalized itself along streams and ditches in the Eastern United States, will thrive under ordinary garden culture. The golden flowers, with small pointed standards, are patterned on the falls with delicate brown lines. The graceful stems and long pointed buds indicate its value in arrangements.

21 IRIS GRAMINEA

This spuria iris species, native to Europe, makes itself at home in my shady garden. The beauty of the narrow open flowers with conspicuous metallic pink style-arms is more apparent when cut.

means "smooth," probably refers to the leaves of the type species, *Iris laevigata,* which have no midrib. The Japanese irises are "smooth" in the slang sense, too. They are even easier to grow than the tall beardeds. They require less frequent transplanting, are equally beautiful and they bloom *after* the tall bearded season is over, during that lull in the garden when few perennials are blooming and annuals have not begun. In late June and early July, they highlight my garden, dramatizing even the roses.

All the lovely colors—from pure white through light blue, lavender, delicate pink, and rose to deep reddish-magenta, purple, and blue-violet—which now exist in these irises, were derived by Japanese growers largely from the red-violet Manchurian species, *Iris kaempferi.* The achievement of such variation in color and petal pattern is a monument to the persistence, skill, and patience of many generations of Japanese breeders.

Perhaps the reason that American gardeners have not availed themselves more freely of this unrivaled source for midsummer garden beauty is the myth that Japanese irises must be grown in pools or bogs, or kept flooded during their growing period. Few gardeners want to provide a flood basin for finicky flowers. Luckily for our gardens, the story is false. The wild ancestor, *I. kaempferi* is *not* a water plant and neither are kaempferi descendants, the modern strains of Japanese irises. In soil that is enriched annually and well watered in season, these irises make splendid clumps and flower freely.

I have a vigorous stand of the kaempferi species that I have grown from seed in a humus-rich and consequently moisture-retentive area in my garden—watered artificially only during periods of drought.

In the United States, W. A. Payne of Terre Haute, Indiana, and Walter Marx of Boring, Oregon, developed their own strains of Japanese, largely from the famous Higo strain. Marx named his strain Marhigo, and began to introduce it in 1953. Among his introductions are some of my favorite varieties, including the single 'Hoyden', with white falls and pert violet standards, and the double, white 'Snowy Hills'. His 'Blue Pompon' and 'Sorcerer's Triumph' won Prize of Honor in the 1963 International Gartenbau Ausstellung in Hamburg, Germany. For the beginner, collections of unnamed Marhigo seedlings are offered in the catalogue at low prices.

Since Mr. Payne's death, his nursery has been discontinued. Though not identified as Payne originations, a number of his introductions, priced to suit the general gardener, are available from the A. H. Hazzard garden in Kalamazoo, Michigan (see Appendix

B). Mr. Payne, who worked eighteen years before introducing even one variety, concentrated on developing strong stems and good branching. His originations included a number of the lovely, graceful singles. I look forward to growing his large single 'Joyous Cavalier', in which a pure white center radiates out in broad veins almost to the edge of the three purple-bordered falls. Style-arms and the small standards are white, narrowly edged with purple—and both stand up to form a little cup.

In the international competition at Hamburg, Mr. Payne's 'Blue Nocturne', 'Fashion Model', and 'Orchid Majesty' won, respectively, gold, silver, and bronze medals.

Inexpensive, long-time favorite Japanese irises, listed in catalogues of large general nurseries, include the double white 'Gold Bound', violet 'Eleanor Perry', and blue-violet 'Lucia Marshall'. The superiority, for gardens, of the Marhigo and Payne strains to these older varieties lies in certain characteristics that might not be noticed by general gardeners: the stiffer flower stems are better branched, resulting in more flowers per stalk and longer bloom. The flowers themselves, though no larger than the old favorites, have improved substance, are rain-resistant, and last much longer in the garden.

A planting that includes both early and late blooming varieties will, of course, produce the longest show. Single varieties, with three large, wide falls and three small, semiupright standards, tend to bloom earliest. Doubles and what I call triples usually come mid-to-late season. In the double varieties, standards are as large as falls and lie horizontally. Triples are the same as doubles with the addition of a central cluster of petaloids, in the manner of some peonies.

Patterns include selfs and bicolors, and marbling, mottling, stippling, and penciling or veining in a second or third—usually darker —color on a white or light ground. The yellow signal patch on the falls varies from large to tiny.

Culture of Japanese Irises

Although Max Steiger in Germany is working to produce a strain of lime-resistant Japanese irises, the varieties now available to American gardeners demand slightly to moderately acid soil. Both lime and bone meal are fatal. Nor should wood ashes be used.

They need a soil rich in humus, more food than any other iris, and—during the growing period—plenty of moisture. After flowering the need for water is greatly diminished, although like most perennials they should not suffer drought. In the North they must have good drainage, for they cannot survive alternate freezing and thawing with wet feet. In the South, they can be grown in low marshy ground.

My own method of maintaining sufficient moisture, which works well enough to satisfy me though it does not produce ten-inch "dinner plate" flowers, was to sink a large cracked tile about eight inches deep in the middle of the small planting space. When we have an April drought, all I need do is poke the hose nozzle into the tile and let the water run slowly for several hours.

The favorite food of these hungry irises is well-rotted or dried manure, which may be supplemented with a commercial fertilizer prepared for azaleas and rhododendrons. I feed the plants generously in early spring and again about the end of May.

I like to do necessary transplanting of overgrown clumps by late August. This allows time for plants to adjust before cold weather. Spring planting, advised for this region, means loss of bloom for that season. I dig out planting space to a depth of at least ten inches, and mix about 50 per cent peat moss and compost or leaf mold into the soil. Rhizomes are set two inches deep and *must* be kept moist until they become established.

Plants are little troubled by disease, though they are said to be susceptible to wheat rust. Wheat or oat straw, which might carry the spores, should not be used as a mulch. A year-round mulch of pine needles, well-rotted sawdust or ground corncobs is advised. As protection against winter heaving, I leave the mass of dead foliage on the plants until early spring when the tenacious leaves should be cut rather than pulled off. Plants may be sprayed at this time with malathion, chlordane, or DDT to guard against thrips or borers.

The varieties in this list are inexpensive. Almost all are originations of either Payne or Marx. The letter "S" indicates single flowers.

RECOMMENDED JAPANESE IRIS VARIETIES

White

Flying Kite
Ivory Glow
Miss Simplicity (S)
Snowy Hills

Red-Purple

Fiery Steed
Good Omen
Pillar of Fire (S)
Red Titan
Royal Sapphire (S)

Rose to Lavender

Butterfly Prince (S)
Confetti Showers
Orchid Majesty
Pink Frost
Princess Aurora
Rose Tower

Blue to Violet

Blue Pompon

Enchanted Lake (S)
Fashion Model
Hisakata
Jeweled Kimona
Silken Parasol
Sky and Water

PATTERNED VARIETIES

Flying Tiger
Gay Gallant
Joyous Cavalier (S)

Shimoyo
Sorcerer's Triumph

Spurias

Several of the dozen or so known species of spuria irises are among the most exciting of the wild irises. They flourish under varying conditions in meadows and mountains of Europe, the Near East and the Middle East. (One species grows along the edge of salt marshes.)

They come in shades of blue-purple, yellow, and white marked with yellow. Some species are low-growing with rather spreading habit; some are of medium height; others are tall and stately. They are suitable for wild and rock gardens, formal perennial borders, and informal, naturalistic plantings. One or two species are vigorous enough to hold banks.

The rhizomes of spurias differ from those of other irises in their greater length and creeping habit. Flowers resemble those of the xiphium irises in shape and coloring, but here the resemblance ends. The spurias produce several flowers on each bloom-stalk, held one above another, close to the stem, and the foliage—in marked contrast to that of xiphiums—is luxuriant and decorative. Even the seed pods are valuable for dried arrangements.

The tall species are most widely known and grown. White and yellow flowered *Iris ochroleuca,* native to the Near East, is a favorite among the world's gardeners because of the vigor and

23 CLUMP OF SPURIA IRIS VARIETY SUNNY DAY

Long-lasting golden flowers on forty-inch stalks enliven the garden in
late June.   Sass. Nies Award, 1957.

adaptability of the plant and the beauty of the butterfly blossoms. It is said to have naturalized itself in England, grows like a weed in California, and flourishes in my New York garden where, in mid-June, it blooms prolifically on forty-inch stalks. *I. aurea* blooms a couple of weeks later. The golden-yellow flowers, similar to those of *I. ochroleuca* in size and shape, are frilled at the edges. Plants are vigorous. The cream-and-yellow 'Shelford Giant', a well-known hybrid between these two species, is the tallest spuria. It reaches the awesome height of six feet.

Iris monnieri—which is probably a natural hybrid rather than a species—has been immortalized by that most celebrated painter of flowers, Pierre-Joseph Redouté. I have not seen this iris, but Redouté has portrayed a flower of such style and finish that I intend to add it to my garden. Dykes described it as soft yellow, of smooth texture. It is said to be early blooming. I take this to mean it would bloom in the Northeast in May.

My favorite among the dwarf spurias is the foot-tall *Iris gram-inea,* the grass iris, which flourishes among a collection of violets in my shady wild garden, blooming at the end of May. Blossoms are narrow of parts and half-hidden among leaves; even so, the leaves are narrow, graceful, and shining; and the sweet-smelling flowers, seen close up, are exquisite, with pinkish-violet standards and burnished metallic-pink style-arms which arch over the falls, revealing only the rounded white blade, heavily veined in deep blue. The long-lasting flowers are ideal for cutting: one narrow cauline leaf extends several inches above the flower and forms a graceful line in an arrangement. (*Caution:* An old variety of the April-blooming miniature dwarf bearded irises was named 'Gram-inea' and is still listed in some catalogues.)

The flowers of *Iris urumovii*, the Bulgarian Iris, and *I. sintenisii*, similar to *I. graminea* in color and form, are less perfectly proportioned, and the plants are even smaller. Bloom stalks of *I. sintenisii* vary from four to ten inches.

Iris spuria is a complex of closely related forms rather than a single species. All the known forms bear smallish flowers in shades of blue-purple on slender plants that are, at most, two feet tall. Some are garden-worthy—notably the form 'Halophila', called "salt-loving" because it is native to the salt marshes of Iran and Turkestan. It is hardy and vigorous; the small, narrow-segmented flowers are produced in profusion. Some forms are unattractive, and growing plants of the spurias is a gamble. I recommend this "species" to adventurous gardeners only.

Until recently so little breeding work had been done on spurias that a few hybrids produced in England at the turn of the century are still grown in gardens. The light cobalt 'Monspur Cambridge Blue', probably still the bluest spuria; rich blue-purple 'Lord Wolsely', and the yellow 'Monaurea' are some of these.

Carl Milliken of California originated the famous creamy yellow 'Wadi Zem Zem' and 'White Heron', but it was not until Eric Nies, also in California, began to devote himself to working with spurias that important results in this hybridizing appeared in any quantity. Flowers are larger, with wider segments and increased color variation. Some are ruffled, some tailored, and all are beautiful. Height averages forty inches.

Today's foremost breeders are Marion Walker and Walker Ferguson. The talented Tell Muhlstein, of Idaho, has introduced the first one with laced edges—a feature still new in tall bearded flowers.

Because almost all spuria breeding has been in mild climates, there may be a question as to hardiness. I have little information on the behavior in cold climates of the newest varieties; but it is reported that they winter successfully in many northern states, including Maine and Montana. I do know that California-bred Nies and Milliken varieties are hardy in this area, and are grown for sale in Massachusetts—where they are winter-minded with salt hay. I do not know that such protection is essential; it is not necessary in southern New York except for new transplants. The vigor of spurias is amazing. I have seen 'Sunny Day', the most popular of all, blooming prodigiously in a thick stand of weeds in a friend's abandoned border.

Spurias are as easy to grow as Siberians. In fact, their sole defect is that they resent transplanting and sometimes take a year —occasionally two years—to settle down and bloom afterwards. A minor black mark, considering their permanence. Once acclimated, plants continue to grow—given proper feeding—in the same place indefinitely because the long rhizomes grow out in a straight line without producing tangled masses. I never do dig up a whole clump; when I want to start a new planting, I merely scrabble a few rhizomes from the perimeter of a large clump, and fill in resulting cavities with fresh, fertile soil.

In the Northeast, spurias are best planted in September, though I have moved them successfully in spring. In the Southwest, where September may be very dry, gardeners are advised to postpone planting until October or even early November. Spurias grow in full sun or partial shade, in all types of neutral to slightly acid, well-drained soil—the richer the better. Set rhizomes about two inches deep in soil to which bonemeal and peat moss or other humus have been added. Keep roots moist while out of the ground, and for two to three weeks after planting. In dry spring seasons, plants will benefit from an occasional deep watering. And they should be side-dressed each spring with a balanced commercial fertilizer, well rotted barnyard or commercially dried manure.

In this area, spurias are little troubled by disease, though they may be attacked by the mustard-seed fungus. In warm climate, this may be more of a problem. (Chapter 12 discusses Pests and Diseases.)

Color variations in modern hybrids include bronze, chocolate, buff, lavender, and chartreuse, in addition to the blue, violet, yellow, and white found in the species. Recent winners of the annual Eric Nies award for the best spuria are the frilly 'Lark Song', with wide, horizontal yellow falls and palest cream standards and style-arms; 'Dutch Defiance', violet-blue with a yellow signal; the rich coppery-brown 'Cherokee Chief', 'Golden Lady', a large, ruffled clear yellow; and 'Thrush Song', dark-purple with brown and yellow signal.

Here is a list of inexpensive varieties, a combination of my own favorites with those most popular in the Spuria Iris Society.

RECOMMENDED SPURIA VARIETIES

White and Yellow

El Camino
Fairy Light
Golden Lady
Good Nature
Lark Song
Wadi Zem Zem

Blue, Violet, Purple

Blue Pinafore
Cambridge Blue
Premier
Ruth Nies Cabeen
Saugatauk
Sunlit Sea

Blend

Dutch Defiance
Katrina Nies
Two Opals

White

Morningtide
Wake Robin
White Heron

Bronze

Bronze Butterfly
Cherokee Chief
Driftwood

Minor Miniature Apogons

Three other Eurasian Apogon species are worth trying: *Iris ruthenica* from Romania, Turkestan, and China; *I. unguicularis (I. stylosa)* from Algeria and Greece (each the sole representative of a series); and *I. minutaurea (I. minuta)* found in Japanese gardens.

The Pilgrim iris, *I. ruthenica,* is a charming plant—very dwarf, never more than eight inches, with narrow leaves and comparatively large dark blue-purple flowers, which appear in May in New York. It is hardy, but should be transplanted in spring when it is in full growth. It is said to be easy to raise from seed. (See Appendix for seed sources.)

The only tender beardless rhizomatous species is *Iris unguicularis,* the winter-blooming iris. On the West Coast, one or another of its various forms will be in flower in rock gardens from October to March. According to a correspondent in Houston, Texas, it blooms for prolonged periods along the Gulf Coast; in England, it is a highly favored species; but in the Northeast, it can be grown only in a cold frame or cool greenhouse. It likes limey soil—one of the few beardless irises that do. Those who have suitable facilities for bringing it to flower are lyrical about the beauty of its smooth silken flowers—bright lilac in the common form, but varying from ivory white, banded with gold on the falls, to a deep rich violet in the honey-scented Greek form, known as *I. speciosa.* In all forms, according to Dykes, the narrow style branches appear to be dusted with gold. Both standards and falls are wide on the blade and very narrow at the haft. The flowers, stemless like those of the miniature dwarf bearded *I. pumila,* are held aloft on a six-inch perianth tube. After blooming, plants are said to produce huge tufts of leaves. Once established, this iris should be left alone, for it resents transplanting. Perhaps, like *I. ruthenica,* it should be transplanted in spring.

Finally, the hardy *Iris minutaurea* (or *I. minuta*) that is from Japanese gardens is a delightful small thing when it blooms; the leaves, though mercifully short when the flowers appear on four to six inch stems, grow to at least a foot later in the season. May-blooming flowers are small, with short, cream standards and round falls marked with brown.

Gardeners who are interested in growing Eurasian apogen species will find others described in Dykes' *Handbook of Garden Irises.* And they will enjoy tracking down sources of seed.

CRESTED IRISES

Irises of the subsection Evansia are usually called crested irises. Botanically, this group is on a par with the Apogon subsection; but for gardens, its importance is considerably less. Only a few species are hardy. Even so, the flowers of these few are so exceedingly handsome that no gardener should deny himself the pleasure of growing at least one or two crested irises. I grow three species and consider them all indispensable.

The common name is derived from the raised crest, with proliferations rather like those of a cock's comb along the center line of each fall. The flower is similar in form to the Japanese irises, though much smaller. With the exception of three American species (discussed in the following chapter), the crested irises are native to Southeast Asia.

The low-growing roof iris of Japan, *Iris tectorum*, ranks high as a foreground plant for semi-shady borders. There are blue and white forms. A clump of the yellow-crested *I. tectorum album* in bloom is one of the most beautiful sights in a garden; the more common white-crested blue form is less striking, but more vigorous —though neither form is at all difficult to grow. Both have comparatively large, slightly ruffled flowers with all parts on one plane. The broad-bladed standards are so extremely narrow at the haft that they seem to float free in space.

I grow these irises in rich soil at the sunniest end of my shady garden, where they get at least a half-day of sun. The rhizomes, which creep along the soil surface, send out short feeder roots. This means they quickly exhaust the food within their reach and must be fed and transplanted more frequently than most irises. Transplanting is best done in midsummer, about the end of June. When I am too busy to transplant, I dig in some additional fresh rich soil around the clumps. 'Paltec', a hybrid between *I. tectorum* and the bearded iris 'Edina', is desirable for the foreground of the sunny June border, and is easy to grow. It has the plant characteristics of tectorum and many smooth blue flowers.

Equally delightful, especially for the lover of miniature plants, is *Iris gracilipes*, which Dykes calls "the most fairy like of all irises." The tiny surface-growing rhizomes, and the fans of narrow, gracefully arching leaves, provide a perfect background for the numerous pinkish-mauve blossoms with conspicuous orange crests.

24   IRIS GRACILIPES

This dainty crested species, native to Japan, is a treasure for the shady
rock garden. The lilac flowers, crested in orange, are hardly larger than
the johnny-jump-up blooming at the left. The leaves are narrow; the
stems slender and branched. Blooms in late May.

25   IRIS TECTORUM ALBA

My favorite form of this low-growing crested species, native to China.
The exquisite shape of the white flower, and the narrow delicate yellow
crests, show clearly against heuchera leaves at the sunny edge of my
shady garden.

These appear on wiry multi-branched stems in late May. There is also a white form, said to be less robust.

I grow the mauve form in rich acid soil in the shade of a boulder, and let it alone. When the rhizomes become matted, transplanting is necessary and should be done in early spring while the leaves are still in the bud stage. I have not found *I. gracilipes* difficult to grow. One November, our dachshund took it into her head to dig up a fine clump. Several days later I found the dried rhizomes, the leaves badly wilted, scattered over the ground. I went through the motions of replanting, without any hope that the plants could survive. When spring came, they put forth leaves *and* flower buds.

The tender species of crested irises are seldom seen in cold climates, where they must be grown either in greenhouses or as pot plants. Even in California and the southern states, where they can be grown outdoors, they are not used in gardens as much as they deserve to be. Both *Iris japonica* (which is not a "Japanese" type) and *I. wattii* flower profusely on many-branched stems. The latter is taller, tenderer, and effective when planted in shade, among begonias, camellias, and ferns. It fairly covers itself with lavender-flushed white blossoms about the size of a silver dollar. The prominent lavender style-branches are deeply feathered at the ends; the orange crests are surrounded by an orange blotch. Like *Belamcanda chinensis* (blackberry lily), it produces a leafy stem, with flowers at the top. *I. japonica,* said to be hardy in England, is similar to *I. wattii* but the flowers are more deeply colored.

Only sporadic attempts at hybridizing crested iris species have been made. In addition to 'Paltec', available hybrids include 'Nada', a hybrid between *I. japonica* and *I. confusa,* and 'Darjeeling', from Nada × self. 'Queen's Grace', a recent lavender hybrid between *I. wattii* and the hardy *I. tectorum,* was bred in New Zealand by Jean Stevens. To my knowledge it is not yet for sale in this country.

9

Native American Beardless Irises

Our native irises were grown in European gardens long before they were known to American gardeners. A number of species from the Atlantic seaboard were described in European botanical works in the 17th and early 18th century so that Linnaeus was able to include *Iris versicolor, I. virginica,* and *I. verna* in his *Species Plantarum.* However, later, American horticulturists searched Asia and Europe for new irises while remarkable species waited undiscovered, at home.

CRESTED IRISES

All the American species are rhizomatous and beardless. Almost all belong to the smooth-falled Apogon subsection, but three dwarf species with linear crests on the falls belong to the Evansia or crested iris subsection.

One of these, *Iris lacustris,* the lake iris, I mention just for the record. It is too difficult for general garden use, though it is said to grow well in Wisconsin and to be at home in English gardens. The tiny plants with three-inch leaves and small slate blue flowers are found in great numbers in sandy woods and bogs around Lake Superior.

A second species, *Iris cristata,* in appearance a larger, brighter *I. lacustris,* is different in behavior—adaptable and undemanding, first favorite among our natives. It is at its best in a lightly shaded, woodsy, and well drained soil where it spreads over large areas, carpeting the ground with rather broad six-inch leaves. In May the matted growth is nearly hidden beneath flat lavender flowers patterned in deep blue and white with a yellow toothed crest on the falls. White, lavender, and almost pink variants have been reported. The long thin rhizomes creep about over the soil surface,

26   IRIS CRISTATA

A delightful miniature crested iris for planting in a cool pocket of
the rock garden. Flowers, opening in May, are blue with golden crests.

and I plant them so, covering only the roots, protecting the whole with a light litter until plants have taken hold. Each spring, I top-dress them with an inch of fresh humusy soil; otherwise *I. cristata,* takes care of itself.

The hardy little *Iris tenuis,* found only along the Clackamas and Molalla rivers in Oregon, has recently been transferred (Lenz 1959) to the Evansia subsection. According to Lenz, it is most closely related to the two crested species *I. lacustris* and *I. cristata* and to the Japanese *I. gracilipes,* differing from them significantly only in the smoothness of the yellow ridge on the falls. It is said to grow in leaf mold and decaying moss among dense underbrush or under Douglas firs. In leaf, growth habit, and in the color and shape of the tiny flowers, this dainty species resembles *I. cristata;* the forked stems, like those of *I. gracilipes,* produce two or three flowers. A charming plant for the shady wild border.

APOGONS

The iris gap between Asia and America is bridged by *Iris setosa,* the Arctic iris, one of the two species belonging to the Tripetalae series. This little iris grows wild in Siberia, the Kamchatka Peninsula, Alaska, Labrador, the Gaspe Peninsula, and the state of Maine. I grew two forms in my garden from Alaskan seed, which germinated easily in a moist shaded spot where plants grew without difficulty. Leaves are broad and shorter than flower stems which, in one form, are only nine inches tall; in the other they are nearly two feet. The floriferous dwarf form is highly ornamental as a border edging. June flowers are violet-blue with a white area in the wide flat falls; standards are so tiny that flowers appear to be three-petaled.

A delightful small silken thing is *Iris verna,* sole representative of the series Vernae, and native to mountains from Kentucky to Georgia. The solitary periwinkle-blue flower is almost stemless, rising above short, almost evergreen leaves. In shape it is similar to bearded irises, and the slightly pubescent bright orange area on the falls might be mistaken for a beard. I had always read that the vernal iris should be planted in moist humusy soil in partial shade, but I found huge clumps of it in North Carolina on a red clay bank in full sun. Subsequently I planted it in both sun and dappled shade, but it would have none of my garden. Though winter-hardy, it refused to bloom and I finally discarded the plants. I shall try it again.

Another pleasing little Eastern native, which grows along the

coast from Maine to the Carolinas, is *Iris prismatica,* the only
species in the series Prismaticae. It looks like a small slender
Siberian iris and is closely related to that group. Light blue or
lavender flowers, veined white on the round-bladed falls, are carried
on tortuously curved and wiry branched stems above tufts of leaves
that come up here and there at the ends of creeping rhizomes.
Though difficult to transplant, once acclimated it grows well in full
sun and acid soil. It comes easily from fall-sown seeds—as does
I. versicolor, Edna Millay's "blue flag of the bog," so familiar in
swamps from New Brunswick to Georgia as to seem unexciting
to Eastern gardeners. This American representative of the series
Laevigatae grew so well in my garden that I moved it to an uncul-
tivated spot where it could take over as it pleased. Seeds of various
color forms, the red-violet 'Kermisina' and the pink 'Rosea' are
available, and pale blue and white forms have been reported. The
similar but even more robust *I. virginica* grows from Indiana to
Louisiana. Heavily veined fragrant flowers, dark blue and bright
pink to white, are produced on branched two-foot stems. Collected
forms are available. 'Giant White' is a fine clone with large flowers.

The Louisiana Irises

In the bayou country of southern Louisiana, where land ends in
a world of salt marshes and twisting bayous, miles of blue, orchid,
wine-purple, yellow, pink, rose, red, bronze and copper-colored
irises choke the swamps in spring. Though botanical mention of
one or another species of these irises belonging to the series Hexagonae had been made from time to time, the "discovery" of the
beautiful Louisiana irises belongs to the 20th century.

In 1925, Dr. John K. Small of the New York Botanical Garden
saw them in all their wealth of natural hybrids and was so enthusi-
astic that he is said to have called southern Louisiana "the iris center
of the universe." He spent years collecting plants, and his published
descriptions introducing Louisiana irises to the world became news.
In 1930, they even made *The New York Times.* Soon the swamps
were full of ardent collectors, and southern gardeners began to
improve the hybrids that nature had already so abundantly
produced.

Though Louisiana irises grow most luxuriantly in the Deep
South, the Southwest, and California, they must not be dismissed
as plants for warm climates only. They are winter-hardy (with
some protection) and give adequate bloom as far north as Canada.
A theory that the large corky seeds "floated down the river" from

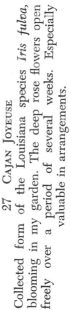

28 White Siberian iris varieties, showing different flower forms. Top and lower left: Snow Crest, with vertical flowers. Gage. Morgan Award, 1963. Lower center: Snow Wheel. Small, neat, flaring flowers. Hodson. The three broad horizontal flowers are White Swirl. Cassebeer. Morgan Award, 1961.

27 Cajan Joyeuse
Collected form of the Louisiana species *Iris fulva*, blooming in my garden. The deep rose flowers open freely over a period of several weeks. Especially valuable in arrangements.

cooler climates would, if true, satisfactorily explain their hardiness. All gardeners who love graceful and unusual flowers and arrangers who grow their own material should try these irises.

The large number of species named by Dr. Small has since been reduced to four. The three species involved in the Louisiana hybrids are *Iris fulva, I. brevicaulis,* and *I. giganticaerulea.*

I. fulva that grows as far north as Missouri and Ohio has rather small drooping flowers of no great beauty, but the "Abbeville irises" called super-fulvas, discovered in southwestern Louisiana near Abbeville by W. B. McMillan in the 1930's, are giant-flowered and spectacular. Colors range from yellow through red, copper and bronze to purple. Wide flaring falls, velvety in texture, leathery in substance, are sometimes smooth, sometimes marked with a conspicuous yellow crest. In my garden, plants grew to three feet; in Louisiana, they may reach four feet.

The smallest species is *Iris brevicaulis (I. foliosa)* which, though commonly twelve to eighteen inches tall with flowers hidden in the foliage, has miniature forms only six inches high with flowers carried above leaves. These are desirable as edging plants. Typically the leathery blue flowers with horizontal falls and upright standards are borne along the zigzag stems. As many as six may open at once, one stem providing a handsome natural arrangement. This iris, which grows in Louisiana pastures and along river bluffs, adapts easily to gardens.

The tallest of the Louisianas is *Iris giganticaerulea,* found only at the edges of fresh water bays and salt marshes along the Gulf Coast of Louisiana. The large blue, purple, or white flowers with broad flaring falls and upright standards are borne at different levels on erect stalks, which may reach six feet in the wild.

Though the wild iris fields have been sadly diminished by the clearing of swamps, many beautiful wild clones have been collected and made available to us—as the white *Iris giganticaerulea,* 'Her Highness', with light green style-arms and a raised yellow signal patch. In 1957 this won the Debaillon Award given annually for the top Louisiana Iris.

It was not until the early 1950's that I began to experiment with these unusual flowers. I bought plants from a Massachusetts nursery and both seeds and plants from Louisiana. I planted the seeds in a cold frame and set the plants in my garden and also along a path bordering the small swamp in our woods. That experiment was a failure, not because the plants failed to grow and bloom but because our deer eventually discovered the plants and cropped the leaves to the ground.

In the garden, my bed of Louisiana irises flourished. I dug out clay soil to a depth of one foot and filled in to within an inch of the top with about 75 per cent peat moss and compost liberally mixed with dried manure.This gave me a slightly sunken bed that could be soaked during the pre-bloom season. Later I discovered that these "swamp" irises needed extra watering only in a very dry spring or fall. They must have good drainage to withstand northern winters. And they should not be planted too deep—an inch and a half of soil over the rhizome is about right. In southern gardens a half day of sun is sufficient; in the North, the Louisianas flourish in full sun.

I bought only inexpensive hybrids and named varieties; all were beautiful, though I most admired the rose and red varieties. When I finally decided to dispose of them because of my desperate need for space to accommodate my own median bearded seedlings, my husband was cross, for the Louisianas are, of all the irises I grow, his favorites. The only one I have left is the violet, almost prostrate but floriferous, 'Dorothea K. Williamson', that survives, neglected, in an odd corner; also, a few rhizomes keep coming up and being pulled out of the original bed, remade and generously limed though it is. I know that Louisiana irises are not only hardy—they are persistent. I had no trouble with disease, though some varieties are said to be subject to rust.

If you want to adventure with these natives, you would enjoy membership in the Louisiana Iris Society.

In this list I make no attempt to bring you up to date on "best" varieties. Those I have grown and enjoyed are all inexpensive and most of them collected

RECOMMENDED LOUISIANAS

Bronze, Red Rose

Bayou Sunset
Cajan Joyeuse
Cherry Bounce
Wheelhorse

Yellow

Abbeville Yellow
Dixie Deb
Kraemer Yellow

Blue and Purple

Haile Selassie
Holleyblu
The Kahn
Violet Ray

White and Cream

Barbara Elaine Taylor
Gheen's White
Her Highness

The Pacific Coast Irises

For 700 miles along the West Coast, from Washington south to central California, there grows a group of the prettiest and most diversely colored little flowers a gardener could ever hope to see—the Pacific Coast irises. Species and wild hybrid swarms flourish on the western slopes of the Cascade and Sierra Nevada ranges, on shaded foothills and sunny ocean bluffs. This important group of American native irises belongs to the series Californicae, is closely related to the Asiatic Siberians, and blooms just ahead of them. According to Dr. Lee W. Lenz, their ancestors may have reached America eons ago, via the Bering Strait and moved southward to their present position as the mountain ranges were being formed.

The flowers, about the same size as those of the Siberian irises, are of different proportion—more compact, more poised, crisper. The rippled horizontal falls are frequently broad and rounded, though some are narrow and pointed, giving a starry effect; standards are commonly held at an angle instead of upright. The color range is wide—from cream, buff, apricot or golden-yellow to orchid, lavender, deep purple, blue violet, and, rarely, true sky-blue and white. Color is even more diversified in the countless wild hybrid forms, where bronze, chocolate, rose-crimson, and fuschia are found. Falls are usually patterned with rich texture veining in brown, maroon, or red.

Both species and garden hybrids of these irises are increasingly popular in England (where one famous seed house offers seeds of hybrids as well as species) but are rarely found in American gardens except along the Pacific coast. Even there popularity is way below that of the beardeds. A probable reason is that, though they grow easily from seed, the Pacific Coast irises are difficult to transplant, and many gardeners prefer bloom-sized plants to the trouble of growing them from seed. Modern packing techniques are solving this problem.

Late fall, when new roots are forming, is the time recommended for transplanting, but my limited trials with hybrid plants sent from the Northwest in September have been unsuccessful. I think fall is a poor time to move plants to a more severe climate and I intend to try my luck with plants shipped in early spring when they are just starting into growth.

A thorough study of the series Californicae has recently been completed (Lenz 1958), and eleven species are now recognized:

29 IRIS INNOMINATA

A yellow form of this low-growing Pacific Coast species with open
frilled flowers veined tawny-orange. May-blooming in its native Oregon.

*Iris bracteata, I. chrysophylla, I. douglasiana, I. fernaldii, I. hart-
wegii, I. innominata, I. macrosiphon, I. munzii, I. purdyi, I. tenax,
I. tenuissima*—plus several subspecies. Nearly all are in cultivation.

The three species best suited to border and rock garden, are
I. douglasiana, I. tenas, and *I. innominata.* I have grown these three
from seed in neutral to slightly acid soil. They were successful in
both full sun and part shade in my garden.

Iris douglasiana grows wild on bare headlands and grassy coastal
hills along the seacoast from southern Oregon to Santa Barbara
County in California. In gardens, the stems are about a foot high
and bear several heads of three to four flowers. Colors are cream
through lavender and dark purple with an occasional skyblue or
white. The rippled standards are of the same color, though the
center of the fall is usually paler in tone and patterned with darker
veins. Named selections include the white 'Agnes James' and
'Amiguita', a soft lilac.

The graceful *Iris tenax,* common on sunny or lightly shaded hillsides in Washington and Oregon, was the first Pacific Coast species
to be cultivated and is the easiest to grow. Plants form dense clumps
of slender, light green, tough-fibered leaves. Each of the numerous
ten-inch bloom stalks bears two handsome, rather large flowers with
wide crisped segments. The usual colors are lavender or purple
marked on the falls with gold or white. Occasional yellow-flowered
plants are found.

The diminutive *Iris innominata* grows abundantly on sunny or
lightly shaded hillsides in several counties along the Rouge River
valley in Oregon and in Del Norte County in California. It has
become the most popular of the California series. One look at the
jaunty, crisp, perfectly proportioned flowers tells why. Their color,
though sometimes lavender or purple, usually is yellow—either
clear yellow without veining, golden orange with darker veins, or
occasionally apricot. Flowers are carried on numerous slender,
unbranched stems that rise four to ten inches among a profusion
of curving, narrow dark green leaves.

Two other species, more narrowly useful to gardens, are worth
mentioning. They are the little *Iris bracteata,* perhaps the most
beautiful in the series, and *I. munzii,* which according to Lenz
is the nearest to a true blue iris in the whole genus. The problem
with *I. bracteata* is that it is hard to transplant. The plant, which
grows naturally in dry shady areas, produces only a few polished
dark green leaves that occur singly rather than in a fan. They are
unusually thick, rigid, and narrow. The large, ruffled yellow flowers,

30   AMIGUITA

A selection of *Iris douglasiana,* one of the Pacific Coast species. The soft lilac-blue flowers are flushed purple on the falls and along the centers of the style arms.

two to each twelve-inch stem, are patterned on the falls with
maroon.

The rare *Iris munzii*, found in moist shade in only a few places
among the foothills of the Sierra Nevada, is the least cold-tolerant
species of the series. Above short, grey-green leaves, eighteen-inch
flower stems each produce four flowers. In the wild they are usually
violet in tone, with an occasional clone showing an electric-blue
flush on the falls; in some garden plants the flowers are pure
sky-blue.

Several hybrids, mostly between *Iris douglasiana* and *I. innominata*, have been produced in recent years. Mrs. M. Brummitt and
H. S. Fothergill, in England, and Lee Lenz and Richard Luhrson,
in the United States, have originated such varieties as 'Banbury
Beauty', lavender and purple; 'Banbury Butterfly', cream and
maroon; 'Elfin Motley', chrome and ruby-red, 'Fairy Flight', brick
with old gold etching on the falls; 'Ivory Maiden', ivory and rose;
'Pacific Splendor'—really splendid—a greyed buff flower with
very wide rippled falls beautifully patterned in darker veining;
'Selma Sunlight', pale buff-yellow; 'Tranquil Dale', pink with a
heliotrope flush; and 'Woodmont Rose', cream-white and fuchsia.
Of course, these can be increased only by vegetative reproduction
and sources are hard to find. I know of none in the United States
for the English varieties.

The Pacific Coast irises are eminently suited to West Coast
gardens and, to a lesser extent, to those of the Atlantic states; but
conditions in the Central and Rocky Mountain states are less
favorable. A packet of species or hybrid seeds will contain a good
color selection, and *may* contain something entirely new. They
should be planted in late fall in pots, flats, or cold frames and
left outside over winter to germinate in spring. The little seedlings
can be moved to permanent positions as soon as they are large
enough to handle. Once established, plants form large clumps that
require little care; in their season they are fairly smothered with
flowers.

The Longipetalae

Two other species, *Iris longipetala* and *I. missouriensis,* are native
to our western states. Two that were formerly considered species,
I. arizonica and *I. montana,* were reduced by Dr. Foster to varieties
of *I. missouriensis*. Both are easy to grow in sunny gardens; both
vary in height from fifteen to thirty inches, bear several terminal
flowers, and like situations that are moist in spring and dry in

summer. The almost everygreen *I. longipetala,* native to California, forms tight clumps with stiff grey-green leaves. The large, attractive white flowers with close violet veining are characterized by blunt standards. The similar, but deciduous, *I. missouriensis* is native to most western and southwestern states at elevations from 11,000 to a few hundred feet along the Snake River where it joins the Columbia. Typically the flower is lavender or white with precise blue-purple veining on the falls, but both white and purple-flowered forms are known. This hardy species, so vigorous that it will grow almost anywhere, is considered a weed by western stockmen.

10

Bulbous Irises

All the irises that have been discussed so far are rhizomatous, and belong to the subgenus Iris. Now let us discuss the three other subgenera: Xiphium, Scorpiris, and Nepalensis—even though *Iris decora*, sole member of the subgenus Nepalensis, is not bulbous.

SUBGENUS XIPHIUM

Various species and forms of hardy bulbous irises, native to far parts of the world, provide important and unusual plants to enhance our gardens. Some are as easy to grow as crocuses, and yield lavish return for little effort; many of the more difficult ones are beautiful enough to be worth extra care.

The subgenus Xiphium is divided into two sections: the naked bulb section, also called Xiphium, consisting of the Spanish, Dutch, and English irises; and the netted bulb section, called Reticulata, in which the bulb is covered with a fibrous tunic.

The Reticulatas

Among irises that bloom in the open ground in the northeast, the Reticulatas are the earliest. Though hardy bulbous plants are mainstays in gardens, these hardy and permanent little irises appear in few gardens. It's a great pity. I do not understand why these delightful flowers have not as yet caught public fancy. I can only suppose that gardeners simply don't *believe* these irises until they see them, for almost everyone who sees them blooming in my garden immediately orders bulbs for his own planting. They are as effective as the crocus; they should be equally popular.

All the instructions emphasize the necessity of planting these bulbs in gritty well-drained soil in full sun for a thorough baking

114

in summer. Perhaps it is fortunate that I read the books *after* planting the bulbs, for I put them everywhere: in the open border, where they must compete for sun with larger plants; in the rock garden, where ground covers intrude; on a semiwild wooded slope; and in a sheltered nook on the south side of our house. They multiply most rapidly and bloom earlier in the drier, protected positions. Like almost all bulbs, they must have good drainage; otherwise they seem indifferent to soil characteristics.

The blue-violet form known as the species *Iris reticulata* is spectacular planted in drifts. The flower is crisp in texture, with narrow, long-hafted, upward-slanting falls, marked on the broad blade with a golden central spot.

The light blue bitone 'Cantab' increases more slowly than *Iris reticulata,* but contrasts effectively with the deeper colors. My favorite light blue variety, 'Clarette', a Van Tubergen seedling from the species *Iris bakerana,* grows and blooms well. The flower is very lovely; standards are a clear sky blue, the blade of the darker falls a blue with the white base color showing in the center of the fall as it does in the species parent. The intensely blue 'Harmony' and 'Joyce', more violet toned, are hybrids between *I. reticulata* and *I. histrioides major,* as are the violet-colored varieties, 'Wentworth' and 'Violet Beauty', and the deep blue 'Royal Blue'. 'J. S. Digt' and 'Velvet' are the only red violets I find in catalogues. 'Hercules' is violet with bronze shadings. I grow them all, but just four or five different colored varieties provide a wonderful display.

They bloom with the snowdrops, winter-flowering crocuses, and winter aconite. Most years, I can count on having flowers by the ninth of March. Sometimes they are buried under several inches of snow, but emerge unharmed when the snow melts. Leaves are slender four-sided columns terminating in horny spikes. They are shorter than the flowers at the beginning of the bloom season, but they grow to a height of about eighteen inches before they die down in May. Like daffodil leaves, they should not be removed while they are still green; unlike daffodils, they die quickly and tidily.

Other species and varieties in the Reticulata group bloom even earlier than *Iris reticulata. I. histrio* is said to flower in winter, but I have not been able to find a source for it or for *I. histrioides.* In my garden, the tiny *I. vartanii alba* is first to appear, usually in late February. *I. bakerana* and *I. histrioides major,* said to be larger and more desirable than the type, flower around the first

31 *Left.* IRIS RETICULATA. The four-sided leaf spears of this bulbous species top the blue-violet flowers. Blooming in my garden on March 12th.

32 *Center.* IRIS DANFORDIAE. Only yellow-flowered reticulata species blooms before the leaves appear.

33 *Right.* IRIS MAGNIFICA. An April- blooming Juno species with palest blue flowers borne in the axils of broad shining leaves. Daffodils and single early tulips in the background.

of March. To bloom each year, precocious species must have protection in colder regions. I cover them lightly, as soon as the ground is well frozen, with evergreen boughs over the oak leaves that blow onto my garden. A mulch of salt hay would serve the same purpose, which is to inhibit too early emergence. Left to themselves, they might bloom in January and be unable to survive the remaining long weeks of winter.

The most beautiful of all reticulatas are *Iris bakerana* from Mesopotamia and *I. histrioides major* from the Caucasus. The flower of the first is a deep, rich blue bitone with standards of ultramarine and falls of a velvety blue-violet with a pale yellow ridge and white central area flecked with a few dark spots. The leaves are cylindrical spears with eight ridges. The flower of *I. histrioides major* is a lighter but not less brilliant blue with wide falls. It stands only three to four inches tall and blooms almost before leaf points have pierced the ground. The horizontal falls are ridged in orange-yellow and show the white base color in an irregular area.

If the tiny Palestinian *Iris vartanii alba* bloomed, say, in late April, it would not be especially exciting; but in late February its flowers are a delight, narrow of parts but pure white and crested in yellow. It is not permanent in this region or even, according to my correspondents, in the Northwest or California, but it is not expensive. Every three or four years I replace my few bulbs of this species and of the much lovelier four-inch yellow *I. danfordiae,* which blooms in March before its leaves emerge. Its bulbs split into many bulblets after a year or two but it is charming enough to be welcomed even as a sort of biennial, planted in fall to bloom in spring. Tulips share this tendency to split into bulblets—a tendency that I have been able to curb by planting about twice the recommended depth. I wonder whether planting *Iris danfordiae* six instead of three inches deep would reduce its inclination to split. I shall try it.

There is one more Reticulata species that I mention for the sake of those who may become as fascinated with these little irises as I am. This is *Iris winogradowii,* a costly rarity from the Caucasus. I know of four gardens in which it is grown—one in Seattle, one in New Mexico, one in California and one in England—but I have not seen its large flowers in various shades of yellow. In photographs they resemble those of *I. reticulata,* though the falls appear to be nearly as broad as those of *I. danfordiae.*

The Reticulatas will grow in most sections of this country. They are planted in September or October, preferably in full sun and

about three inches deep. Space the bulbs two to three inches apart,
depending on whether you want an immediate effect, or to postpone the chore of transplanting. I leave them in the ground until
they become crowded. I have had no evidence of the dread ink-
fungus infection, a disease that sometimes blackens these bulbs,
and I have never seen a bulb so affected. Nevertheless, a caution:
any bare spots in a planting may indicate that some bulbs have
become infected. Any bulbs that show sooty areas on the coat
should be destroyed.

Inexpensive species and named varieties suitable for the average
garden include:

I. *danfordiae*—yellow   Joyce—brilliant blue
I. *histriodies major*—brilliant   J. S. Digt—red-violet
   blue   Royal Blue—dark violet-blue
I. *reticulata*—blue-purple   Violet Beauty
Cantab—light blue   Wentworth—dark violet
Harmony—brilliant blue

The Xiphiums

These are the Spanish, the well known hybrid Dutch, and the
English irises. Use of the name Xiphium (from *xiphos* meaning
sword) to describe plants with narrow, deeply channeled leaves is
mystifying.

Spanish irises are known to have been grown in Europe since the
middle of the sixteenth century. Modern varieties are descendants
of the blue-purple *Iris xiphium,* native to Spain and North Africa.
The modern Dutch hybrids resulted (according to Dykes) from
crossing a large and early flowering form of I. *xiphium* with two
closely related species, the red-purple I. *tingitana* from Tangiers
and the bright blue I. *fontanesii* from Morocco. The English varieties are all derived from blue-flowered I. *xiphioides,* native to the
Pyrenees. This species is unusual in that large wings project from
either side of the hafts and rise above the style-arms.

The species from Tangiers and Morocco are too tender to be
grown outdoors in the Northeast. They might flourish in a warm
section of the Southwest.

The large-flowering Dutch irises, tallest and most popular of
bulbous irises, have rather crowded the smaller-flowered Spanish
irises from the garden picture. These hybrids are much used by
florists since they transport well and can be forced for winter bloom.

To my mind the most important use of these handsome flowers is to provide material for arrangements. They last well in water; there are two flowers per stem, and they may be cut while in bud. I plant them in the cutting garden.

Varieties that have performed well for me include:

Blue Giant—deep indigo blue
Joan of Arc—white with yellow
blotch
Melody—white standards,
yellow falls
Lilac Queen—lilac standards
white falls
Wedgwood—very early light
blue
White Excelsior—pure white

A correspondent in Salt Lake City, who specializes in bulbous irises, has rated for me some Dutch varieties growing in her garden: tops—'Blue Champion', 'Harmony', 'Lemon Queen'; excellent—'Ankara', 'Delft Blue', 'H. C. Van Vliet', 'King Mauve', 'Le Mogul', 'Panamint', 'Princess Beatrice'. She comments that yellow varieties are planted by themselves because they soon take over a bed of mixed colors. No Xiphium variety of any color has grown that well in my garden. I prefer the dainty, smaller-flowered Spanish irises, which bloom two weeks later than the Dutch varieties, at a time when the tall beardeds and Siberians are fading. Several clumps of a half-dozen or so Spanish irises perk up a tired garden. Not many Spanish varieties are available, but there are some blended smoky varieties and several are pleasantly fragrant. They start growth in the fall, usually with a single spear like leaf.

Varieties that I have found most attractive include:

Blue River—blue bitone
Canarybird—bright yellow
Delft Blue—blue bitone
Heracles—smoky blend
King of the Blues—deep blue
L'Innocence—late pure white
Menelik—blue standards, white
falls
Prince Henry—smoky blend

Culture for Spanish and Dutch irises is the same. Although the bulbs are hardy and they flourish in only slightly milder climates than that of New York State, there are ifs, ands, and buts about growing them here. The reason is that in the fall they insist on producing leaves which are subject to a long winter of viciously alternating temperatures. This means that they need the protection of a salt hay mulch or evergreen boughs. Plant them with four inches of soil above the top of the bulb in the Northeast. October is the best time to plant. In regions with less severe winters, shallower setting will suffice. In the South, they are dug as soon as foliage withers and left "as is" to cure. They can be separated after they have dried out thoroughly, stored and replanted in fall. Probably the same treatment would benefit them here, but I leave them in place.

The "English" *Iris xiphioides* was brought from moist, cool, upland meadows in the Spanish mountains to the English port of Bristol by traders—probably in the sixteenth century—and grown in gardens there. Dutch nurserymen, who imported them from Bristol and gave them the name, must have assumed they were native to England.

These irises are far more at home in the English climate and its American counterpart, the Pacific Northwest, than in New York State; but the saying that English and Dutch irises will not grow in the same garden is not altogether true. They do not thrive in my garden, but I can coax them into bloom at least one year—sometimes two—in a semishaded area where slightly acid soil is moist and well drained—the coolest spot I own. English irises do not produce foliage in fall and are hardy. Dormancy is brief. Top size bulbs are almost as large as single-nose daffodils; they are rather soft and do not store well so plant them six inches deep, as early as possible in fall. They like to begin root growth in September.

Available colors run from white through light blue to deep blue, and from lilac through rosy purple to dark red-purple. Good mixtures contain a fair sampling of the available colors. I have had two years of bloom from the following varieties—two of which came from Holland, two from the Northwest:

Montblanc—pure white   Prince of Wales—marine blue
Prince Albert—silver blue   Tricolor—mottled orchid

SUBGENUS SCORPIRIS: JUNO IRISES

The Junos, as the irises in this subgenus are called, have been included in and removed from the genus *Iris* several times by several botanists. I cannot quarrel with any scientist who has decided that Juno irises are not irises; no one would be apt to identify a Juno plant as an iris until it blooms.

The plants resemble miniature corn plants in form. The broad channeled and shining leaves alternate on the stem, giving a two-dimensional effect to the plant. Leaf points are visible in early March, and grow rapidly. Flower buds that develop in the leaf axils and stand vertically against the central stem add to the plant's charm. Even the flower is unusual; the standards, though sometimes horizontal, usually hang below the falls or swirl around the base of the bloom. This habit is not particularly noticeable, because the standards are small and narrow, in marked contrast to the falls and the style-crest. Juno flowers are beardless, except for *Iris tubergeniana,* in which the crest breaks up into a few straggly hairs. In all other Junos, falls carry a golden central crest.

Hybridizers have hardly touched this subgenus, and few Juno hybrids exist. The two that I grow are not more beautiful than the species—nor do they need to be; every species I have seen is exquisite.

Among the Junos I grow, the earliest to bloom—about the first week in April—is *Iris aucheri* (*I. sindjarensis*), from northern Mesopotamia. It bears light, almost turquoise-blue flowers on an eight-inch stalk. Like those of English Irises, the hafts of the falls bear large wings which curve up over the style-arms.

Only a week later, *Iris graeberiana* opens a terminal flower on a ten-inch stalk (in Junos, the terminal flower always opens first). This newly discovered species, with cobalt blue flowers, was named for P. L. Graeber, who collected many bulbous plants for Van Tubergen and Co. in Tashkent. It is distinguished from other Junos by long, glossy, medium-green leaves, less than an inch wide. In all the other Junos I grow, leaves are at least two inches wide.

Near the end of April, *Iris magnifica* and *I. bucharica* open. The newly planted hybrids, 'Sindpers' and 'Warlsind', which should bloom early, sometimes open last. The seven flowers of *I. bucharica,* are pale cream with a large overlay of golden yellow on the blade of the falls, and black, vertical parallel lines (or veins) on either side of the central orange crest. (All my Junos have these lines, which extend deep into the throat.) The stem of this vigorous species is eighteen inches tall; leaves are light green.

Iris magnifica is most imposing, growing almost two feet tall. It also produces seven flowers that seem white at first glance, but a closer look shows them to be delicately tinged with lavender. This species, too, has great vigor.

The hybrid 'Sindpers' (*I. sindjarensis* × *I. persica*) produced large, ruffled turquoise-blue flowers on a four-inch plant the first year, and was able to ripen its bulbs for second-year bloom.

'Warlsind' (*I. warleyensis* × *I. sindjarensis*), is even more charming and colorful than I had expected from the catalogue description. It has blue standards, white falls edged blue, and a golden crest.

There are other hardy and easy-to-grow Juno irises, such as the lemon yellow *Iris orchioides* and the hybrid *I. willmottiana alba;*

but the ones I long to grow, and can find no source for, are two more difficult dwarf species—the nearly stemless and narrow-leaved Persian iris *I. persica,* and the spinster iris, *I. rosenbachiana.* Both are sufficiently hardy to be grown in the Northeast, and bloom with the crocuses. Dykes called the latter "one of the most brilliant of all irises." The flower varies from white to violet, except for the blade of the falls, which is a deep crimson-purple around a conspicuous golden crest. The drooping standards are large for a Juno iris.

The Persian iris, subject of the first plate in Curtis's *Botanical Magazine* in 1787, was known to Parkinson in 1629—he wrote that it will "hardly abide to be noursed up." It is said to be difficult to grow because it needs a heavy soil and a thorough baking in summer. I long to try this exquisite little species in the heavy soil along the south wall of our house. I know that *I. persica* has been flowered for a number of years in *sandy* soil on the south shore of Long Island, and I have a hunch it would succeed here better than in England.

The flower of this species is described as palest sea-green except for the ruffled blade of the falls, which is brownish crimson with an orange central ridge. The style-crests are large, ruffled, and fluted; and the narrow, spoon-shaped standards stand out like spokes below the falls. A number of color forms of this species, including a bright yellow, have been discovered in the Taurus mountains.

Two dwarf Juno species, the blue-flowered winged iris, *I. planifolia* (*I. alata*) from Spain and North Africa, and the yellow-flowered Palestine iris, *I. paleastina* from Syria, are tender. Even in New Mexico, a correspondent reports growing them in pots. It is said that *I. planifolia* will bloom outdoors in California for a year or two but is not permanent. It might be grown successfully in southern California.

The root system of Junos is unusual. Attached to the bulbs are several storage roots, shaped like the old fashioned long varieties of garden radish. These are brittle and are said to break off easily when bulbs are dug or shipped. All the warnings I had read about the difficulty of keeping these food reservoirs attached to the bulbs frightened me and, for years, kept me from ordering Juno bulbs. Perhaps I have been lucky, but only one of the bulbs I received had lost all the storage roots. Several have had only one root but most have arrived with roots intact. (Nor have I broken off any in planting.) I have ordered bulbs from three sources, and each nursery has done an admirable packing job. I think the dire warnings must have been written before the wonderful modern packing facilities were available.

The taller, later-flowering species are easiest to grow. They come from the eastern part of Turkestan where, according to Laurence Neel in *The Iris Year Book* for 1957, "the soil is light and sandy." The difficult winter-flowering dwarf species, also according to Mr. Neel, "mostly grow (in the wild) in a very heavy calcareous red loam which˙gets baked hard in the summer and ensures proper ripening of the bulb."

I plant Junos in full sun in a raised bed of well-limed clay soil against the south wall of our house, and keep the surrounding soil bare of other plants in summer so it will be as hot and dry as possible. What's a summer bare spot compared to April beauty of a Juno iris? These are recommended species:

I. aucheri (I. sindjarensis)	*I. orchioides*
I. bucharica	*I. magnifica*
I. graeberiana	*I. willmottiana alba* (hybrid)

SUBGENUS NEPALENSIS: IRIS DECORA

I can't honestly say that *Iris decora* is a choice garden species, but it is more than a botanical curiosity. It has charm, is very easy to grow from seed, and persists in my garden with almost no care.

The unique rootstock consists of several long fleshy roots attached to a growing point. There is no visible bulb or rhizome—a truly unique iris. Even the seeds with a white excrescence at one end are fascinating.

Plants are graceful and pleasing. The surfaces of the leaves, stems, and bud spathes are all satin smooth and glaucous. The narrow leaves have one central ridge on one side and two ridges on the other, so that a cross-section of the leaf would zigzag slightly like a very wide and shallow letter W. They die down completely in fall, and start into growth very late indeed—so late that one year I thought my plants had died. There was still no sign of leaves in early May, I remember, but I don't know exactly when growth began. Luckily I had no chance to cultivate the bed until June or I might have lost my plants.

Bloom starts in late June. The flowers of *I. decora*, like those of hemerocallis, last only one day, but the fifteen-inch stems branch, and each head produces two or three light red-violet flowers in succession. Standards and falls lie in a horizontal plane, while the style-arms with large deeply cleft crests stand almost erect. Falls are decorated with several parallel white striations in a precise pattern on either side of a raised and exceedingly ruffled white crest, which is tipped with gold in the throat of the flower.

Gardeners who would like to grow this interesting species from the southern slopes of the Himalayas can obtain seeds from at least one English seed-house.

11

Progression of Bloom

It is not possible to make an accurate chart of blooming periods for all the groups of irises that can be grown in such a vari-climated country as the United States. My chart gives average periods for Rockland County, New York. This is just above the New Jersey line, where I have grown irises for more than a quarter of a century. Eastern gardeners north or south of this area can add or subtract a few days from the dates for first flowers.

PEAK BLOOM DATES FOR TALL BEARDEDS

Dates for the flowering of tall beardeds in various parts of the United States string out over three months, from the beginning of April in southern Texas to the end of June in Maine. Although freakish weather may postpone or advance the season as much as a week, peak bloom usually can be expected about mid-june in Montana, North Dakota, New Hampshire, Vermont, and Massachusetts. Memorial Day week end usually coincides with the height of the season in southern parts of Michigan, Connecticut, and New York, central areas of Colorado and Ohio, and northern parts of Indiana and Utah. Mid-May brings peak bloom to Nebraska, Missouri, Oregon, Washington and Northern California. Late April is the time for iris shows in the southern tier of states—Alabama, Louisiana and Mississippi—and in southern Tennessee.

125

BLOOM SEQUENCE IN SOUTHERN NEW YORK

	Feb.	Mar.	Apr.	May	June	July	Aug.	Sep.	Oct.
Reticulata	x	xxxx	xx						
Miniature dwarf bearded		xxx	x						
Juno		xx	xx						
Standard dwarf bearded			xxxx						
Aril and arilbred		x	xxxx	x					
Intermediate bearded			xxxx						
Evansia			xxx	x					
Tall bearded			x	xxx					
Border bearded			x	xxx					
Siberian			x	xxx					
Dutch, Spanish, English				xxxx	xx				
Louisiana				xxx					
Spuria				xx	xx				
Japanese				xx	xxx				
I. dichotoma						xxxx	xx		
Reblooming bearded						x	xxxx	xxxx	x

THE IRIS PAGEANT IN SOUTHERN NEW YORK

In my garden the iris pageant opens somewhere between the seventh and the fifteenth of February with the flowering of *Iris vartanii alba,* a tiny member of the reticulata section of bulbous irises. The February date does not count the winter-blooming *I. unguicularis* (*I. stylosa*) which needs coldframe protection in this northern climate.

One after another, in late February and early March, the small, brilliant flowers of the various reticulata species and hybrids join snowdrops and native winter-flowering shrubs to bring pre-spring bouquets into our often snow-covered gardens. These early irises have a notably long flowering period; they continue along with the early daffodils, and often last until the miniature dwarf beardeds appear at the height of the daffodil season.

The Juno irises start to bloom here about mid-April. These are interesting but are grown infrequently in this country though they should succeed in many regions. They always attract attention with their brilliant blossoms and unusual plant form. Before the Juno flowers fade, the later miniature dwarf bearded hybrids come into peak bloom, and color begins to show in the buds of the earlier regelia species—such as *Iris korolkowii*—and in the earliest varieties of the standard dwarf beardeds.

From the beginning of May, the iris pageant becomes a four-ring circus. With the late miniature dwarf beardeds still flowering, the species and early standard dwarf beardeds and the arilbreds blooming, and the intermediate bearded irises beginning to open among the ranks of tulips and early May perennials, the gardener hardly dares turn his head for fear he will miss something. One year, I almost missed the miniature crested *Iris gracilipes*, which does not flaunt its very definite attractions.

As May progresses, the dwarf crested irises, *I. cristata, I. gracilipes,* and *I. tectorum,* flower in that order. More and more varieties of intermediate beardeds and arilbreds come into bloom, and the season of standard tall bearded, border bearded, and miniature tall bearded (table iris) begins. At the same time beardless irises, including the Pacific Coast species, are in flower. In this region, the season of tall bearded and Siberian irises usually coincide, through a few Siberian varieties continue to bloom until mid-July. The standard tall beardeds most popular of all irises, dominate the scene, but their shorter, slightly smaller-flowered brothers, the border beardeds, are beginning to be seen in gardens.

Before the end of the tall bearded season, spuria iris species, such as *Iris graminea* and *I. ochroleuca,* the Dutch varieties of bulbous irises, and the Louisiana irises begin to bloom. Spuria hybrids continue to bloom until the end of June. In mid-June, they are joined by the bulbous Spanish group. The English irises bloom in very late June and early July.

Towards the end of June the earliest of the Japanese irises open first flowers, coinciding with the pre-peak daylily season and the second burst of roses. Later varieties continue through July. In early July, *Iris decora,* sole representative of the sub-genus Nepalensis, offers small fleeting flowers, similar in form to the Japanese.

Obviously a gardener in lower New York can easily have continuous iris bloom from the beginning of March to the end of July— a five-month period. He can extend the period through August if he likes (and I do) by growing the beardless species, *Iris dichotoma*— and even into September by planting some of the September reblooming bearded irises. Those varieties that come into second flowering in October are seldom satisfactory in this region where frost almost surely nips buds before they open. So there are seven months of possible bloom outdoors. I hear that winter-flowering *Iris unguicularis* can be grown successfully in a coldframe here for flowers from December into January, but I have not tried it.

A FEW OTHER REGIONS

Throughout much of continental United States, the iris procession is essentially the same as it is here in the Northeast. In some regions, variations in time are most surprising.

Pacific Northwest

In Oregon and Washington, where the climate makes possible the best plant nursery in this country, all the bearded irises grow spectacularly well. Several famous specialists in the tall beardeds are located in this region. *Iris unguicularis* can be grown outdoors as far north as Vancouver, B.C. The bulbous English irises, Pacific Coast natives, Japanese varieties, and other moisture-loving types, such as *I. chrysographes* and *I. forrestii* of the Siberica group, all flourish in this area. Even the dwarf bearded species, including *I. subbiflora,* grow well. In the drier climate of the eastern part of Washington, the arils are easily grown. In fact, almost any iris will grow somewhere in the Northwest.

California

In southern California, the tall bearded season starts in mid-April. In that fabulous state it is possible to have one iris or another in bloom the year round. Many tall bearded varieties, not so prodigal in less favored climates, continue to send up bloom stalks over an extended period in spring and summer or rebloom in early and also in late autumn. Some even flower in December.

The year opens with the little reticulata species which, in Los Angeles, show color almost before the bells have announced the New Year; and various forms of *Iris unguicularis* bloom in rock gardens all winter long.

I arrived in Los Angeles in late February one year, just in time to see the last of these charming flowers in my host's garden and the first of the Juno species, *Iris bucharica,* and the tender crested *I. japonica.* All of us were enchanted with the lavender flowers of a small beardless iris which my friends had transplanted from the wild and which we were able to identify as *Iris douglasiana,* one of the native Pacific Coast irises. The various species in this group bloom in California between March and May.

In April and May, the aril irises—oncocyclus and regelia—the bulbous Dutch varieties, spurias, Siberian, and Louisiana irises join the iris pageant.

Southwest

The sequence in parts of the Southwest (Arizona, for instance) is, according to my correspondents, similar to that of California. In New Mexico, bulbous irises including the Junos will flourish; Siberian irises do not, although, together with the American native species *Iris missouriensis,* they grow well through most of the Southwest. Louisiana and spuria irises grow luxuriantly in this whole region. Aril irises are very successful in many areas, even as far north as Utah. In Texas, Dallas is the heart of the tall bearded area, though these irises are grown as far south as Houston and San Antonio. Dutch irises bloom along with the median beardeds, which perform poorly in comparison to their vigorous growth in Colorado and Utah. In eastern Texas, the arils grow well.

The Carolinas

This is another iris paradise. Bearded, beardless—including the native *Iris virginica*—and bulbous flourish in this region. And, of course, the crested irises and tiny *I. verna.* This one and *I. cristata,* both native here, bloom in April.

Reticulatas begin in January or early February in the Carolinas; Junos, in March. The Dutch irises, very popular there, flower in April, as do the aril species and intermediate beardeds. The peak of tall bearded bloom comes in early May.

In one garden in southwestern North Carolina, I saw a luxuriant naturalized planting of Japanese irises in shaded, swampy ground along a meandering stream. They flower in May; Louisiana and spuria irises in May and June: Siberians in June.

12

Diseases and Pests

There is probably no plant on earth that is not susceptible to attack by some pathogenic organism—some fungus, some bacterium, some virus; but irises are hardy plants and the few diseases that may damage them are seldom fatal. I have lost a few plants of various species, but not from disease: I was trying to make them grow in an environment they could not tolerate. Occasionally, one of my young bearded seedlings fails to survive its first winter, but I have lost only one named tall bearded iris in all the years I have grown them. However, I have come close to losing a few.

Plants growing in fertile, well-drained soil, in a weed-free garden where air can circulate freely, are seldom seriously damaged by the various pathogenic micro-organisms that attack irises. The best—though not perfect—insurance against disease lies in preventive measures, such as producing vigorous plants and removing and burning all dead leaves and other debris in the fall. No diseased material should ever be composted. The only iris plants I ever add to the compost heap are healthy young seedlings not distinctive enough to keep. Some growers compost all vegetative material, healthy or not, and report no increase in disease. I look at such reports with a skeptical eye. I am especially wary of composting material that might contain pathogenic fungi or pest eggs.

Different diseases appear in different regions; seldom are iris plants in any given locality attacked by more than two or three. I discuss here the various diseases and pests that sometimes attack irises not to worry you or turn you into a plant hypochondriac, but to give you a basis for early diagnosis. Informed vigilance is the price—for gardeners—of healthy irises.

FUNGUS DISEASES

Diseases caused by fungi are Heterosporium leaf spot, winter rot (botrytis), and crown rot or sclerotium rot—also called Southern blight.

HETEROSPORIUM LEAF SPOT is most common here in the Northeast and in other humid or rainy regions. It attacks only the leaves— never the rhizomes—and is more unsightly than debilitating; though, of course, any disease weakens a plant. In a dry summer, leaf spot is hardly evident, and it is interesting that some varieties in a group of irises are not affected even in a rainy season. Fungus spores are spread by splashed water. In early summer many oval yellow spots begin to show on the upper parts of the leaves. Later the whole leaf may turn brown and die prematurely.

Control: Carefully remove all dead leaves and debris, and cut off infected green leaves below the lowest visible spots. Burn all this material. The disease may be prevented or at least greatly reduced by weekly use throughout spring and summer of a dust or spray containing Zineb. (DuPont Vegetable Garden Dust and Ortho Vegetable Dust contain Zineb; so do a number of spray materials.)

SCLEROTIUM OR CROWN ROT: Another pathogenic fungus, commonly called the mustard-seed fungus, is usually present in soil and affects many kinds of plants. It may attack irises during very warm wet periods in summer, especially if adequate air circulation and drainage are lacking so that moisture gathers around the base of plants. This fungus attacks leaves at the base, where they develop a dry rot; they die at the tips and sometimes collapse on the ground. A dry pithy rot develops in the rhizomes. A web of fine white mycelial threads may be visible on the immediately surrounding soil. In a later stage, the threads form small hard brown structures, which look like mustard seeds and are called sclerotia. These represent the resting stage of the fungus; they can endure for a long time until a favorable opportunity for growth occurs.

Though this disease is, of itself, not likely to kill a plant, control measures should be taken at once, lest rot-producing bacteria invade the injured tissues and destroy the rhizome.

Control: Diseased leaves and rotted portions of rhizome should be cut away and burned. The clump and surrounding soil may be disinfected by drenching with a bichloride of mercury solution (one tablet dissolved in a pint of water, or one ounce dissolved in a little hot water, then diluted with cold water to make seven and one-half gallons). The tablets may be purchased in garden supply and drug stores. *Caution:* Bichloride of mercury is a virulent poison. And according to U. S. Department of Agriculture Home and Garden Bulletin No. 66, bichloride of mercury solution should never be mixed or applied near rose bushes because the vapors are injurious to them.

Dr. A. W. Dimock, in the A.I.S. *Bulletin* for July 1959, writes of a new fungicide which I have not yet had occasion to use. "Drenching the bases of the plants with a preparation containing one level tablespoon of . . . Terrachlor 75 in a gallon of water has provided good protection against sclerotium rot." This chemical is produced by Olin-Mathieson Chemical Corp. of Baltimore, Maryland.

WINTER ROT: This disease is caused by a cool-weather fungus which is active in fall, winter and spring. It attacks rhizomes; roots are badly rotted, rotted portions of rhizomes are shriveled and dry, and there may be a felt-like fungus growth on the rhizome surface. Plants may fail to grow as spring advances, or symptoms may be slight—and very persistent. Only wounded rhizomes can be infected; it is thought that mechanical injuries to rhizomes due to alternate thawing and freezing provide entry for this fungus.

Control: Cut off and burn all diseased rhizomes, and soak those of healthy appearance for about ten minutes in a suspension of one ounce of mercurous chloride (calomel) per gallon of water. (The calomel will sink to the bottom, and constant stirring is required to keep it in suspension.) Use a winter mulch to reduce rhizome injury due to frost action.

BACTERIAL DISEASES

The two iris diseases caused by bacteria are soft rot and bacterial leaf blight. Leaf blight is not serious; soft rot, common in iris gardens, may be. Both apparently occur in warm weather under moist conditions.

SOFT ROT: This is the one disease that the iris gardener in the Northeast must really watch out for. In my garden, it seems more likely to attack in early spring than midsummer, but that may be because I am most alert for signs of it at that time. Gardeners unfamiliar with the symptoms of soft rot may not notice the presence of the disease until the green leaves topple over. In the pre-bloom season, I watch rhizomes carefully. The disease seems to have an infuriating predilection for the central rhizome, and if unchecked will destroy the bloom point, though usually not the whole plant. A new plant, consisting of one central rhizome and small side shoots is in real danger. The one tall-bearded variety I have lost was 'Galilee', on which I had spent all my tall-bearded iris money the previous year—and which I had planted in my sunniest and quickest draining garden spot. Yet, in the spring, the rhizome had degenerated into a custardy mess. (The originator, Mr. Orville Fay, graciously replaced the plant.) It may be that in my zeal to keep the surrounding area weed-free, I had nicked the rhizome with my sharp trowel.

Control: No sure cure for soft rot is known, but several remedies are effective, provided the rot has not progressed too far. An eagle eye and a testing finger can diagnose bacterial rot in an early stage. I test the rhizomes for firmness with a gentle pressure. If one seems soft, I pull away a little of the surrounding soil and explore further. (I am not one to dig up a plant except as a last resort.)

Though references say otherwise, this rot seems to start at the end of the rhizome farthest from the leaf fan. If there is only a small soft area, I cut off this soft part of the rhizome with a sharp paring knife, leaving the plant in the soil; if there is a good deal of mushy pulp, I scrape it out with a spoon. In either case, I finish the treatment by pouring a half cup or so of Clorox (diluted with the same volume of water) over both the affected rhizome and the immediately surrounding soil, and leave the injured "toe" exposed to the sun and air until it heals. It always does heal, and the plant continues to grow.

There is remarkably little rot among the irises in my garden, considering the fact that it is surrounded by woods, with consequent reduction in air circulation and slow evaporation of moisture. This happy condition I attribute to the use of antibiotics. Certainly the percentage of bacterial rot has been reduced since I began to use Pfizer's Agrimycin 100 several years ago. I mix the solution according to the highest concentration recommended in the directions on the bottle (four tablespoons per five gallons of water) in a watering can, add a trace of detergent, and drench the plants and surrounding soil. I have no regular program, but start in early spring and repeat during hot and humid periods in summer.

I used this antibiotic first to combat a case of bacterial leaf blight which came into my garden on some gift rhizome and spread to several nearby plants.

BACTERIAL LEAF BLIGHT turns a fan of iris leaves into a horrifying sight, but does not attack the rhizome. Some authorities describe

it as similar in appearance to fungus leaf spot, but it is much uglier:
the leaves look as if they were covered with sores in large irregular
spots and streaks, from which a sticky gluey liquid oozes.

Control: You may as well cut off and burn affected leaves at
once. And take care to sterilize scissors or knife blade by dipping
in a lysol solution—or by boiling—before using on non-infected
plants.

Bacterial leaf blight flourishes in wet weather, and symptoms are
said to disappear of their own accord during dry weather. Spraying
plants and drenching soil with Pfizer's Agrimycin 100 plus careful
sanitation appears to have eliminated the disease in my garden. At
least, during very rainy summers none of my irises show signs of it.
And as I have said, I treat all incoming plants to a thorough soaking
in a bactericide-fungicide solution.

OTHER DISEASES

The most widespread disease of irises appears to be a mosaic,
caused by a single type of virus. Most varieties of iris are tolerant
of the virus and show, at most, only moderate symptoms; many
infected varieties show no symptoms at all.

Characteristic symptoms are a light green-and-yellow streaking
and mottling of leaves. In the most susceptible varieties the plant
may be stunted—though so susceptible a variety is rarely put on
the market. This would happen only in the unusual circumstance
that a seedling failed to show susceptibility through the years of
observation in the field.

More distressing than the effect on leaves is an ugly streaking or
blotching that sometimes occurs on flower petals. This symptom is
similar to "breaking" in tulips, in which flowers are attractively
feathered and flaked as a result of a virus infection. The streaking
and blotching of the iris flower is of irregular pattern, usually in a
darker color—and most unattractive. A white flower may be
streaked and smeared with purple. This symptom is not apt to
occur except in a rainy period; if the weather clears, flowers opening later may be clean.

Control: Mosaic is incurable. Elimination of aphids that spread
the disease is recommended as a control. Since it is very likely that
bearded irises have already acquired the disease, this suggestion
seems to me optimistic, to say the least (though aphids should be
eliminated for other reasons). Iris hybridizers are now alert to the
necessity of breeding for resistance to mosaic, and future varieties
will be even more tolerant than current ones.

SCORCH: There is one mystery disease of tall-bearded irises; if it occurs in other irises, I have not seen or read of it. Though a few sporadic attempts have been made to find the culprit, nobody has a clue to the cause, and the only name it has is the popular one: scorch. Once in a while, among some fancier's tall-bearded irises, I see a clump that looks as if it had been burned in a fire. The dead leaves are very short (because they had been unable to grow properly) and reddish brown in color. The rhizomes, though plump and firm, are also reddish. I have found no evidence of this disease in my own garden (I hope I never do) and consequently have had no opportunity to watch its progress. The first symptom is said usually to be die-back in the central leaves of a fan. Roots are said to rot, beginning at the end furthest from the rhizome and progressing up to the rhizome. It seems logical to suppose the leaf die-back is preceded by—and caused by—the unnoticed rotting of the roots.

What is left when the mysterious culprit has done its work is a group of rootless and leafless but still firm rhizomes. What does one do with such a plant—if it can still be so called. Many fanciers, considering the disease to be fatal, discard all affected clumps; others try out various treatments. In *The Iris Year Book* for 1962, L. W. Brummitt reports a "simple and infallible cure (obtained) by lifting the plant, cutting off any top growth, as well as the dead roots, and then burying it about six inches deep, treading down firmly and, of course, marking the spot." Mr. Brummitt claims 100 per cent success for this "cure." "Following this treatment, if the old plant was large, there will appear above the ground a crop of small growths resembling seedlings which, without disturbance, will require one more year to form normal independent rhizomes at ground level."

Last year, in the garden of an iris-fancier friend, one iris clump showed symptoms of scorch. I suggested that he experiment, trying out Mr. Brummitt's cure with half the clump, and leaving the other half in place as a control. He liked the suggestion but was too busy. Later, he told me that a clump of another variety had shown the same symptoms the previous year but had returned to apparent health the next year. Conclusion? I have none; but I hope some iris growers will experiment with clumps that show symptoms instead of destroying them. To draw valid conclusions from such an experiment, it is essential to use part of the clump as an untreated control.

This strange disease is apparently not infectious. Even if several clumps in a field are affected, they seem never to be found in a group, but occur here and there throughout the planting. I can't help wondering if the cause could be a combination of unfavorable environmental conditions affecting the physiology of the plant rather than some pathogenic micro-organism.

INSECT PESTS

THE IRIS BORER. From Canada to Washington D.C. and west to Iowa, the iris borer is the major pest-hazard of all rhizomatous irises —and the bogeyman of all gardeners who grow even a few of them. The majority of gardeners and even some specialists seem to have fanciful and inaccurate ideas about *the borer* and how to combat it. I have given more impromptu lectures to more gardeners on this subject than any other—and probably uselessly, because I suspect they quickly return to their original fears. The solution preferred by a surprising number is to dig up and destroy the plants. One summer a physician phoned me and said his iris bed was riddled with borers. I asked him how he knew. Because the leaves were brown, he said. (I refrained from exploring the possibility of fungus leaf spot; that would have been too confusing.) He proposed to dig up all his irises and replant them on the far side of the house. Why? To get rid of the borers. I asked him what would prevent the borer moths, when they emerged in the fall, from flying around the house and laying their eggs on the iris leaves there. Then he really wanted to know the whole story.

Because the control of iris borers consists, basically, of interrupting the life cycle of the insect, an understanding of this cycle is a necessary preliminary to dealing effectively and efficiently with this major pest. The course of action taken can depend on the number of irises grown. In the small garden, where a few are used in combination with other plants, the iris borer can be controlled manually, if you prefer that method.

The borer story may well start in midsummer, at transplanting time—the time when most gardeners are acutely concerned with "doing something" about the borer. At this season the life cycle can be interrupted successfully, though laboriously. The procedure is to dig up the clump, examine the rhizomes, and extract and crush any borer larvae—which have become big and fat (but not lazy) on the tissue in the interior of the rhizome.

If this is not done, each larva emerges in late July or August from the rhizome and, several inches below the soil surface, changes into the pupal or chrysalis stage. The inert pupa is shiny chestnut brown, slightly smaller than the inch-and-a-half larva. The life cycle can

34. *Above, right.* Showing fat, pink, fully mature larva of iris borer resting, in late July, on the hollow shell of rhizome it has destroyed. (Rot was involved here, too.)

35 *Center* Shiny chestnut-brown pupa of iris borer, recovered from soil in late August. It measured one and a quarter inches long.

36 *Below, right.* Moth of iris borer, with wings extended, measuring one and three-quarter inches across. Head and thorax of this seldom seen moth are black; fore wings are dull brown, hind wings light tan.

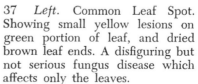

37 *Left.* Common Leaf Spot. Showing small yellow lesions on green portion of leaf, and dried brown leaf ends. A disfiguring but not serious fungus disease which affects only the leaves.

be interrupted at this stage, too, by destroying the pupae, but the likelihood of finding all pupae in the soil is small. However, when transplanting is done after the end of July, and freshly tunneled rhizomes are found, but no larvae, the soil should be searched for pupae.

In the fall, the moth emerges from the pupa. The adult moth lives only a short time, is secretive in habit and seldom seen. Soon after emerging, the female lays her eggs on the old basal iris leaves, on any nearby debris, or even on the surrounding soil. The eggs, only one-fiftieth of an inch in diameter, are not easily observed. The life cycle can be interrupted here with a thorough late fall clean-up job.

When the soil warms in spring—usually April in the Northeast— the eggs begin to hatch, and hatching continues until after the tall beardeds bloom. The new-born larvae make straight for the outer surfaces of the young iris leaves, crawling upward, chewing pin-holes and eating the edges, producing the characteristic saw-tooth appearance. The damaged leaves become stained with a shiny, watery exudate. In a few days, the young larvae enter the leaf sheath where they are safely hidden.

The iris leaf is a sheath, open like an envelope on the side toward the center of the fan. You can open the damaged leaf and find the tiny larvae on the inside surface, busily eating their way down toward the rhizome. Instead of destroying the leaf sheath in which they are hiding, the larvae feed on the tender edge of the younger center leaf, which projects into their hiding place. Several larvae are usually found in one leaf sheath, and more than one leaf in a fan may be attacked.

I have never found more than one borer (adult larva) in a rhizome. This puzzled me until I came across a statement in an old A.I.S. publication, *The Iris, An Ideal Hardy Perennial*, that "only one borer, the 'survivor of the fittest,' is found alive in a rhizome."

In a small planting, young larvae may be exterminated by squeezing affected leaves firmly between thumb and forefinger, beginning at the ground and pulling upward. A surer method, which I prefer, is to cut off affected leaves in late April or May just above the rhizome, and burn them. This is a good time to interrupt the life cycle of this pest—*before* the larvae have reached the rhizome where their most destructive attack occurs. I have even cut off a whole fan of leaves when it was badly infected—on the theory that the loss of leaves is less damaging to the plant than a hollowed out rhizome.

However, just as the iris leaves can survive being nibbled by deer, the rhizome can—and usually does—survive being partly devoured by the borer. The injury, like a cut finger, is only mechanical. Both heal quickly, unless infection occurs. A new skin forms over the tunnel made by the borer, and the rhizome continues its growth— looking very like a doughnut but perfectly healthy. This is what happens if the micro-organism causing bacterial rot does not invade and destroy the injured rhizome before it has a chance to heal. To eliminate this possibility, soak valuable rhizomes in the bichloride of mercury solution, already described. I prefer to use the less poisonous antibiotic-fungicide solution mentioned in Chapter 5, under transplanting.

Control: In addition to these measures, a complete clean-up of old iris leaves and all debris is essential in late fall, or in *early* spring before leaf growth starts and borer eggs begin to hatch. Iris leaves should be cut three to four inches above the ground, and the refuse burned.

A dust or spray containing malathion (combined with Zineb to combat fungus leaf spot) gives a high degree of protection when applied weekly during the pre-bloom period, starting when leaves are six inches high. The dust or spray job must be thorough, covering all leaf surfaces.

Tests of various insecticides for borer control made by the Purdue University Department of Entomology in 1956 and 1957 indicated the superior effectiveness of malathion, endrin and several other new insecticides over DDT.

MINOR PESTS

A few other pests may be occasionally troublesome.

APHIDS, commonly found in gardens, sometimes feed on iris leaves in spring. They suck the juices from the plant, and may transmit the virus causing iris mosaic. Control: Spray leaves with malathion, using enough detergent to wet the aphids thoroughly. If they reappear, repeat.

THRIPS, controlled by malathion or DDT, sometimes attack irises, especially Japanese varieties.

VERBENA BUD MOTH is a menace to breeders because it destroys iris seeds within the pods. This pest is difficult to control for it has several host plants (including goldenrods, snapdragons and penstemons) and produces several broods each year. Recommended controls are the pesticides, DDD and methoxychlor, plus general garden cleanliness.

COMMENTS

All the insecticides and fungicides recommended above are poisonous and must be used judiciously and carefully. You must make your own decision, admittedly difficult, in regard to their use on your property. "It has now become clear," states the 1963 Report on Pesticides by the President's Science Advisory Committee, "that the proper usage is not simple and that, while they destroy harmful insects and plants, pesticides may also be toxic to beneficial plants and animals, including man."

As a rule, I employ the more laborious methods outlined here and in Chapter 5, and use pesticides as conservatively as the garden situation permits. The health of songbirds is as important to me as that of garden plants. However, in a "bad" season I use chemicals more frequently. I *always* protect new and expensive rhizomes, promising seedlings, and varieties in short supply.

13

Hybridizing Irises for Fun

"Pollen daubing" has become a popular sport among iris fanciers, and has spread over the back yards of all countries in which irises are grown and admired. The hobby may be indulged in casually or pursued with determination. Theoretically, that is. In practice, many a mildly curious gardener has made one cross, "just to see what will happen," and before he quite knew it, he had purchased the vacant lot next door as "a sensible business venture." Then "temporarily of course," he transplanted there the tremendous batches of seedlings that were crowding his flats.

The trouble—or the joy—is that iris seeds are so easy to produce and seedlings are so fascinating. Any one of them might turn out to be more beautiful or more unusual than any iris yet created. It is not at all likely that this will happen; the days when a magnificent surprise could result from careless dusting of pollen from one iris onto the stigmas of another chosen at random are almost gone. In his heart, the amateur hybridizer knows this. But it *could* happen. Once in a very great while, it does. But even without such luck it's easy to produce attractive seedlings; I've done it myself. In fact, it would be hard to avoid producing seedlings that your gardening friends will covet.

If you have the impulse to make an iris cross, give way to it— at least once. It is not necessary to know a chromosome from cortisone. Just brush pollen from one fresh iris flower onto the three stigmas of another fresh flower, a procedure called crossing or cross-pollinating. (Selfing or self-pollination involves transferring pollen to the stigmas of the same flower or to another flower of the same variety.)

The future pollen-dauber may ask questions:

What's pollen? We might answer that pollen is the dust on that little paddle-like thing below each of the three style-crests, and leave it at that.

What's a stigma? The easiest way to answer is to point to the stigmas. They are shown in Figure 7. In most flowers the stigma or stigmas are conspicuous, but in iris flowers they are hidden beneath the huge style-crests.

Brush pollen from any iris onto any other iris? It would depend on circumstances. If only tall-bearded irises are grown, the answer is yes, but if you are a beginner play it safe and cross two blues or two whites or two yellows. (You will probably do as you like.) But if you grow some Siberian and, say, some crested irises, the answer is, No. Cross two varieties of a kind—tall-bearded or Siberian or whatever. To be sure this is a partial truth, but it will do for a start. Chances are that you will want to cross tall-bearded irises, anyway: most people do—pollen-daubers and professionals alike.

With this information, plus some hints on technique and a few recommendations as to labeling, record keeping, and harvesting,

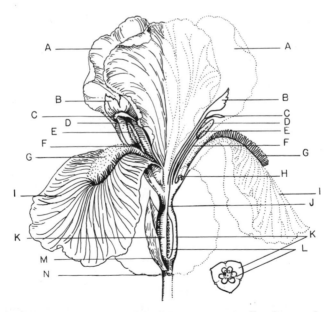

FIGURE 7   TALL BEARDED IRIS FLOWER, partially dissected to show essential parts: A—standard; B—style crest; C—stigma; D—style branch; E—anther; F—filament (anther and filament together make up the stamen); G—beard; H—nectary; I—fall; J—perianth tube enclosing style; K—ovary; L—ovules; M—spathe; N—stem.

storing, and planting seed, the gardener can proceed to produce his own seedlings. Perhaps eventually you will be stimulated to learn more about the processes you have set in motion, perhaps not. Almost certainly you will enjoy yourself. And poetry has been created by poets who did not know the alphabet. I make no plea for ignorance, but it *is* possible for a hybridizer who knows nothing about genetics or even botany, but who has highly developed powers of observation, what I call intuition, and excellent taste, to produce seedlings superior to those created by a scientific breeder who has little artistic judgment and imagination. The great hybridizers are superior in all these areas; they are gifted, inspired, informed—and full of curiosity.

REPRODUCTIVE STRUCTURE OF THE IRIS FLOWER

The beautiful standards and falls, known collectively as the perianth of the iris flower, enclose another kind of beauty. Within their circle, at the heart of the flower, lies its reason-for-being—the structures that contain the sources of the next generation.

Strip off the perianth to lay bare these reproductive structures. The conspicuous central structure is the female *pistil*. It is surrounded by three small male *stamens*. The pistil consists of ovary, style, and stigma. In the iris it is compound, made up of three adhering parts. Within the slightly swollen ovary, which is located below the perianth, are numerous ovules, each containing one egg cell. Each egg cell lies inside a tiny embryo sac. Above the ovary, the pistil continues as a slender columnar style which divides into three large curving style-branches. Stylar tissue runs through the center of each of these broad bands of petaloid tissue and terminates in the stigmatic lip or shelf beneath each style-crest.

Each male stamen consists of an inconspicuous two-lobed pollen-bearing anther carried on a slender "stem" or filament. The lower end of the filament is attached to the inner wall of the fall just below the beard, and curves back against the style-branch. The important anther rests slightly below the stigma, behind and just above the beard. Theoretically this placement ensures cross-fertilization; the entering bee will brush another flower's pollen from her back onto a stigma. As she goes deeper into the flower, she brushes against the anther and collects more pollen to deposit on the stigma of the next flower visited. Actually, in modern tall-bearded hybrids, the very large style-branches press so close against the falls that bees are said to enter flowers from the side and thus avoid the pollen altogether. And it is true that few seed pods form on modern tall-bearded irises.

CHOOSING PARENTS

It is important to select breeding material with care. The basic reason for crosing two irises is to combine the most desirable characteristics of each in one plant. Even the tyro hybridizer will notice whether the flower substance is thick, or thin and papery; whether the color holds throughout the life of the flower, fades out after a day, or burns white in the sun. He will notice whether standards are weak and floppy, or strongly arched and touching at the tips. But he may fail to consider other characteristics that will affect the quality of his seedlings. The vigor and rate of increase of variety, resistance to disease, size and color of leaves, strength and length of stem, number and type characteristics of branches, and number of buds per socket. These are all inheritable tendencies.

For instance, if from among several blue irises in the garden, two are to be chosen as parents, which varieties should you select? We will suppose that all have enduring color and perfect shape but the stems of one are weak and need staking, and the substance of the flowers is so thin that they don't hold up well in rain. Another variety has heavy-substanced flowers and increases rapidly, but the branching is inadequate. A third is perfect except for slowness of increase. In making your choice, try to offset a weakness with a strength. A few years ago, in a hybridizer's seedling patch, I noticed that many otherwise fine seedlings from several crosses involving a popular light blue variety had inherited its one fault—weak stems. I went home and crossed it with a favorite light-blue variety that had the opposite fault: stems too thick to be pleasing, but ramrod-strong. Every seedling from this cross had strong, sufficiently slender and tall stems, adequate branching, and attractive flowers. None was good enough to name, because the seedlings were not improvements on existing varieties; however, they do grace a friend's garden.

There's more to the business of choosing parents than all this indicates. Some beautiful irises make poor parents, producing consistently mediocre seedlings. Botanists say the *phenotype* (appearance) of these varieties is superior to the *genotype* (genetic constitution, often partly latent). This works in reverse, too; some varieties with ordinary flowers carry latent characters that, expressed in its seedlings, spell beauty.

How can you as a beginning breeder find out these things? One way is to become familiar with the parentage of favorite varieties, and with their performance as parents. (For instance, the variety 'Chivalry' crops up again and again as a parent for blues; so does 'Snow Flurry'.) Such research makes a wonderful winter pastime. I once filled a notebook with such data, charting the records of many varieties as pod and pollen parents. In the process I discovered for myself that some varieties are used only as pod parents, and others only as pollen parents. Frequently, but not always, such a variety is sexually imperfect—i.e., it produces no pollen, or refuses to set seed. Knowing such things will keep you from planning to use 'Snow Flurry', for instance, as a pollen parent. It produces no pollen but freely sets seed.

Then, from among the known good parents in your garden, list various combinations to try. Such a list will almost certainly be so long that, if all the crosses were successful, an embarrassment of seed-riches would result. A second list will probably be more realistic.

MECHANICS OF CROSS-POLLINATION

Pollination, which in nature is usually accomplished by insects or wind, is the first step in fertilization. When the hybridizer deposits pollen on a stigma, he—in a sense—makes himself a tool of nature. It is not necessary to protect a cross of tall-bearded irises from contaminating insect-borne pollen. Other types of irises, commonly insect-pollinated, must be protected, either by bagging the bud or by removing stamens and falls from the pod parent.

Many hobbyists merely go into the garden, pluck a stamen and immediately brush the pollen onto the stigmas of the chosen pod parent. Make sure the pollen is dry. I go out early—before breakfast, if possible—to collect stamens from freshly opened flowers. A small forceps or eyebrow tweezer is an excellent tool for pinching off the stamen near the point of attachment. The filament is thus preserved to be used as a handle.

Place all the stamens from one variety, pollen-side up, in one open container, already labeled with the variety name. Keep in an airy room until the pollen is dry. (I wash and save milk bottle caps for this purpose.) Treated thus, pollen grains remain alive for some time. When a flower first opens, the anthers are still closed and no pollen is visible; don't worry—they soon split open. If pollen is not to be used for several days, stamens can be folded in unglazed paper, labeled, and stored in a closed jar in the refrigerator. I have not found it necessary to use a drying agent for short-term storage but many breeders use some material such as silica gel in the bottom of the jar.

It is convenient to have a hybridizing basket or pan, outfitted at the beginning of the season and kept supplied. In mine, I carry a small notebook for recording each cross, several lead pencils, two eyebrow tweezers (in case I lose one), a supply of small paper tags on strings for labeling the pollinated flower, and a stack of clean milk bottle caps. Every hybridizer chooses his own tools.

Prepare labels and record crosses just before pollinating. If labeling is delayed, even briefly, you may forget which is what. (This has happened to me when I have been interrupted in the middle of a pollinating session.) I use one line of the notebook to record the date, cross number, and names of parents, as Snow Flurry × Chivalry. The name of the pod parent is always written first—a touching courtesy to females—and I pollinate at least two flowers for each cross. About a week later, I examine the ovaries. If fertilization has occurred, they will be visibly plumper, and I will write "T" (for "take") in my record. If the ovaries are withering, I write "X" and repeat the cross.

I like to do my pollinating about 10 o'clock on a sunny morning, but I have made successful afternoon and evening crosses. When pollinating, I find it convenient to hold the stamen filament between thumb and forefinger. With the other hand, I turn back each style-crest of the pod flower until the top surface of the stigma is visible, and gently brush a small amount of pollen on each stigma. (Pollinating one stigma is usually sufficient, but I take no chances unless the pollen is in short supply.) Then I fasten a label on the stem of the flower, and stake the stalk—to protect the hoped-for pod from pets and people.

Water destroys pollen grains, but it is possible to protect them from moisture. When rain is predicted, I cover newly-opened flowers—or buds about to open—with plastic freezer bags supported on bamboo sticks tall enough for clearance above the blossom. During even excessively rainy seasons I have obtained a fair percentage of takes by this method. I remove anthers from, and deposit pollen on, protected flowers under cover of an umbrella. It's awkward but it works.

FERTILIZATION

A pollen grain is a minute sphere containing in its protoplasm the hereditary male material. At first it is a single cell, but by the time it reaches a stigma it has become two cells, one within the other. When the iris stigma becomes receptive to pollen, it secretes a sugary sticky substance. Each of the many pollen grains that come in contact with this fluid swells and swiftly thrusts out a slender delicate tube formed from its large cell. The smaller cell within the pollen tube divides into two cells, and the tube grows down the style-branch almost as a root pushes its way into the soil. It continues down the style until it reaches the ovary. There the tip of each pollen tube penetrates an ovule, enters the embryo sac, and discharges the two male cells it has been carrying near its tip. One of these unites with the egg cell, mingling the hereditary factors of the male and female parents, and creating the next generation; from the fusion of these two cells is formed the minute living embryo of a totally new, never-before-known iris plant. No wonder the novice looks at the first flower of his first seedling with the awe and delight approaching that of parenthood.

The second male cell unites with *two* other nuclei existing within the embryo sac—but outside the egg-cell—to produce the endosperm, which provides food for the embryo. Now the flower has accomplished its purpose; the seed is set. The walls of the ovule develop into seed coats. The tiny seeds grow and swell the walls of the ovary, now called a seed pod. If, as happens in some crosses, the endosperm fails to develop properly, the embryo will not be able to grow into a plant unless food is supplied by artificial means, as in embryo culture, where the embryo is removed from the defective seed and transplanted to an artificial nutrient medium.

THE LIFE CYCLE

The essential life cycle of every living thing, a cycle endlessly repeated, is the story of immortality. The following is a simplified version of the iris life-cycle.

No matter how many times the rhizomes are divided, each healthy iris plant of a given variety remains the same, with the same flower and beard color, the same degree of flare in the falls, and the same ruffled, tailored, or crinkled edges. The agents that control the development of a variety—holding it, with rare exceptions, to the same form—are contained in the chromosomes, which are present in the nuclei of the body, or somatic, cells. (*Soma* means "body.") The number of chromosomes in each healthy somatic cell of each growing plant of any variety is almost always the same, and the chromosomes in each cell are identical with those in every other somatic cell of that variety. Exceptions are of rare occurrence —somatic mutations, etc., are the result.

In each type of iris, the chromosomes occur in sets of a given number. Each chromosome in a set is different from every other chromosome in the same set. H. W. Rickett, in *Botany for Gardeners*, uses this comparison, "Just as a deck of cards is a set, a definite number of definite kinds of cards, each different from all the rest."

In bearded irises, the basic set number may be twelve, or it may be eight. In modern tall bearded irises, each somatic cell contains four sets of twelve chromosomes, a total of forty-eight. Two sets came from the male and two from the female parent. In some aril irises, the set number is ten; in others, it is eleven. Both number and kind of chromosomes are maintained through millions of somatic cell divisions by a complicated process called *mitosis*, which occurs in each cell division.

Cell division begins in the nucleus. A cell is a little box of protoplasm enclosing a spherical nucleus in its center. As the nucleus begins to disintegrate, all the chromosomes congregate across the center of the cell, and each splits lengthwise into identical halves. The two halves move to opposite ends of the cell, and a new nucleus is formed around each of the two groups of chromosomes so that for a moment the protoplasmic box contains two nuclei. Then it divides across the center to form two new cells, each containing one of the just-formed nuclei. Thus each of the new cells is an exact duplicate of the old. The complete story of this dramatic and beautiful process is told in clear and interesting fashion in Dr. Rickett's book.

Germ cells are formed by a similar process, in which the preliminary division is called the reduction division, or *meiosis* (from the Greek "to make smaller"). In this division, the number of chromosome sets per cell is reduced from four to two, and the number of chromosomes from forty-eight to twenty-four, by a variation of the mechanism of mitotic division. As a preliminary to division, each chromosome of a set seeks out and pairs closely with a like chromosome from another set. Dr. Ricklett's deck of cards is again apt; but this time there are two decks, and each card of one deck seeks a like card from the second deck—an ace of hearts seeks out the second ace of hearts, etc. The lengthwise split occurs, just as in mitosis, but this time one whole chromosome of each pair moves to one end of the cell, and one whole chromosome moves to the other end—twenty-four chromosomes to each end. When the cell division is complete, the new cells thus contain but twenty-four chromosomes. These are the germ cells.

This division takes place within the anthers and the ovary some time after the flower bud is formed, but certainly while it is still deep within the plant, and while anthers and ovary are still very small. When, at the culmination of the fertilization process, a pollen cell unites with an egg cell to form an embryo plant, the full number of chromosomes is restored, and the cycle is complete.

Now, however, unless the flower has been self-pollinated, half the chromosomes of the tiny embryo are "foreign"—that is, they carry inheritance factors from the pollen parent that may cause the new plant to be different from either parent in some respects, or like one or the other parent in other respects.

HARVESTING AND PLANTING SEEDS

After seeds are set, all side branches are cut off flush with the stem, and spathes (modified leaves which shelter the flower buds) carefully removed. Moisture, which may contribute to stem-rot, can be caught and held in the angle of stem and branch, and in the cuplike spathes.

Seeds mature in about eight weeks after pollination. Thus seeds of June-blooming irises ripen in August while those of April irises ripen at the end of June. Sometimes accidents occur before harvest time. If a pod-bearing stalk is broken, or if stem-rot sets in after the pod is fully developed, the stalk can be cut off above the break or rotted area and kept in water in a sunny window. Usually the seeds will ripen. Normally pods are gathered after they turn brown and just before they split. Seeds from each cross are shelled out into individual shallow dishes or mesh bags and air-dried at room temperature.

Seeds of most irises can be planted outdoors at any convenient time in the fall, or in flats or coffee cans in the winter, whenever you have time. (Containers are then set outdoors to freeze.) When garden space is limited, seeds are not planted in the open ground, which might tie up space for two to three years if germination is slow. My own practice is to start planting seeds immediately after Labor Day, a few crosses at a time.

I divide the crosses into two groups, those which have produced many seeds of uniform size, and those in which few seeds—or seeds varying greatly in size—have formed. In all likelihood the first group will give a high percentage of germination the first year, and I plant these seeds early in a "cold frame"—which amounts to a restricted seed bed since I do not use the glass covers. I don't worry if seeds germinate in fall: with a light cover of oak leaves, even tiny seedlings live over winter.

I plant seeds of the second group which may be very slow to germinate—or many never germinate—in small flats, or in coffee cans with drainage holes punched in the bottom, and one in the side for wiring on a label. In both cold frame and container, I use garden soil mixed with a little peat moss and sand. I sink the coffee cans almost to the rim in out of the way spots where they can be left for two to three years, and set the flats in the shrubbery border for the winter. (In early spring I move them to full sun— the hottest place available.) After planting, better germination is obtained if seeds are kept *continuously moist until winter sets in.* And it is necessary to keep seedbeds moist from about April first, here, until germination seems to be complete—about May fifteenth.

And I keep records. My method is amateur and personal. I describe it here only to emphasize the necessity of keeping records for even the most casual hobby hybridizer. It is heart-breaking to get a batch of wonderful seedlings and not be able to repeat the cross, or to back-cross, because you can't remember what the parents were. Each hybridizer develops his own methods. Some like to use file cards. I keep a series of hard-cover bound note-books. Each holds records of two to three years of crosses. Before planting seeds, I prepare a plastic label for each cross, listing the number of the cross, the year (as #21-64), the parents and—so I can check the germination percentage on the spot—the number of seeds. I enter the same information in the current notebook, leaving plenty of space for subsequent notes on numbers and detailed descriptions of seedlings. I also draw plot plans for cold frame and flats—in case labels are lost—and note the locations of coffee cans.

TRANSPLANTING

Seedlings transplanted when very tiny—one to two inches tall—have given me a much higher percentage of bloom the following year than those left to grow in the seedling beds until hot weather comes. In my experience, transplanting shock is much less for small seedlings. If the chore is done carefully, without detaching the seed, which is still providing nourishment for the tiny plant, growth continues unabated. When plants with well-developed root systems are transplanted, growth is checked.

Ideally, beds for seedlings are prepared the previous fall. When this cannot be done, prepare them as early in spring as soil can be handled in order to give beds time to settle before you set out the seedlings. (See Chapter 5 on Culture for soil preparation.) The perfect time to transplant is just before a rain; and seedlings are always watered in with a nutrient solution, such as Miracle-Gro. Tall bearded seedlings are set a foot apart; miniature dwarfs can be planted four to six inches apart, and standard dwarfs six to nine inches.

WHAT WILL THE SEEDLINGS LOOK LIKE?

The seedlings will reflect the parents in plant habit, including strength of stem, type of branching, position of buds, etc.

What flower colors can be expected from crossing two light blues, two dark blues, two yellows, two whites? By and large, the progeny of two irises of the same color will be of that color; but today's tall beardeds are complicated hybrids, and many varieties carry in their germ cells unexpressed directives for other colors.

These directives, carried in the chromosomes, are called genes. Different genes direct the development of every character in the plant—color, vigor, disease-resistance, height, bloom season, and many others. When we speak of a gene for blue, we do not mean that a certain gene discharges a minute bit of concentrated blue dye into the flower tissue. We mean that the function of a certain gene is to cause blue color to develop in a flower. It may not be successful in its mission: when male and female germ cells join, the chromosomes of the one always pair with the corresponding chromosomes of the other, which carry genes controlling the same characters. If in both parents all genes controlling height are for "tall," all seedlings will be tall (unless they are starved); if both parents carry color genes for blue only, seedlings will inevitably be blue. *But* if a blue-flowered variety, carrying only genes for blue, is crossed with pollen from a white-flowered variety carrying only genes for white, the gene for color in one of the pairing chromosomes will direct the future flower to be blue. We will call this gene B. The gene for color from the white-flowered parent will direct the flower of the resulting seedling to be white—and we will call this gene *b*. The genetic constitution, for color, of this seedling will be *Bb*. What color will the flower be? It depends on which gene is the boss, or dominant gene.

If gene *B* is dominant over gene *b*, then gene *b* is said to be recessive to gene *B*. Its directives will not be heeded in any seedling that contains the gene *B*. All such seedlings will be blue-flowered. But if the gene for white turns out to be dominant, then gene *B* will be unable to express itself—it will be unsuccessful in its mission and all the flowers will be white.

A complication here is that two different genes for white are known to exist in tetraploid tall-bearded irises. One is recessive; the other is dominant and will prevent the expression of blue color. 'Snow Flurry', considered to be the greatest tall bearded parent, carries the dominant gene for white. So does its child, 'New Snow'. Two famous recessive white varieties are 'Matterhorn' and 'Jake'.

'Snow Flurry' permits some expression of color in its seedlings, whereas 'New Snow' does not. According to Dr. Randolph, this behavior may indicate that 'Snow Flurry' carries the dominant gene for white in only one of its four sets of chromosomes, while 'New Snow' may carry this gene in two sets. The common term to describe this situation is *dosage*. Thus 'Snow Flurry' would be said to carry a single dose, 'New Snow' a double dose of this gene.

When a gene is incompletely dominant, a compromise is reached and the flower color may be blue-white, ice-blue, or any one of the lighter shades of blue. Two dark blues may produce a dark blue, light blue, and even a few black seedlings. (The dark blue varieties 'Allegiance' and 'Midnight Blue' both have one black parent.) Two yellows may produce creams, light yellows or even pink seedlings. ('Limelight' and 'Waxing Moon' both have one pink parent and one pink grandparent.) Two whites may produce some blue or some yellow seedlings.

Not all the expressions of color possible in a cross of tetraploid tall bearded varieties can be expected to show up among the seedlings from one or two pods of a given cross; the Dykes Medalist

'Blue Sapphire' was chosen from among 500 seedlings of 'Snow Flurry' ✕ 'Chivalry', according to the originator. Such a large number of chromosome combinations is possible that the amateur breeder of tall beardeds may as well relax, enjoy himself, and expect to be surprised. Part of the fun is to use your intuition and develop your powers of observation—to plot and to plan, and to learn from each batch of seedlings.

SELECTING SEEDLINGS

When the seedlings bloom, what is the next step? Unless you are already an expert judge of irises, you will—momentarily at least—regard each seedling as incredibly beautiful. When you come down to earth again, you may decide to continue making crosses for sheer delight in the doing—as valid a reason as any—without any ambition to name and register future seedlings, or compete with experienced hybridizers for awards.

If you take this hobby seriously, you will need to learn to evaluate the characters that contribute to, or mar, the beauty of an iris. You are almost certain to concentrate on the color of the flower —a characteristic that is almost the *least* important, for the reason that (with certain exceptions) it is easier to improve the color of a flower than the vigor of the plant, and the sturdiness and branching of the bloomstalk. The most beautiful blossom in the world has only potential value if the plant that bears it is weak and spindly. (I'm talking to myself, too: I have a little seedling in my garden with a smooth well-shaped flower of so beautiful a shade of rose-red that I call it "Glorious," and I don't like to admit how few leaf fans it has produced during two years of "growth".)

Blooms are sparse on first-year plants. The majority will not bloom until their second year—but a beginning evaluation is possible. Making a complete record of each seedling will help the beginner to attain some degree of objectivity.

Number of fans. The hybridizer can tell himself that a favored seedling has few fans because fertilizer was spread unevenly in the seedbed and it didn't get a fair share. (He may be right; he can prove it by supplying a little extra fertilizer for the second year's growth.) Some iris plants produce leaves so tall, broad and lush as to dwarf the flowers—in my opinion an undersirable characteristic.

Bloomstalks. Stems of some varieties are so thick as to be ugly, but they should be strong enough to hold up without staking.

Branching. Ideally, there should be three branches and a terminal. Candelabrum branching is most admired, but short branches function well if they are not held so close to the stem as to squash the flowers against it. Both types of branching should begin about halfway down the stem. Wide high branching produces a top-heavy plant that will blow over in the wind. The worst branching fault is toeing in—branches bend inward so that flowers open against the stem.

Number of buds per socket. Superior varieties have three to four, under good cultivation. Buds open in succession: the more buds, the longer the season of bloom.

Proportion of plant and flower. Size of flower and leaf fans, and height and thickness of stem, should balance. Your personal taste will determine your estimate. Arbitrary standards cannot be set up.

Flower shape is a matter of personal preference, too. Standards may be arching and touching or overlapping, slightly open and cupped, or conical and tightly closed. Falls may be rounded or pointed; they should be broad at the haft, and smoothly pendant or flaring, not pinched or hanging limp. Size of falls and standards should balance—again a matter of taste.

Substance and texture. The shape of the flower is dependent on the substance of the segments, which cannot always be judged by the appearance. Some flowers look fragile and delicate, yet hold their shape well in rain and are not tattered by wind; others, seemingly thick and strong as leather, go to pieces in bad weather. A flower should hold its shape for at least three days.

Clear colors are preferred to subtle blends by most gardeners and iris specialists. Again a matter of preference, as is the texture, though roughness of texture usually dulls the color. Velvety, silky, and satiny textures are all admired.

CROSSES BETWEEN SPECIES

In the iris genus, related species cross much more readily than in most other genera. Among diploid species, those with the same number of chromosomes cross most easily and are most apt to produce fertile hybrids. When both parents are tetraploids, the resulting hybrids are apt to be fertile whether or not the two parents have the same number of chromosomes.

All the dwarf-bearded species may be combined with either diploid or tetraploid tall bearded varieties to produce hybrids of varying heights and bloom seasons. The well-known tetraploid tall bearded hybrid 'Wide World', a reverse bicolor with light blue standards and white falls, was obtained by crossing a tetraploid tall bearded variety with the tall diploid species *Iris imbricata;* and the recently introduced 'Mellite' resulted from a similar cross of tall bearded and the diploid *Iris mellita* 'Vandee'.

Usually a cross between a tetraploid and a diploid results in a sterile triploid hybrid containing three sets of chromosomes—two from the parent and one from the pollen parent. Sometimes, as in the above varieties, during the process of forming the diploid male cells the normal reduction division fails to occur. The diploid germ cell, which normally has one set of chromosomes, then—like the tetraploid germ cells—has two sets. Sometimes the triploid hybrid is fertile—as in 'Chancelot', the thirty-two chromosome hybrid that came from a cross of the 16-chromosome *Iris attica* and the tetraploid tall bearded 'Golden Hind'. *Iris attica* contributed one set of eight chromosomes; 'Golden Hind', two sets of twelve. A triploid hybrid in which the single set has the smaller number of chromosomes is more likely to be fertile than when the reverse is true.

Species with *almost* the same number of chromosomes may be more difficult to cross than those with a greater difference in the chromosome number. The sixteen chromosome *Iris attica* (two sets of eight) crosses like a breeze with the twenty-four chromosome diploid tall bearded varieties (two sets of twelve); but I have used pollen of the twenty chromosome oncocyclus species *Iris susiana* (two sets of ten) on both diploid and tetraploid tall bearded varieties for a number of years without success. One year, two seed pods formed and I hoped for a seed or two from each pod but both were empty. It can be done, if you try long enough and hard enough; many successful crosses between the tetraploid tall bearded 'Purissima' and *I. susiana* have been reported, and a number of named hybrids exist.

Making difficult species crosses—which either fail, or produce few viable seeds—is a good field for the amateur with enormous curiosity and little garden space for growing seedlings. Of course, such a program *could* result in no seedlings at all!

The bearded species *Iris pumila*, a miniature tetraploid thirty-two chromosome dwarf, is a real treasure trove for breeding all sorts and sizes of bearded hybrids. Any of its numerous forms combined with tetraploid varieties of either tall bearded or arilbred irises will produce quantities of May-blooming standard dwarf hybrids in the ten- to fifteen-inch range. *Iris pumila* may be used as the

pod parent if you can find an amiable warm-region grower of tall
bearded or arilbred irises willing to gather, dry and air-mail pollen
to you in April. Or you may store pumila pollen in the refrigerator
until your own tall bearded irises bloom. The pollen should be
air-dried, folded in labeled, unglazed paper and kept in a closed
jar. Because the stamens are tiny, a good supply should be
gathered.

The fun is to mix up the colors of the parents, using any color
of pumila on any color of tall bearded. *Iris pumila* carries an in-
hibitor that partially suppresses the expression of tall bearded color,
and all sorts of blends, odd patterns, and surprising colors result.
A black tall bearded seedling ('Black Forest' × 'Storm King')
crossed with the famous cream amoena pumila, Cook 1546, produced
both the tan-gold, lavender-bearded 'Zing' and the black 'Shine
Boy'. My own standard dwarf, 'Blue Ivory', is from the yellow
border bearded 'Primrose Bonnet' × yellow pumila. Crossed
with a sister seedling, 'Moon Spinner', it produced a red-flowered
seedling. ('Primrose Bonnet' has a red-brown parent.)

The first generation of hybrids can be intercrossed or selfed to
give further generations of standard dwarfs; or they can be played
up or down the height-and-bloom-season scale; back-crossed with
pumila, to produce miniature dwarfs; or crossed onto tall beardeds
for taller, later-blooming intermediate hybrids. The intermediate
seedlings in turn may be selfed, intercrossed, back-crossed onto the
original pumila-tall bearded hybrids, or crossed again onto a tall
bearded variety. This last cross, a difficult one, might produce a
few medium-sized hybrids that bloom in the tall bearded season.

This breeding is endlessly fascinating, though one runs into
sterilities—or partial sterilities—once in a while. Sometimes a bee
will come to the aid of the frustrated hybridizer. Two of my cream-
colored bearded seedlings from ('Twilight Sky' × 'Fantasy') ×
yellow pumila crosses had a curious deep brown-rose flush on the
standards. These seedlings would not self, cross with each other or
with any of their cream-colored siblings, though I tried all these
combinations for several years. Finally, when I was about to call
it quits and toss them on the compost pile, one produced a bee
pod. I planted the seeds and last year bloomed one ivory seedling
with a slight rose flush, one with solid rose standards and cream
falls, and one with brown-rose standards and henna-rose falls. (It
looks as if that bee crossed sister seedlings.) These were intercrossed
successfully and the seedlings sprouted. Luck does play a big part
in this game.

Many other areas of hybridizing offer exciting challenges to the beginner. The development of beardless irises is still in an early stage. Among American native irises, both Louisiana and Pacific Coast groups offer easy opportunities to the amateur; and some enterprising gardener who has access to wild stands of *Iris cristata* could undoubtedly acquire enough different color forms to build up a very fine breeding project. If I had not already produced more inter-specific hybrids than I can develop properly, I would be tempted to start work with some of the forty-chromosome Siberian species. This seems to be a most promising field.

14

People Behind the Plants

The United States, which leads the iris world in number of hybridizers, seedlings raised, and varieties introduced, leads also in hybridizing advances. Our climates are so varied that, in one region or another, almost any iris can be cultivated successfully. But we have no monopoly on enthusiasm for irises. Dedicated irisarians in many countries work to increase the beauty, garden value, and popularity of their favorite flower.

The work of scientists is carried on so unassumingly behind the scenes that most gardeners are unaware of the enormous contributions made by these quiet men to the steady improvement in quality and variousness of garden irises, to increased knowledge of the genus, and the creation of valuable tools for hybridizers.

SCIENTISTS

Dr. Werckmeister, of the Botanisches Institute, Geisenheim am Rhein, has analyzed the pigments present in iris flowers with results of important genetic implications. He is active also in hybridizing oncocyclus irises and discovering the secret of their culture in cold climates. G. I. Rodionenko of the Komarov Botanical Institute, Leningrad, USSR, published in 1961 *The Genus Iris,* a scientific work embodying the results of a ten-year study of irises including their morphology, biology and classification. Dr. Lee W. Lenz, Director of the Rancho Santa Ana Botanic Garden in Claremont, California, has significantly increased our knowledge of irises and their relationships. His published material on spuria species and revision of the Pacific Coast irises have been mentioned in the chapters on beardless irises.

Dr. L. F. Randolph, internationally known for his cytogenetic studies of corn, is now Professor Emeritus of Botany at the New York State College of Agriculture, Cornell University, Ithaca. Few individuals in recent years, I dare say, have contributed more to the advancement of irises. He served for eleven years as chairman of the important Scientific Committee of the A.I.S. and, more recently, as president of the society. He has traveled extensively studying the geographical distribution of irises and collecting bearded species for experimental study. He has perfected a method of embryo culture and somehow has found time to breed garden irises of high quality, including the delightful intermediate 'Barbi' and the tall bearded 'Exotic Blue'.

In Italy, Mrs. Flaminia Specht, vice-president of the Italian Iris Society, has done much of the planning for the annual international tall bearded competition in Florence. In 1963 she organized an International Symposium on Irises in Florence—a city that has been linked with irises since the Middle Ages. According to the report in *The Iris Yearbook* for 1963, iris notables who contributed were Mr. Harold Cole, Mr. H. Castle Fletcher and Mr. Patrick Synge of England, Dr. Marc Simonet of France, Dr. Peter Werckmeister and Mr. Max Steiger of Germany, Mr. Michael Hoog of Holland, Dr. Gian Luigi Sani of Italy, Dr. Suichi Hirao of Japan, Dr. G. I. Rodionenko of the USSR, and Dr. Lee W. Lenz and Mr. Hubert Fischer of the U.S.A.

HYBRIDIZERS

Jean Stevens

Mrs. Jean Stevens of New Zealand, 1953 recipient of the Foster Memorial Plaque of the B.I.S., is internationally admired for her work with the difficult amoena pattern. Her efforts—and those of Jesse Wills of Tennessee—have resulted in greatly improved yellow amoenas.

According to W. F. Scott (A.I.S. Bulletin #152), Jean Stevens was introduced to irises in 1923 when she was a young girl, became enchanted with the beauty of imported English hybrids, and decided to produce seedlings of her own. In 1929, only six years after she had made her first cross, she produced the variety 'Destiny', which won a Bronze Medal when it was shown in England.

The most widely known British hybridizers are H. Senior Fothergill and Harry Randall, both former presidents of the British Iris Society, and Leonard Brummitt. All three have received the Foster Memorial Plaque of the BIS. Two of Mr. Brummitt's introductions have won the English Dykes Medal: 'Golden Alps', 1957 and 'Headlines,' 1959. Mr. Fothergill's 'Arcady' won this award in 1963. Mr. Randall's originations have won it three times: 'Seathwaite', 1952; 'Tarn Hows', 1958, and 'Patterdale', 1961.

In the United States, the list of hybridizers of tall bearded irises is a long one. Those whose names appear consistently on recent award lists include Clifford Benson, Paul Cook, Orville Fay, David Hall, Mrs. J. R. Hamblin, Mrs. Georgia Hinkle, Tell Muhlestein, Gordon Plough, Brother Charle Rechamp, Robert Schreiner, Mrs. Neva Sexton, W. B. Schortman and Chet Tompkins. Other bright new stars are rising.

Leading hybridizers, all of whom have received the Hybridizer's Medal of the A.I.S. are:

Paul Cook

Paul H. Cook has received all the highest honors of the iris world. His death in 1963 does not eliminate him from the list of today's hybridizers, for his genius has given tools to hybridizers for years to come; and from his Indiana seedling fields, varieties will continue to be introduced. Mr. Cook read Liberty Hyde Bailey as a boy, and began breeding irises as a young man, starting with the difficult red and black color lines. His first introduction in 1937, was the famous 'E. B. Williamson'; the black 'Sable', 1938, is still used in hybridizing. 'Sable Night' and 'Allegiance', won the Dykes Medal (DM) in 1955 and 1964, respectively.

To improve the blue color in tall beardeds, he collected wild species and started working them into his lines. From a yellow *Iris reichenbachii* seedling crossed with the tall bearded 'Shining Waters' came the ugly little seedling Progenitor, that produced the blue amoena, 'Whole Cloth', probably the greatest advance in modern irises and winner of the Premio Firenze in 1961 and the Dykes Medal in 1962. I am told that beautiful orchid-pink amoenas and bicolors with yellow standards and blue falls abound among his seedlings.

Orville Fay

Orville Fay of Illinois started breeding irises in 1931. His early training on his father's farm where certified seed grain, certified seed potatoes, and pedigreed Aberdeen Angus cattle were raised and then in a technical school for teachers of biology and agriculture made him aware of the importance of exactness in himself and quality in material. His first cross was made with the objective of producing a true white iris hardy in the Chicago region. The best white varieties of the time were half tender, but 'Katherine Fay', which he introduced in 1945, fulfilled his requirements.

Mr. Fay was quick to sense the breeding potential of 'Snow Flurry'. In 1939 he paid a considerable sum (for depression days) to acquire it. Only five years later, 'Snow Flurry' gave him the hardy, disease-risistant 'New Snow', and the cream-colored 'Desert Song'; other breeding produced 'Zantha' and 'Pink Cameo' the same year. All four received the Award of Merit.

In 1945, Mr. Fay planned a ten-year breeding program to obtain white irises with red beards: he crossed 'Snow Flurry' with pink varieties, and the progeny with *Iris pallida*. Within the ten-year period he had obtained his objective—a row of 200 red-bearded white seedlings, plus dividends of red-bearded violets and fine new pinks, all with the blue-green leaves of *I. pallida*. The first seedlings of his new orange line were introduced in 1964.

So far, this hybridizer's introductions have received twenty Awards of Merit, and two Dykes Medals (for 'Truly Yours' and 'Mary Randall'; from England several AM's from the trial gardens at Wisley, a first class certificate for 'Cliffs of Dover', and the Foster Memorial Plaque.

David Hall

David Hall, also from Illinois, originated the Hall strain of flamingo pink irises that have made him famous. He received the Foster Memorial Plaque in 1949. Mr. Hall is a devotee of line breeding, and well he may be; the majority of his originations have received AM's and 'Cherie' won the Dykes Medal in 1951. Mr. Hall has specialized in flamingo pinks and variations—yellows, apricots, and orchid pinks.

It was a long road, but triumph came; four pink irises with tangerine beards finally appeared in his seedling rows. Mr. Hall still continues line-breeding the descendants of these four seedlings. Vigor, he says, has increased rather than decreased. Two of the latest descendants to win AM's are his golden 'Bravado' and apple-blossom pink 'Spring Festival'.

Recently, he began to introduce from a new plicata line. His "black and white" plicata 'Dot and Dash' is generally admired.

Tell Muhlestein

Tell Muhlestein, of Provo, Utah—known affectionately as "Tell" by numerous admirers—fell in love with irises as a small boy. The love grew and flowered into 'Swan Ballet' (Premio Firenze 1958 and Dykes Medal 1959); 'June Meredith', still the pinkest iris, and runner-up for DM in 1958 and 1959; blue 'Praiseworthy', never properly honored; and the newer 'Cream Crest', blue 'Wonderful Sky', and bronze 'Doctor K'.

In 1935, when the young Tell left the little Colorado mining town where he was born, to enter college in Utah, he took his irises along and planted them in his aunt's garden. He owned four varieties: an old purple that a neighbor had thrown on the trash pile, a white (Tell says it must have been 'Albicans'), a yellow, and 'Madam Chereau', the prize of the "collection."

In the big town he found excellent collections of modern iris varieties, and bought all he could afford. In 1943 he saw one of David Hall's original pink seedlings and knew that a new race of irises had been born. On learning from Mr. Hall that 'Golden Eagle' was one of the parents, Tell crossed Loomis' SQ72 with 'Golden Eagle' to start his own series of fine pinks. His 'Pink Enchantment' carries 'Gold Ruffles' blood.

Even if Tell had never gained prominence as a hybridizer, he would still be regarded as an important irisarian for the inspiration and help he has given freely to so many novice hybridizers. His enthusiasm for irises—*all* irises—continues unabated; his breeding at present includes spurias, arilbreds and the smaller bearded irises—border and standard dwarf-beardeds, in addition to tall bearded selfs of many colors, sultry blends, and plicatas. Perhaps this man of zest and enormous curiosity spreads himself too thin; almost certainly he has a rich and happy life.

Robert Schreiner

Robert Schreiner, with his sister Constance and brother Bernard, inherited their father's Minnesota iris nursery. Robert began to breed irises while he was still a boy, and put in ten years of intensive work before he registered his first variety. About 1946 Schreiner's moved their nursery to Oregon where they now grow twenty-five acres of tall bearded irises and raise from 10,000 to 35,000 seedlings annually. They save only 250 of the best each year, and even these are progressively culled until, after several years of observation, a very few are selected for introduction.

From this huge nursery, where even the hybridizing is a joint enterprise, have come many of our finest blue, black, red, bronze, yellow, and orchid varieties, plicatas, and blends, including two Dykes Medalists, 'Blue Sapphire' (1958) and 'Amethyst Flame' (1963); and twenty-some Award of Merit winners. Robert Schreiner received the Foster Memorial Plaque in 1963. The Schreiners are aware that irises are first and foremost for gardens. Their orchid-colored introductions are exceptionally fine—'Lavanesque', 'Crisp-ette', and the new 'Imperial Lilac'.

No formula for becoming a high-ranking iris hybridizer can be evolved from such a small sample, but it is interesting to note the essential similarity of background, including some familiarity with the biological sciences, and the fact that all of them became fascinated with irises very early in life.

15

Shows and Arrangements

Many gardeners thoroughly enjoy showing their irises in competition with other iris growers. Even those who lack the competitive drive may, in a spirit of loyalty to the group or to the flower, contribute their finest blooms toward the success of a show.

The two main show divisions are the horticultural, or specimen, and the arrangement, or artistic sections. I will discuss only the first.

Show dates usually coincide with the peak bloom period of tall bearded and Siberian irises. Some shows include classes for border, table and arilbred irises, and occasionally species and Dutch varieties.

EXHIBITING

It is not necessary to exhibit the latest novelties to win a prize. Specimens are judged according to the characteristics of a variety. Thus a perfectly grown stalk of an older variety with three open flowers would win out over a fair specimen of a new variety with one open flower.

Judges evaluate individual flowers for color, size, substance, and form according to the norm for that variety. An iris show, or iris section of a flower show, should always be judged by A.I.S. judges, who are familiar with the characteristics of both current and older varieties.

The specimen is rated according to the number of open flowers, the placement of buds, and the placement and balance of branches. Finally, cultural perfection is considered. The care given a plant is reflected in the quality of the flowers, height of stem, and even the number of branches.

To win a prize, it *is* necessary to take care in choosing, preparing, and transporting entries. I have seen specimens on the show bench that would have won a prize if their exhibitor had been aware of the penalties judges are required to impose. Bruised or torn petals, flowers which show the least sign of folding up, leaves—and even flowers—spotted with spray residue, ugly stubs of branches where dead flowers have been removed, all must be penalized. Don't let this information frighten you into keeping your beautiful irises at home; instead, let it inspire you to get your entries to the show in good condition. No stalk is perfect; every exhibit will have some fault.

Choosing Entries

The first essential is forethought. Look over the iris planting several days before the show, and tag the stalks with the best branching and largest number of buds. Select more stalks than you think you will need, and include as many different colors and patterns as possible. Sometimes a specimen you had hesitated to enter will take a prize in a class with few entries. Cut the stalks a day before show; if bad weather threatens, it is safer to cut them two days ahead. Late afternoon or early evening is the best time for cutting. The stalks should be plunged deeply into cool water, to harden or condition them. The containers should be narrow enough to hold them upright.

If you have a cool dark basement, keep the stalks there. (I use our dark moist well-house.) Otherwise, keep them in the refrigerator. If there is no basement and insufficient refrigerator room, cut the stalks *early* on the morning of the show and condition them for two or three hours in the coolest place available.

Preparing or Grooming Stalks

Remove faded flowers carefully with a sharp knife or razor blade; cut off the branch-stub flush with the stalk, working carefully so as not to damage the spathe which, smoothed back in position, will cover the wound. Wrap each soon-to-open bud loosely in tissue paper, and fasten at the stem with a plant tie or pin. When the tissue wraps are removed at the show, buds will unfurl almost immediately.

Even leaves come in for their share of grooming. Make sure they are clean. When a leaf is brown at the tip, cautious trimming may remove the brown area. Cut in a long slanting line on either side of the leaf to produce a new tip.

Once show plans are made and the date is set, it cannot be

changed. Exceptionally hot or cold weather that advances or holds back iris bloom can bring anguish to prospective exhibitors. Veteran show enthusiasts, in a frequently successful attempt to outwit nature, may cut stalks several days ahead of the show and keep them in cold storage to hold back bloom—or at the other extreme, sit up half the night before the show encouraging stalks with laggard buds to open in a warm, constant-temperature bath.

Transporting Irises to the Show

Separate stalks must be placed firmly so individual flowers will not touch each other. Exhibitors of hard-to-handle tall bearded irises use ingenious methods. A perfectionist friend has acquired a strong florist-type cardboard box, five feet long, thirty inches wide and about a foot deep, which he uses year after year. He punched four small holes in each side of the box, six inches above the base, a foot apart and starting a foot from either end. Through the holes and across the inside of the box, he laced strong cord to form a sort of cradle, on which he lays the stalks with tips pointing in alternate directions. He fastens each stalk with a plant tie to two separate cross cords. The flowers, thus suspended in air, ride safely over the bumpiest road.

An easier method is to collect from the supermarket those boxes with twelve sections in which glass jars have been packed, and place containers in alternate sections, like a checkerboard, with one iris stalk in each jar. Each box will hold six tall bearded stalks safely, especially if paper is wadded in around the stalk in each jar.

Irises with fewer flowers per stalk, such as arilbreds, the various medians, Siberians, and species are much easier to transport.

Every exhibitor should plan to have all his entries on the show bench at least fifteen minutes before judging is to begin. A last minute rush almost inevitably results in mistakes.

Show Schedules

The Schedule Committee makes schedules available far enough in advance so that prospective exhibitors can study it carefully, become familiar with the rules, and decide on the classes they wish to enter.

The exhibitor should fill in entry tags legibly, making sure to use the correct name of each variety. If in doubt as to the proper class for any entry, he can ask a member of the show's classification committee. Even a small show may have twenty-five to thirty classes.

RULES AND REGULATIONS OF AIS-SPONSORED SHOWS *

1. Exhibition privileges are available to all persons, and are not limited to A.I.S. members. (In case of a shortage of space, the show committee may limit exhibition privileges to A.I.S. members and local club members.)

2. Horticultural entries may include registered cultivars, numbered seedlings, and species.

3. Cultivars, species, and numbered seedlings must be correctly and clearly identified and labeled. Unregistered cultivars and unidentified irises may not be exhibited.

4. The number of entries which an exhibitor may make in any one class is left to the jurisdiction of the local show.

5. All horticultural entries must have been grown by the exhibitor.

6. A show must list at least twenty classes in the horticultural division to qualify for awards, and an adequate number of entries must be shown in a majority of the classes comprising the horticultural division to ensure fair competition.

7. All registered cultivars and species are eligible for all ribbons, rosettes, certificates, medals and other awards offered for entries in the horticultural division.

IRIS FLOWERS INDOORS

Right off, I disavow any professional knowledge of flower arranging. I am merely a gardener who, from childhood, has enjoyed bringing flowers and leaves and branches from the garden and from the woods and fields into the house, particularly during the early spring months when my dried bouquets seem as dull and dead as the autumn leaves still blowing across my garden. It is in March that I am most appreciative of the fragrance and form of a flower —any flower. And of the luminous iris colors that man has never been able to equal in his paints and dyestuffs.

I like to combine them into pleasing patterns according to my own fancy, and for my own pleasure. The only time I ever entered an arrangement in a show was in response to an urgent SOS from an iris show chairman. It won a red ribbon, and would have won a blue—or so one of the judges told me—if I had not broken a leaf

* From A.I.S. *Bulletin* Number 169, April, 1963.

38   FOR MARCH

Four green-speckled yellow flowers of *Iris danfordiae* and one early yellow crocus accent the bronze leaves and greenish bud-clusters of *Pieris japonica*. Arranged in a brass tea caddy, they capture a hint of spring for my living room.

in getting the arrangement to the show. Even if it had won Best in Show, I would not be tempted to repeat that experience. Exhibiting arrangements is fun for many, but not for me.

The real joy of flower arranging, like that of creating a garden picture, lies in assembling diverse plant elements and making them live in harmony. I consider any flower arrangement successful when the ingredients are combined so as to please the *arranger's* sense of scale, color, and pattern; in other words, when you succeed in pleasing yourself. Copies of others' triumphs, even if technically correct, are dull indeed because they fail to reflect the personality of the copyist. If you are pleased with the appearance of several stalks of iris flowers poked into a vase and left to lean at whatever angle gravity dictates, there's no reason in the world why you should bother to place them differently. They may be specimen stalks of your best seedlings, and your pleasure may come from

40 *Below*. FOR MAY
Arrangement by Win
Whyte. The graceful sprays
of the May-blooming snow-
flake are just the right size
to go with the crisp small
flowers of the ten-inch
standard dwarf iris, Lilli
White, for a sparkling
white and green arrange-
ment. Short, curved iris
leaves were chosen. Flow-
ers from my garden.

39 *Above*. FOR JUNE
White Siberian irises are
arranged with their own
foliage in a shallow blue-
brown pottery container
with the velvety brown of
inverted shelf fungi. The
flowers at the top are of
Snowcrest; the broad flowers below, of White Swirl.

gloating over their perfection of form and branching. If you think they deserve a better setting, if you wish you could assemble them in a pleasing pattern, you need only try—using whatever equipment is at hand.

For my own casually furnished house I prefer simple, informal designs of only a few flowers, though occasionally I do enjoy arranging a huge, scintillating mass of bloom. Sometimes, when I rogue out a blooming seedling, I dig the plant, carefully wash the roots and rhizomes, and set the whole thing on a pinpoint holder in a wide dark bowl which will emphasize the beautiful pale roots swirling out in the shallow water. Nothing could be easier and the effect, like that of a well-executed botanical drawing, enchants me.

Cutting

For your house as for a show, irises are cut in late afternoon or early morning, and conditioned for several hours. When the stemless March and April bloomers are brought in out of the cold, a transition period in a cool dim room is essential. It is desirable for all irises.

Spuria and Dutch irises are the best keepers, often lasting a week with proper care. Bearded types and Siberian and Japanese irises will last up to four days. To obtain maximum life indoors for these summer bloomers, I select stalks with buds just about to open, cut them on a slant and plunge them at once into a pail of tepid water.

Containers

While it is pleasant to have handsome bronze, pewter, old hand-wrought copper and delicate porcelain containers, don't let the lack of them hamper you. The plainer and less competitive the setting, the better for displaying irises. Numerous suitable containers can be found in every household. Platters, cake-plates, vegetable dishes, soup tureens, pitchers, cups, ashtrays, large juice cans coated with paraffin on the inside and painted with flat paint on the outside—the list is endless. I don't consider wooden bowls, baskets or the plebian bean pot suitable for so elegant a flower as a tall bearded iris. And vases elaborately decorated in color compete with the flowers. I prefer a plain—even dull—medium or dark green, black, white or pewter-grey container, though yellow, orange, beige or brown irises are brilliantly handsome in old handmade copper wash-basins.

Miniature Arrangements

The fragrant, March-blooming bulbous irises and the April-blooming bearded pumilas are perfect material for informal miniature groupings, which I call posies or nosegays. They are inevitably small and intimate, both because the flowers are stemless or nearly so, and because no gardener wants to remove many of these bright treasures from the bare March garden where their colors glow for weeks in the cold. In the warm house, they last two or three days.

I like to arrange mosses with small textured stones or turkey-tail fungi and polypody fern fronds or short sprays of ivy on a small black pottery plate. When I add one or two pale yellow winter aconite flowers, their green ruffs nestling against the deeper green moss, and one violet *Iris reticulata* for height (four inches), I have an indoor garden—six inches across. As the flowers fade, I replace them with fresh ones.

For the March arrangement picture on page 168, I cut four flowers of the yellow *Iris danfordiae* and one Dutch Yellow crocus to accent the bronze-green leaves and green-white flower-buds of *Pieris japonica*. The container is an old-fashioned brass tea caddy, four inches tall. Its inverted lid held the tiny echoing group.

Foliage

The indispensable "greens" in an arrangement may be used sparingly to accent the flowers or give added direction to the line; or they may constitute the mass of the arrangement, with flowers providing the accent—especially when few flowers are available or when the gardener is unwilling to cut more than a stem or two.

While tall bearded irises look well with their own foliage, in some arrangements the taller leaf fans of hybrid spuria irises are more effective; or the curves of daylily leaves may add grace. When foliage is used for the mass of the composition, some variation in size, shape, and texture of leaves will help to produce a more vibrant design. Every garden will provide an abundance of material. I think fine feathery foliage looks fussy with large-flowered irises. Peony leaves are attractive, but I prefer smooth-edged rather than deeply cut leaves. In combination with fans of iris leaves, I have used the large heart-shaped leaves of redbud trees, magnolia leaves, and various hostas including the variegated types. Leaves and green berries of the early-blooming *Viburnum carlesii* set off white tall beardeds. As a background for an arrangement of cream tall beardeds I have often used a plant of false Solomon's seal, with its terminal raceme of tiny cream-white flowers. The dark green alternate leaves stand out horizontally from a central stem. The holder for the arrangement is concealed by a few individual leaves.

The use of non-iris foliage in an arrangement of little, early-blooming bulbous and bearded irises is next to necessary: the small leaves have not attained their maximum growth and I am reluctant to deprive the tiny, heavy-flowering plants of their food factories. Even in March, my garden provides young daffodil leaves, fronds of the evergreen polypody fern, ivy and periwinkle. In April, the pleated leaves of alchemilla, furls of lily-of-the-valley and blood-root leaves begin to unfold and fern fiddles of various kinds appear. From my house plant window I have cut the velvety leaves of mint geranium, small begonias, and fat, curving, purple-leaved stems of zebrinas. Once in a blue moon I cut a few glistening undulating fronds from my one bird's nest fern.

With Other Flowers

More lively and vibrant arrangements are obtainable if two kinds of irises, as tall bearded and smaller more open-flowered Siberians, are used together; or if irises are combined with other flowers. Some of the garden and wild flowers I like to combine with various irises are:

MARCH—RETICULATAS

Daffodils—*Narcissus minimus,*	Polypody fern fronds
Forsythia—forced	Pussywillows, wild
High-bush blueberry—forced	Snowdrops
Pieris japonica, leaves and buds	Winter crocuses

APRIL—MINIATURE DWARFS

Chionodoxas
Daffodils—small hybrids, as April Tears and Bee Bop
Forsythia
Grape hyacinths
Primulas—small-flowered *P. juliae* hybrids

Bleeding heart—common garden and wild types
Daffodils—small-cupped varieties
Lily-of-the-valley
Phlox divaricata
Snowflakes *(Leucojum aestivum)*
Tulip—*T. clusiana*
Violas and johnny-jump-ups
Wood hyacinth *(Scilla hispanica)*

LATE MAY—INTERMEDIATES

Azaleas	Columbine	Tulips

JUNE—TALL BEARDED, DUTCH, SIBERIAN AND SPURIAS

Baptisia	Lilacs	Peonies	Roses
Beauty-bush	Lupin	Poppies	Viburnums

JULY—JAPANESE HYBRIDS

I use a clematis flower or two, or sprays of an ever-blooming stemmed violet, as a sort of grace note. No other flowers.

Appendix

A. AVAILABLE SPECIES

Bloom periods, heights, planting times and cultural directions are all based on performance in southern New York State.

Unless otherwise indicated, these species should be planted in full sun.

"Normal" means culture generally advised for herbaceous perennials.

174

	Height in Inches	Bloom Season	Predominating Color	Planting Time	Remarks on Culture
BULBOUS					
I. bakerana	4	Feb.	blue	Oct.	Normal. Sheltered site.
I. danfordiae	4	March	yellow	Oct.	Normal. Sheltered site.
I. histrioides major	4	Feb.-March	blue	Oct.	Normal. Sheltered site.
I. reticulata	4	March	purple	Oct.	Normal.
JUNOS					
I. bucharica	15	April	white and yellow	Oct.	Normal. Sheltered site.
I. graeberiana	12	April	light blue	Oct.	Normal. Sheltered site.
I. magnifca (I. vicaria)	18	April	lavender	Oct.	Normal. Sheltered site.
I. sindjarensis (I. aucheri)	9	April	blue	Oct.	Normal. Sheltered site.

TRUE BEARDED

	Height in Inches	Bloom Season	Predominating Color	Planting Time	Remarks on Culture
I. aphylla	10	May	purple	June or August	Normal.
I. chamaeiris	6–8	April-May	yellow or purple	June or August	Lighten heavy soil with sand and stone chips.
I. mellita	4	April-May	yellow or purple	June or August	Lighten heavy soil with sand and stone chips.
I. pallida	16–30	May-June	blue	July-Aug.	Normal.
I. pumila	4	April	various	June or August	Normal.
I. variegata	18	May-June	yellow and brown	July-August	Normal.

ARILS

	Height in Inches	Bloom Season	Predominating Color	Planting Time	Remarks on Culture
I. arenaria	5	May	yellow	June or August	Very sandy soil.
I. hoogiana	18–30	May	blue	Oct.-Nov.	Sharp drainage. Summer dryness not essential.

	Height in Inches	Bloom Season	Predominating Color	Planting Time	Remarks on Culture
I. kamaoenensis	6–8	May	purple	Oct. (seeds)	Sharp drainage.
I. korolkowii	15	May	various	Oct.-Nov.	Sharp drainage. Summer dryness not essential.
I. stolonifera	15	May	blue and brown	Oct.-Nov.	Sharp drainage. Summer dryness not essential.
I. susiana	18	May	grey, veined purple	Oct.-Nov.	Sharp drainage. Dry in summer.
CRESTED					
I. cristata	3–4	May-June	lilac	April or Sept.	Humus. Part shade.
I. gracilipes	6–8	May-June	lilac	June	Humus. Part shade.
I. tectorum	10	May-June	blue or white	June or August	Sun or part shade. Normal.

BEARDLESS

	Height in Inches	Bloom Season	Predominating Color	Planting Time	Remarks on Culture
I. aurea (I. crocea)	36	June-July	yellow	Sept.	Normal.
I. bulleyana	16	June	lilac	Sept.	Normal.
I. chrysographes	15	June	purple	Sept.	Moist border or pool-side.
I. clarkei	24	May-June	purple	Sept.	Moist border or pool-side.
I. delavayi	45	June	violet	Sept.	Moist border or pool-side.
I. dichotoma	24	Aug.	lilac	Oct. (seeds)	Normal.
I. foetidissima	18	June	purple; seeds scarlet	Sept.	Moist, humus, shade.
I. brevicaulis	12	June	purple	Sept.	Normal, moist, humus.
I. forrestii	18	June	yellow	Sept.	Normal, moist.
I. fulva	24–30	June	rust	Sept.	Normal, moist, humus.
I. giganticaerulea	36	June	blue or white	Sept.	Normal, moist, humus.
I. graminea	12	May-June	purple	Sept.	Normal. Tolerates part shade.
I. kaempferi	24–30	June-July	purple	April or Sept.	Moist, humus. Tolerates part shade. Normal or pool-side.

	Height in Inches	Bloom Season	Predominating Color	Planting Time	Remarks on Culture
I. laevigata	24–30	June-July	blue or white	April or Sept.	Moist, humus. Tolerates part shade.
I. longipetala	24–30	June	white	April or Sept.	Normal.
I. pseudacorus	30–60	June	yellow	Sept.	Normal. Pool-side.
I. ruthenica	4	May-June	purple	Sept.	Normal.
I. setosa	6–12	June	blue	Sept.	Normal. Tolerates part shade.
I. siberica	28	June	blue	Sept.	Normal. Tolerates part shade.
I. spuria var. lilacina	30	June	lilac	Oct. (seeds)	Normal.
I. unguicularis (I. stylosa)	4	Nov. to March	lilac	Sept.	Cold frame in this region.
I. verna	4	May	blue	June	Humus, part shade.
I. versicolor	18	May-June	blue	Sept.	Normal, moist or pool-side.
I. virginica	18–24	May-June	blue	Sept.	Normal, moist or pool-side.
NEPALENSIS					
I. decora	12–15	June-July	purple	Oct. (seeds)	Normal.

B. SOURCES OF PLANTS AND SEEDS

Most catalogues of herbaceous plants or bulbs offer only a few varieties of a few kinds of irises. Specialists' catalogues, usually unknown to the general gardener, are often the only sources for unusual species and new varieties. From one or another of the sources listed below, plants, bulbs or seeds of almost all the kinds and varieties of irises mentioned in this book may be obtained. Because catalogues are increasingly expensive to produce, a small charge—often deducted from the first order—is made for the more elaborate ones.

After a variety has been in commerce for a few years, it may be listed in several catalogues. The year of introduction, it is available only from the introducer, who may or may not be the originator. Schreiner's originations, for instance, are introduced by Schreiner's; Gibson's by Cooley's Gardens. I have listed one or more of the hybridizers for whom each nursery introduces, without attempting to present a complete list.

A. H. Hazzard, 510 Grand Pre Ave., Kalamazoo, Michigan 49007
Grower of Japanese irises. List on request.

Brown's Iris Gardens, 12624 84th Ave. N.E., Kirkland, Washington 98033
All classes of bearded irises. Features own introductions. List on request.

Cooley's Gardens, 301 S. James Ave., Silverton, Oregon 97381
Tall bearded. Introduces for Gibson. Catalogue in color.

De Jager and Sons, 188 Asbury St., South Hamilton, Massachusetts 01982
Dutch, Spanish and reticulata iris bulbs.

Eden Road Iris Gardens, P. O. Box 117, Wenatchee, Washington 98801
All classes of bearded irises. Features Plough introductions.

Fleur de Lis Gardens, P. O. Box 670, Canby, Oregon 97013
Tall bearded irises; a few smaller bearded varieties. Features Tompkins originations.

Gilbert H. Wild and Son, Inc., Sarcoxie, Missouri 64862
Tall bearded irises. Features introductions of Georgia Hinkle and James Marsh. Color catalogue.

Melrose Gardens, 309 Best Road South A A, Stockton, California 95206
 All classes of bearded irises; arilbreds; spurias; Japanese; Siberian; Louisiana; beardless species. Features Hager introductions. Color and black/white illustrations.
Mission Bell Gardens, 2778 West 5600 South, Roy, Utah 84067
 Recent varieties of all classes of bearded irises. Features Hamblen introductions.
Moldovan's Gardens, 38830 Detroit Rd., Avon, Ohio 44011
 Specializes in recent tall bearded iris varieties.
Old Brook Gardens, 10 S. Franklin Circle, Littleton, Colorado 80120
 Wide selection of smaller bearded iris varieties; McGarvey, McEwen and Warburton Siberian iris introductions. List on request.
Raleigh Hills Gardens, 5635 S. W. Boundary St., Portland, Oregon 97221
 Tall and median bearded irises. Jones introductions only.
Schreiner's Iris Lovers Catalogue, 3625 Quinaby Rd. N.E., Salem, Oregon 97303.
 Tall bearded iris specialist; medians; Siberians; spurias. Introduces own tall bearded originations and Walker's spuria irises. Color catalogue.
Tell's Gardens, P. O. Box 331, Orem, Utah 84057
 Bearded irises in all classes; arilbreds; spurias.
Walter Marx Gardens, Boring, Oregon 97009
 Specialist in Japanese irises. Features own introductions. Also offers spuria, Siberian and Pacific Coast varieties, and unusual species. Also Dutch, Juno and reticulata iris bulbs. Color catalogue.

SEEDS

G. Ghose and Co., Townsend, Darjeeling, India
 Rare species, including pseudoregelias.
Geo. W. Park Seed Co., Inc., Greenwood, South Carolina 29646
 Some species and hybrids.
Harry E. Saier, Dimondale, Michigan 48821
 Some species and hybrids.
Thomson & Morgan, Ltd., Ipswich, England
 Good list of iris species, forms and hybrids.

C. IRIS AWARDS

AMERICAN IRIS SOCIETY AWARDS

High Commendation (HC): Given annually to seedlings of any origin, named or unnamed, but not yet introduced at time of judging.

Honorable Mention (HM): Given annually to officially registered varieties, of any origin, which have been introduced one or more years.

Award of Merit (AM): Given annually to the twelve eligible tall bearded varieties receiving the most votes. Only those varieties awarded HMs not less than two nor more than five years previously are eligible.

Annual awards parallel to the Award of Merit, for irises in other classes:

Morgan Award: Siberian iris variety

Caparne Award: Miniature dwarf bearded iris variety

Mary Swords Deballion Award: Louisiana iris species or variety

Eric Nies Award: Spuria iris variety

Cook-Douglas Award: Standard dwarf bearded iris variety

Knowlton Award: Border bearded iris variety

Hans and Jacob Sass Award: Intermediate bearded iris variety

Clarence G. White Memorial Award: Arilbred iris varieties with one-fourth or more aril blood

Special awards not parallel to the Award of Merit:

Cook-Lapham Cup: Best red iris in commerce

President's Cup: During the society's annual meeting to the most outstanding variety seen growing in a garden on the regular tour program of the meeting

Clara B. Rees Award: Annually to the best tall bearded white iris in commerce

THE DYKES MEDAL

The Dykes Memorial Medal is the highest award for an iris. It was instituted in 1926 by the British Iris Society as a memorial to William Rickatson Dykes, author of the great monograph, *The Genus Iris,* and of *A Handbook of Garden Irises.*

This award may be given annually by the B.I.S. to two varieties of proven garden merit, one introduced and grown in England, the other in the United States or Canada. The English award is made through the British Iris Society, the North American award through the American Iris Society.

DYKES MEDAL WINNERS
1947-1965

England		North America
	1947	Chivalry
Mrs. J. L. Gibson	1948	Ola Kala
Blue Ensign	1949	Helen McGregor
	1950	Blue Rhythm
	1951	Cherie
Seathwaite	1952	Argus Pheasant
Arabi Pasha	1953	Truly Yours
	1954	Mary Randall
Benton Cordelia	1955	Sable Night
	1956	First Violet
Golden Alps	1957	Violet Harmony
	1958	Blue Sapphire
Headlines	1959	Swan Ballet
Kanchenjunga	1960	
Patterdale	1961	Eleanor's Pride
Arcady	1962	Whole Cloth
Dancer's Veil	1963	Amethyst Flame
Primrose Drift	1964	Allegiance
Mary Todd	1965	Pacific Panorama

THE FLORENCE AWARD

The Premio Firenze is awarded annually to a new tall bearded variety originating in any country, and named and officially registered not more than three years before the year of entry in the contest. The varieties entered are judged, without identification, by an international panel two years after entry. At least two vigorous rhizomes of each variey entered must be submitted.

PREMIO FIRENZE WINNERS

1958　Allaglow　(U.S.)
1959　La Negraflor　(U.S.)
1960　Allaglow　(U.S.)
1961　Whole Cloth　(U.S.)
1962　Indiglow　(U.S.)
1963　Dancer's Veil　(England)
1964　Midnight Waltz　(U.S.)
1965　Lorna Lee　(U.S.)

D. AWARDS OF THE AMERICAN IRIS SOCIETY, 1965

Variety	*Originator*

DYKES MEDAL

| Pacific Panorama | Neva Sexton |

MARY SWORDS DEBAILLON AWARD

| Frances Elizabeth | Sam Rix |

CAPARNE AWARD

| Atomic Blue | Walter Welch |

ERIC NIES AWARD

| Morningtide | Marion Walker |

CLARENCE G. WHITE MEMORIAL AWARD

| Golden Joppa | Jack Linse |

COOK-DOUGLAS AWARD

| Easter Holiday | Dr. J. R. Durrance |

KNOWLTON AWARD

Bayadere   Opal Brown

HANS AND JACOB SASS AWARD

Cutie   Schreiner's

MORGAN AWARD

Violet Flare   F. W. Cassebeer

COOK-LAPHAM BOWL

Tomeco   Mrs. Glen Suiter

CLARA B. REES AWARD

Henry Shaw   Clifford W. Benson

AWARD OF MERIT

Variety	*Originator*
Ultrapoise	Luella Noyd
Wild Ginger	James Gibson
Dark Fury	Walter Luihn
Chinese Coral	Orville Fay
Blue Baron	Schreiner's
Gracie Pfost	Eva Smith
Martel	Tell Muhlestein
Helen Traubel	Clifford W. Benson
Fifth Avenue	Melba Hamblen
Lilting Melody	Dorothy Palmer
Christmas Angel	Fred DeForest
Sparkling Waters	Schreiner's

E. JUDGES' CHOICE, 1965

Irises eligible for this honor are those which have received an Honorable Mention award during the current or previous year.

Tall Bearded	*Originator*
Winter Olympics	Opal Brown
Stepping Out	Schreiner's
Skywatch	Orville Fay
Champagne Music	Clifford W. Benson
Ribbon Round	Chet Tompkins
Sterling Silver	Steve Moldovan
Arctic Fury	Clifford W. Benson
Cross Country	Dr. Frederick Knocke
Coraband	Melba Hamblen
Prince Indigo	Schreiner's
Mission Sunset	Bro. Charles Reckamp
Flaming Heart	Orville Fay
Claudia Rene	Larry Gaulter
Wine and Roses	David Hall
Java Dove	Gordon Plough
Music Maker	Don Waters
Moon River	Neva Sexton
Ellem Manor	Clarence Blocker
Kingdom	Orville Fay
Ever and Ever	Ione Hope
Denver Mint	Maynard Knopf
Gaily Clad	Jeanette Nelson
Gypsy Jewels	Schreiner's
Wenatchee Skies	Luella Noyd
Dancing Bride	Nathan Rudolph

Standard Dwarf Bearded	*Originator*
Blueberry Muffins	Bee Warburton
Circlette	John Goett
Gold Buttons	Melba Hamblen
Nylon Loveliness	Doriot-Reath
Velvet Caper	Bee Warburton

Miniature Dwarf Bearded

Sky Caper	Bee Warburton
Bumble Wings	E. Smith

Arils and Arilbreds

Trisha	Flora McGee
Saffron Jewel	Thornton Abell
Little Sheba	Thornton Abell
Sir Gordon	Flora McGee
Angelique	Clarice Batson

Miniature Tall Bearded

Zimbrakeet	Earl Roberts

Intermediate Bearded

Drummer Boy	Schreiner's
Maroon Caper	Bee Warburton
Dark Eden	A. Brown

Border Bearded

Blue Miller	T. Brown
Small Talk	Neva Sexton
La Nina Rosa	Eugene Sundt
Native Daughter	Luella Noyd
Glacier Bay	B. Jones

F.   IRIS SOCIETIES

UNITED STATES

American Iris Society. Secretary, Clifford Benson, 2315 Tower Grove Ave., St. Louis, Missouri 63110. The A.I.S. publishes a quarterly *Bulletin,* an annual list of iris registrations, and, every decade, a *Check List of Iris Varieties* in book form. Annual Membership, $7.50.

Special Interest Societies

Median Iris Society. President, Anthony Willot, 26231 Shaker Blvd., Beachwood, Ohio

Society for Siberian Irises. President, Dr. Currier McEwen, South Harpswell, Maine 04079.

Society for Japanese Irises. President, Mrs. Troy Westmeyer, 60 Gary Rd., Stamford, Connecticut 06903.

Spuria Iris Society. President, Mrs. Eleanor McCown, P. O. Box 176, Holtville, California 92250.

Reblooming Iris Society. President, Mrs. Wynnaline Stinson, 2035 Alhambra, Dallas, Texas 72517.

Membership in the above societies is open only to members of the American Iris Society.

OTHER COUNTRIES

British Iris Society, 72 S. Hill Park, London, N.W. 3. Publishes annually *The Iris Year Book* (well worth the cost of membership). Americans may send the annual membership fee of $4 through the American Iris Society.

Australian Iris Society, Vic. Reg., 360 Lower Heidelberg Rd., East Ivanhoe 3079, Victoria, Australia.

Australian Iris Society, NSW Reg., 8 Mary St., Longueville, Sydney, New South Wales, Australia.

Canadian Iris Society, 997 Vine St., Preston, Ontario, Canada.

French Iris Society (Société Française des Amateurs d'Iris), 134 Avenue Savorguan de Brazza, La Valette-du-Ver, France.

German Iris Society (Deutsche Iris und Liliengesellschaft), Justinus Kerner-Strasse 11, (14a) Leonberg bei Stuttgart, Germany.

Italian Iris Society (Società Italiana dell' Iris), presso Instituto Botanico, Via Lamarmora 4, 50121, Firenze, Italy.

Japan Iris Society, Manchidani 8-7, Nishinomiya City, Japan.

New Zealand Iris Society, Bastia Hill, Wanganui, New Zealand.

Iris Society of South Africa, P. O. Box 82, Transvaal, South Africa.

Glossary

Amoena. A color pattern of white standards and colored falls. A *reverse amoena* has colored standards and white falls.

Anther. The pollen-bearing part of a stamen.

Apogon. A rhizomatous iris which has no beard or crest.

Aril. The small white collar, on seeds of oncocyclus, regelia and pseudoregelia irises, which surrounds the point of attachment to the seed pod; also, these groups of irises.

Arilbred. A hybrid between aril and eupogon irises.

Backcross. The offspring obtained by the cross of a hybrid to either parent.

Bicolor. A color pattern in which the standards are of one color, and the falls are of a darker color. In a *reverse bicolor*, the standards are of the darker color.

Bitone. A color pattern in which the standards are a lighter shade of the same color as the falls. In a *reverse bitone*, the falls are lighter than the standards.

Blend. A color pattern in which two or more colors are combined in the flower segments.

Chromosome. A threadlike body in the cell nucleus, containing genes arranged in linear order.

Clone. All the vegetatively produced descendants of a single plant, propagated in irises by division of the rootstock or multiplication of bulbs.

Crest. The raised linear ridge on the haft of the falls of crested (Evansia) irises.

Cultivar. A cultivated variety, usually originating and maintained in cultivation.

Diploid. Possessing two sets of chromosomes in each nucleus.

Egg. The female germ cell in the embryo sac of the ovule.

189

Embryo. The rudimentary plant, or germ, within the seed.

Endosperm. The part of the seed that surrounds and provides nourishment for the embryo.

Eupogon. A true bearded iris, distinguished from aril irises by the lack of an aril on the seeds and by a linear instead of a diffuse beard.

Form. Shape (of a flower); also variant of a species, as "a blue *form* of *Iris pumila.*"

Gene. A part of a chromosome responsible for the development of certain characteristics of the plant.

Genetics. The experimental study of heredity.

Genus. A botanical category containing one or more related species (see *species*).

Germ cell. A gamete; a male or female cell, usually with a single set of chromosomes, which can unite with a germ cell of the opposite sex to produce a new individual.

Haft. The narrow inner portion of the standards and falls.

Hybrid. The offspring of parents belonging to differing species, races, etc.

Meiosis. Two specialized cell divisions which result in the production of germ cells.

Mitosis. The normal method by which cells are multiplied.

Mutation. A change in a gene or chromosome, thus causing a permanent (hereditary) change in a characteristic or characteristics of the race.

Nucleus. A rounded or oval body within the living matter of the cell; it contains the chromosomes.

Ovary. The part of the pistil that contains the ovules; after fertilization, it develops into the fruit containing the seeds (the seed pod in irises).

Ovule. The immature seed; it contains, within the embryo sac, the egg or female germ cell.

Perianth. The collective name for the petals and sepals of a flower.

Perianth tube. A slender tube formed of joined petals and sepals; in the iris, it connects the perianth (the standards and falls) with the part of the stem that surrounds the ovary. It may be very short, as in tall bearded varieties, or several inches long, as in *Iris pumila.*

Petaloid. Having the appearance or texture of a petal.

Pistil. The part of the flower that forms the ovules. It consists typically of ovary, style and stigma.

Plicata. A color pattern in which a white or yellow flower is stitched or stippled in a second color.

Pollen. The mass of minute grains formed in the anther and transferred to the stigma.

Rhizomatous. Having a rhizome.

Rhizome. A horizontal stem growing at or beneath the ground surface.

Seed. The fertilized and ripened ovule.

Self. A color pattern in which the standards and falls are the same color.

Species. A group of plants with common characteristics distinguishing them from other such groups and reappearing in their offspring. They may be variable enough to be subdivided into *varieties* or *forms.* Similar species are combined into the higher ranking group called a *genus.* Similar genera form a *family.* The genus *Iris* is one of many related genera, including *Crocus, Freesia, Gladiolus* and *Tigridia,* which together make up the family *Iridaceae.*

Stamen. One of the pollen-bearing organs of the flower.

Stigma. The part of the pistil that receives the pollen. In the iris, it is a lip projecting from the style-branch, below the style-crest.

Style. The part of the pistil that rises from the ovary and bears the stigma. In the iris, it consists of three flat branches, generally colored like the perianth.

Tetraploid. Possessing four sets of chromosomes in each nucleus.

Triploid. Possessing three sets of chromosomes in each nucleus.

Variegata. A color pattern in which the standards are yellow and the falls are brown or red.

Variety. Botanically, a subdivision of a species. Horticulturally, a cultivar. A botanical variety may be brought into cultivation and may thus rank as a cultivar; but most cultivars originate in cultivation and are less stable in reproduction.

List of References

BOOKS—GENERAL

Anley, Gwendolyn. *Irises, Their Culture and Selection.* London, W. H. and L. Collingridge, Ltd., 1946

Cave, N. L. *The Iris.* New York, Chanticleer Press, Inc., 1951

Dykes, W. R. *The Genus Iris.* Chicago, The University of Chicago Press, 1913

————. *A Handbook of Garden Irises.* London, W. Hopkinson, 1924

Dykes on Irises. Compiled and edited by George Dillistone. Printed and published for the British Iris Society by C. Baldwin

Lawrence, W. J. C. *Practical Plant Breeding.* London, George Allen & Unwin, Ltd., 1937

Mitchell, Sydney. *Iris for Every Garden.* New York, M. Barrows & Co., Inc., 1949

Randolph, L. F., editor. *Garden Irises.* Published by The American Iris Society. St. Louis, 1959

Rickett, H. W. *Botany for Gardeners.* New York, The Macmillan Co., 1957

Soil. The Yearbook of Agriculture, 1957. U. S. Department of Agriculture. U. S. Government Printing Office

The Iris: An Ideal Hardy Perennial. Written and published by members of The American Iris Society. Nashville, 1947

CHECK LISTS, PERIODICALS AND PAMPHLETS

Bulletin of the American Iris Society. Nos. 1-174. 1920-1964. Published quarterly by The American Iris Society

Dwarf Iris Society Portfolio, 1955 to 1961. Published annually by the Dwarf Iris Society

The Iris Year Book, 1952-1963. Published annually by The British Iris Society

The Medianite, 1961-1964. Published quarterly by the Median Iris Society

Morrison, B. Y. *Garden Irises.* Farmers' Bulletin No. 1406. U. S. Department of Agriculture, Washington, D.C., 1926

Spuria Iris Society Checklist, 1963. Published by the Spuria Iris Society

Index

Abbeville irises, 2, 106
Abell, Thornton, 187
Acidity (of soil), 50, 51
Alkalinity (of soil), 51
American Iris Society (A. I. S.), 6, 25, 27, 28, 32, 42, 58, 59, 63, 65, 80, 132, 138, 159, 160, 164, 167, 182, 183, 184, 187, 188
Amoena (color pattern), 42, 71, 159
Anther, illus., 142, 143
Antibiotics, 133
Aphids, 134, 139
Apogons, 6, 83, 97, 98, 101, 103
Apricot-flowered irises, 38
Arctic iris, 103
Aril irises, 6, 74, 78, 80, 126, 127, 129, 176, 182, 187
Aril Society International, 188
Austin, Lloyd, 75, 77, 79, 82
Ayres, Mrs. Adda E., 188

Bacterial diseases, 132
Bailey, Liberty Hyde, 160
Bantam irises, 28
Barr and Sons, 24
Batson, Clarice, 187
Beard (of iris), 44; illus., 142
Bearded irises, 5, 6, 10, 23-28, 32-45, 46-57, 58-73, 148, 170, 176; illus., 20
Beardless irises, 5, 6, 10, 83-100, 101-113, 127, 179
Bell, Ian, 88
Benson, Clifford W., 35, 160, 185, 186, 187
Bertolini, Antonio, 61
Bicolor (color pattern), 32, 42-43
Bitone (color pattern), 32, 43
Black iris, 79
Black-flowered irises, 27, 40, 69, 72
Blend (color pattern), 32, 44

Bliss, A. J., 25
Blooming periods, 125-129, Appendix A
Blue-flowered irises, 27, 39, 69, 72, 87, 92, 96, 107, Appendix A
Border bearded irises, 7, 23, 28-30, 65, 126, 127, 182, 187
Border planting, 10; illus., 9, 18
Botanisches Institut, 158
Botrytis, 131
British Iris Society (B. I. S.), 25, 159, 183, 188
Bronze-flowered irises, 96, 107
Brown, Alta, 71, 187
Brown, Opal, 185, 186
Brown, Dr. Percy, 30
Brown, T., 187
Brown-flowered irises, 37, 70, 72, Appendix A
Brummitt, Leonard W., 135, 159
Brummitt, Mrs. M., 112
Buff-flowered irises, 37
Bulb, definition of, 4; illus., 4
Bulbous irises, 4, 5, 6, 114-124, 129, 175; illus., 116, 127
Bulgarian iris, 94

Californicae (series), 108
Caparne, J. W., 70; award, 60, 182, 184
Cassebeer, F. W., 13, 16, 31, 105, 185
Chromosomes: See Genetics
Claw (of iris), definition of, 2
Clusius, Carolus, 1
Cole, Harold, 159
Color classifications (A.I.S.), 32
Color patterns, 32-45
Color planning, 13
Compost, 53
Cook, Paul, 42, 59, 65, 67, 71, 160

193

Cream-flowered irises, 28, 33, 70, 107
Crest (of iris), definition of, 2; illus.,
    3
Crested irises, 5, 98-100, 101-103,
    127, 178; illus., 5
Crossing (cross-pollination), 141, 145,
    154
Crown rot, 131
Culture, 46-57, 81, 90, 95, 117, 119,
    120, Appendix A
Cutting, 165, 170

Dimock, Dr. A. W., 132
Diploid, 25, 42, 73, 155
Diseases, 130-136
Disinfecting, 131
Dividing, 55
Dosage (genetic), 152
Douglas, Geddes, 65, 67, 71
Dusting, 131
Dutch irises, 6, 10, 114, 118, 119,
    120, 126, 127, 129, 170, 173;
    illus., 4
Dwarf Iris Committee (A.I.S.), 59
Dwarf Iris Society, 59, 188
Dykes, Dr. William Rickatson, 25, 58,
    59, 78, 94, 97, 98, 118, 122, 183

English irises, 6, 10, 114, 118, 120,
    126, 127, 128
Eupogons, 6
Evansias, 6, 98, 101, 126

Fall (of iris), definition of, 2, 143;
    illus., 3, 143
Farr, Bertrand, 25
Fay, Orville, 133, 160, 185, 186
Feeding, 49
Ferguson, Walker, 95
Fertilization, 147
Fertilizing, 49, 57, 82
Filament (of iris), illus., 142
Fischer, Hubert, 159
Flag, 1, 21, 23, 70, 104
Fletcher, H. Castle, 159
Florence, Italy, 159, 183
Flower-de-luce, 21, 23
Foetidissima subsection, 83
Foster, Dr. Robert, 112
Foster, Sir Michael, 25
Fothergill, H. Senior, 112, 159, 160
Foucault, Mme. B., 188
French Iris Society, 188
Fungi, 170; illus., 169
Fungicides, 82, 132, 140
Fungus diseases, 131

Genetics, 151, 155
Genotype, 144
Gerard, John, 21
German Iris Society, 188
Germination, 150
Goett, John, 69, 186
Greenlee, Wilma, 71

Hager [Ben], 71, 72
Hall, David, 160, 161, 162, 186
Hamblen, Melba (Mrs. J. R.), 160,
    185, 186; illus., 34, 35
Heterosporium leaf spot, 131; illus.,
    137
Hexagonae (series), 104
Hexapogons, 74
Higo irises, 89
Hinkle, Mrs. Georgia, 160
Hirao, Dr. Suichi, 159
Hoog, Michael, 159
Humus, 51
Hungarian iris, 23
Hybridizing, 141-157, 159

Insecticides, 82, 140
Insect pests, 136-140
Intermediate bearded irises, 7, 65,
    70-72, 126, 127, 173, 182, 187
International Gartenbau Ausstellung,
    89, 90
International Symposium on Irises,
    159
Iris (genus), 4-7
—acuta, 86
—alata, 122
—aphylla, 10, 40, 45, 176; illus., 65
—arenaria, 1, 75, 76, 77, 176
—arizonica, 112
—atrofusca, 79
—atropurpurea, 79
—attica, 155
—aucheri, 121, 123, 175
—auranitica, 79
—aurea, 94, 178
—bakerana, 115, 117, 175
—barnumiae, 79; var. mariae, 79
—benjaminii, 79
—bloudowii, 77
—bracteata, 110
—brevicaulis, 106, 178
—bucharica, 121, 123, 128, 175
—bulleyana, 84, 178
—calcarea, 79
—cengialtii, 29
—chamaeiris, 61, 176
—chrysographes, 84, 85, 128, 178

—chrysophylla, 110
—clarkei, 85, 178
—confusa, 100
—cristata, 10, 19, 101, 103, 127, 129, 157, 177; illus., 4, 5, 102
—crocea, 78
—cypriana, 25
—danfordiae, 4, 17, 117 118, 171, 175; illus., 3, 116, 168
—darwasica, 77
—decora, 6, 114, 123, 127, 179; illus., 4
—delavayi, 178
—dichotoma, 6, 19, 83, 126, 127, 178
—douglasiana, 21, 110, 112, 129; illus., 111
—fernaldii, 110
—flavissima, 77
—foetidissima, 6, 19, 83, 178
—foliosa, 106
—fontanesii, 118
—forrestii, 85, 128, 178
—fulva, 106, 178; illus., 105
—gatesii, 79
—germanica, 24
—giganticaerulea, 106, 178
—gontcarpa, 78
—gracilipes, 2, 19, 83, 98, 100, 103, 127, 177; illus., 99
—graeberiana, 121, 123, 175
—graminea, 94, 127, 178; illus., 5, 88
—hartwegii, 110
—haynei, 79
—histrio, 115
—histrioides, 115
—histrioides major, 115, 117, 118, 175
—hoogiana, 75, 77, 176
—hookeriana, 78
—imbricata, 155
—innominata, 19, 110, 112; illus., 109
—japonica, 100, 128
—kaempferi, 21, 89, 178
—kamaonensis, 78, 177
—kashmiriana, 25
—korolkowi, 75, 76, 77, 127, 177; illus., 3; var. violacea, illus., 68
—lacustris, 101, 103
—laevigata, 21, 89, 179
—leptophylla, 78
—longipetala, 112, 113, 179
—lortetii, 79
—macrosiphon, 110
—magnifica, 121, 123, 175; illus., 3; 116

—mandschuria, 77
—mariae, 79
—mellita, 61, 155, 176; illus., 66
—mesopotamica, 25
—minuta, 97
—minutoaurea, 97
—missouriensis, 112, 113 129
—monnieri, 94
—montana, 112
—munzii, 110, 112
—nazarena, 79
—nigricans, 79
—ochroleuca, 92, 94, 127
—orchioides, 121, 123
—orientalis, 84
—palestina, 122
—pallida, 23, 24, 25, 41, 161, 176; var. dalmatica, 17, 24, 29
—persica, 121, 122
—planifolia, 122
—plicata, 24
—prismatica, 104
—pseudacorus, 1, 21, 87, 179; illus., 88
—pumila, 23, 59, 65, 97, 155, 176; illus., 5, 62
—purdyi, 110
—reichenbachii, 160
—reticulata, 11, 115, 118, 171, 175; illus., 5, 116
—rosenbachiana, 122
—ruthenica, 97, 179
—saari, 79
—samariae, 79
—sanguinea, 84
—setosa, 2, 179
—sibirica, 84, 85, 179
—sikkimensis, 78
—sindjarensis, 121, 123, 175
—sintenisii, 94
—speciosa, 97
—spuria, 94; var. lilacina, 179
—stolonifera, 75, 77, 177; illus., 4
—stylosa, 97, 126, 179
—subbiflora, 128
—susiana, 78, 79, 155, 177
—swerti, 24
—tectorum, 10, 19, 98, 100, 127, 177; illus., 3; var. album, 98; illus., 99
—tenax, 21, 110
—tenuis, 103
—tenuissima, 110
—tingitana, 118
—trojana, 25
—tubergeniana, 121

—*unguicularis*, 97, 126, 128, 179
—*urumovii*, 94
—*variegata*, 17, 23, 24 176
—*vartanii alba*, 115, 117, 126
—*verna*, 19, 101, 103, 129, 179
—*versicolor*, 19, 21, 87, 101, 104, 179
—*vicaria*, 175
—*virginica*, 87, 101, 104, 129, 179
—*warleyensis*, 121
—*wattii*, 100
—*willmottiana alba*, 121, 123
—*wilsonii*, 85
 —*winogradowii*, 117
—*xiphioides*, 118, 120
—*xiphium*, 118
Iris (subgenus), 5, 6, 114
Iris borer, 54, 136; illus., 137
Iris plant and seed sources, Appendix
  B
Iris shows, 164-167
Iris societies, Appendix F
Iris Society of South Africa, 188
Iris varieties
  Abbeville Yellow, 107
  Acuta, 86
  Agatha, 76
  Agnes James, 110
  Ahoy, 38
  Albicans, 1, 70, 162
  Allaglow, 44, 184
  Allegiance, 39, 40, 152, 160, 183;
    illus., 20
  Alpine Rose, 40
  Already, 63
  Amandine, 33
  Amas, 25, 29
  Amethyst Flame, 40, 163, 183
  Amigo, 43
  Amiquita, 110; illus., 111
  Amphion, 77
  Ancilla, 77
  Andromache, 76
  Angel Eyes, 19, 63; illus., 18, 60
  Angelique, 187
  Ankara, 41, 119
  Apricot Dancer, 39
  Apricot Lustre, 39
  April Mist, 61
  April Morn, 19, 61
  Aqua Green, 70
  Aquarelle, 77
  Arabi Pasha, 183
  Arcady, 43, 160, 183
  Arctic Blue, 71
  Arctic Flame, 45
  Arctic Flare, 71, 72

Iris varieties (*continued*)
  Arctic Fury, 186
  Arctic Ruffles, 71, 72
  Arctic Skies, 42
  Argus Pheasant, 37, 183
  Arrangement, 70
  Artemis, 77
  Astralite, 72
  Atomic Blue, 184
  Autumn Queen, 70
  Autumn Twilight, 31
  Azurea, 19
  Azurite, 41
  Baby Snowflake, 67, 69
  Baby's Bonnet, 42
  Banbury Beauty, 112
  Banbury Butterfly, 112
  Bang, 38
  Barbara Elaine Taylor, 107
  Barbi, 72, 159
  Barbizon, 38
  Baria, 70
  Barium Gold, 61
  Bayadere, 29, 185
  Bayou Sunset, 107
  Beau Catcher, 30
  Bee Wings, 63
  Bellerive, 28
  Benton Cordelia, 183
  Benton Susan, 41
  Black Baby, 19, 63
  Black Forest, 28, 29, 156
  Black Hawk, 72
  Black Hills, 27
  Black Magic, 11, 30, 70, 72
  Black Onyx, 41
  Black Spot, 63
  Black Swan, 40, 41
  Black Taffeta, 27; illus., 20
  Blazon, 19
  Blonde Doll, 69, 70
  Blue Baron, 40, 185
  Blueberry Muffins, 70, 186
  Blue Brilliant, 87; illus., 18
  Blue Cape, 87
  Blue Champion, 119
  Blue Crest, 45
  Blue Denim, 67, 69
  Blue Doll, 63
  Blue Ensign, 183
  Blue Fairy, 77
  Blue Fantasy, 42
  Blue Flute, 28, 29
  Blue Fragrance, 71, 72
  Blue Frost, 19, 22, 63
  Blue Giant, 119

Iris varieties (*continued*)
  Blue Ivory, 67, 156
  Blue Joy, 75
  Blue Miller, 187
  Blue Moon, 86, 87
  Blue Nocturne, 90
  Blue Pinafore, 96
  Blue Pompon, 89, 92
  Blue Raven, 39, 40
  Blue Rhythm, 27, 183
  Blue River, 119
  Blue Sapphire, 27, 153, 163, 183;
    illus., 20
  Blue Spice, 77
  Blue Spot, 19, 61
  Bluet, 15, 29
  Bocena, 77
  Bold Contrast, 43
  Braithwaite, 43
  Brass Accents, 37
  Brassie, 67, 69, 70
  Bravado, 36, 37, 161; illus., 20
  Brazilia, 37
  Brigadoon, 44
  Bright Forecast, 37
  Bright Hour, 42
  Brite, 67
  Bronze Armor, 37
  Bronze Beauty, 76
  Bronze Bell, 37
  Bronze Butterfly, 96
  Brown-eyed Katie, 70; illus., 64
  Bumble Wings, 187
  Buriensis, 24
  Butterbit, 72
  Butterfly Prince, 92
  Butterhorn, 28
  Butterscotch Kiss, 37
  Caesar's Brother, 87
  Cajan Joyeuse, 107; illus., 105
  Cambridge Blue, 96
  Camilla, 76
  Canarybird, 119
  Cantab, 115, 118
  Capitola, 80
  Captain Gallant, 38
  Caribou Trail, 37
  Carmela, 37
  Carnton, 37
  Caroline Jane, 41
  Carpathia, 19, 59
  Caterina, 25
  Celestial Blue, 27
  Celestial Snow, 33
  Centerpiece, 70
  Champagne Music, 186

Iris varieties (*continued*)
  Chancelot, 155
  Charmed Land, 45
  Charon, 76
  Cherie, 161, 183
  Cherokee Chief, 96
  Cherry Bounce, 107
  Cherry Spot, 19, 22, 63; illus., 60
  Chewink, 73
  Chinese Coral, 39, 185
  Chinquapin, 41
  Chione, 77
  Chit Chat, 72
  Chivalry, 27, 145, 183
  Chocoleto, 29
  Christmas Angel, 33, 185
  Circlette, 69, 70, 186
  Claire, 63
  Clara, 77
  Clarette, 115
  Claudia Rene, 186
  Cliffs of Dover, 28, 33, 161
  Clotho, 77
  Cloud Dancer, 45
  Cloud Fluff, 71, 72
  Columbine, 29
  Confetti Showers, 92
  Congo Drums, 87
  Cool Comfort, 22, 36, 37
  Cool Spring, 87
  Coraband, 186
  Coreop, 70
  Country Cream, 36
  Cream Crest, 36, 162
  Crinkled Beauty, 39
  Crinkled Ivory, 36
  Crispette, 27, 163
  Crispy, 63
  Cross Country, 186
  Cup and Saucer, 63, 76
  Curl'd Cloud, 33
  Curtsy, 63
  Cutie, 22, 71, 72, 185
  Dainty Dancer, 73
  Dainty Delight, 69
  Dale Dennis, 67
  Dancer's Veil, 183, 184
  Dancing Bride, 186
  Darjeeling, 100
  Dark Chocolate, 37
  Dark Eden, 72, 187
  Dark Fairy, 69
  Dark Fury, 185
  Dark Violet, illus., 64
  Dave's Orchid, 40
  Daystar, 73

Iris varieties (*continued*)
  Decorated Blue Beard, 75
  Decorated Giant, 75
  Delft Blue, 119
  Demetria, 40
  Denver Mint, 186
  Derring-Do, 69; illus., 18, 68
  Desert Song, 161
  Destiny, 159
  Dixie Deb, 107
  Doctor K, 37, 162
  Dogrose, 17
  Doll Type, 72
  Dominion, 25
  Dorothea K. Williamson, 107
  Dot and Dash, 41, 161
  Double Date, 30
  Dream, 15
  Driftwood, 96
  Drummer Boy, 22, 71, 72, 187
  Dutch Defiance, 96
  Early Dusk, 41
  Easter Holiday, 184
  Ebony Echo, 28
  E. B. Williamson, 160
  Echoette, 29
  Edenite, 40, 41
  Edina, 98
  El Camino, 96
  Eleanor Perry, 90
  Eleanor's Pride, 39, 40, 183
  Elfin Antique, 72
  Elfin Motley, 112
  Elfin Royal, 72
  Elizabeth Noble, 42
  Ellem Manor, 186
  Ellesmere, 87
  Elmohr, 80, 81
  Elvira, 77
  Emerald Fountain, 36
  Emma Cook, 33
  Enchanted Lake, 92
  Enchanted Violet, 45
  Engraved, 80
  Eric the Red, 87
  Esther Fay, 38
  Ever and Ever, 186
  Exotic Blue, 45, 159
  Fair Luzon, 22, 38; illus., 34
  Fairy Fable, 38
  Fairy Flax, 67; illus., 18
  Fairy Flight, 112
  Fairy Jewels, 29, 30
  Fairy Light, 96
  Fall Primrose, 30, 31
  Fantasy, 156
  Fashion Lady, 63
  Fashion Model, 90, 92

Iris varieties (*continued*)
  Fiery Steed, 91
  Fifth Avenue, 185; illus., 35
  Fire Chief, 43
  Firenze, 45
  First Lilac, 72
  First Violet, 27, 183
  Flame Kiss, 42, 45
  Flaming Heart, 186
  Flaring Ivory, 36
  Fleeta, 39
  Florentina, 70
  Fluff, 29
  Flying Kite, 91
  Flying Tiger, 92
  Foxfire, 13; illus., 14
  Fox Grapes, 40
  Frances Elizabeth, 184
  Frenchi, 29, 30
  Front Page, 37
  Frost and Flame, 44, 45
  Frosty Lemonade, 71, 72
  Full Reward, 28
  Gaily Clad, 186
  Galilee, 133
  Garden Flame, 28
  Garden Party, 38, 39
  Garnet Royal, 38
  Gatineau, 87
  Gaucho, 29
  Gay Gallant, 92
  Gay Lassie, 19
  Gaylord, 42
  Gene Wild, 41
  Germanica, 70
  Gheen's White, 107
  Glacier Bay, 30, 187
  Glittering Amber, 39
  Glowing Amber, 41
  Gold Bound, 90
  Gold Buttons, 186
  Gold Piece, 36, 37
  Gold Ruffles, 162
  Golden Alps, 160, 183
  Golden Anniversary, 37
  Golden Bow, 30, 70
  Golden Butterfly, 77
  Golden Eagle, 162
  Golden Fair, 69, 70
  Golden Garland, 28
  Golden Hawk, 28
  Golden Hind, 155
  Golden Holiday, 184
  Golden Lady, 96
  Golden Masterpiece, 36, 37
  Golden Spice, 41
  Golden Sunshine, 28
  Golden Years, 36

Iris varieties (*continued*)
  Good Nature, 96
  Good Omen, 91
  Gracie Pfost, 185
  Graminea, 94
  Gravure, 77
  Great Lakes, 27
  Green Crest, 36
  Green Spot, 67, 69
  Gypsy Flair, 72
  Gypsy Jewels, 186
  Haile Selassie, 107
  Halophila, 94
  Hanselmayer, 61
  Happy Birthday, 22, 27, 31
  Harmony, 115, 118, 119
  H. C. Van Vliet, 119
  Headlines, 60, 183
  Heart's Content, 63
  Heigho, 80
  Helen Astor, 87
  Helen Collingwood, 43
  Helen Hayes, 33
  Helen Louise, 27
  Helen McGregor 83,
  Helen Traubel, 185
  Henry Shaw, 33, 35, 185
  Heracles, 119
  Herald Angel, 45
  Hercules, 115
  Her Highness, 106, 107
  Hindu Wand, 44
  Hisakata, 92; illus., 18
  Holleyblu, 107
  Holy Smoke, 44
  Hoogie Boy, 77
  Hope Divine, 40
  Hoyden, 89
  Immortal Hour, 33
  Imperial Lilac, 163
  Indeed, 71
  Indiglow, 40, 184
  Innocenza, 24
  Interim, 71, 72
  Irish Linen, 33
  Irma Melrose, 36
  Isolda, 77
  Ivory Glow, 22, 91
  Ivory Maiden, 112
  Ivory Satin, 36
  Jack of Hearts, 67
  Jake, 152
  Java Dove, 186
  Jay Kenneth, 72
  Jean Sibelius, 39, 40
  Jersey Beauty, 40
  Jeweled Kimona, 92
  Joan of Arc, 119

Iris varieties (*continued*)
  Joyce, 115, 118
  Joyous Cavalier, 22, 90, 92
  J. S. Digit, 115, 118
  Judean Charmer, 79
  Judean Silver, 79
  June Bride, 27
  June Meredith, 38, 162
  Jungle Bird, 44
  Jungle Fires, 38
  Jungle Shadows, 29, 30
  Juniata, 25
  Kahili, 43
  Kanchenjunga, 183
  Kashmir White, 25
  Katherine Fay, 161
  Katrina Nies, 96
  Keepsake, 76
  Kermisina, 104
  Kingdom, 186
  Kinglet, 73
  King Manor, 119
  King of the Blues, 119
  Kiss Me Kate, 11, 71
  Kochii, 70; illus., 64
  Kraemer Yellow, 107
  Lady Kay, 30
  Lady Mohr, 31, 80, 81
  La Negraflor, 41, 184
  La Nina Rosa, 187
  Largesse, 36
  Lark Song, 22, 96
  La Rosita, 39
  Late Amethyst, 75
  Lavanesque, 163
  Le Mogul, 119
  Lemon Flare, 69, 70
  Lemon Queen, 119
  Lenna M, 69
  Licorice Stick, 41
  Lilac Festival, 40
  Lilaclil, 69
  Lilac Queen, 119
  Lilligoldput, 72
  Lilli-Green, 69
  Lillipinkput, 71, 72
  Lilli-Var, 70
  Lilli-White, 67; illus., 169
  Lilting Melody, 185
  Limelight, 11, 28, 152
  Lime Ripples, 72
  L'Innocence, 119
  Little Angel, 71, 72
  Little Charmer, 61
  Little Dude, 30
  Little Grackle, 69
  Little Helen, 73
  Little Reb, 29

Iris varieties (continued)
Little Sapphire, 67, 69
Little Shadow, 67
Little Sheba, 187
Little Sir Echo, 29
Little Witch, 70
Lord Wolsely, 95
Lorna Lee, 184
Lovely Diana, 39
Lucia, 76
Lucia Marshall, 90
Lula Marguerite, 44; illus., 20
Luna, 77
Lutetia, 77
Lynn Hall, 39
Mme. Chereau, 24, 162
Magnet, 39
Main Event, 38
Margot Holmes, 85
Marine Wave, 70, 72
Maroon Caper, 72, 187
Marriott, 39, 40
Martel, 185
Mary McClellan, 80
Mary Randall, 39, 161, 183
Mary Todd, 183
Matterhorn, 152
Mauve Mink, 39
May Hall, 27
May Magic, 27
Melbreak, 44
Melissa, 40
Mellite, 155
Melodrama, 43
Melody, 119
Memphis Lass, 41
Menelik, 119
Midnight Blue, 22, 27, 152
Midnight Waltz, 184
Mildred Presby, 25
Millionaire, 37
Miss Indiana, 42
Miss Simplicity, 91
Mission Sunset, 186
Mocha Polka, 41
Mohr Lemonade, 80
Mohrning Haze, 80, 81
Monaurea, 95
Monspur Cambridge Blue, 95
Montblanc, 120
Moonblaze, 70
Moonchild, 71, 72
Moongate, 41
Moon River, 186
Moonspinner, 67, 69, 156; illus., 18, 66
Morningtide, 96, 184
Mountain Lake, 87; illus., 20

Iris varieties (continued)
Mrs. J. L. Gibson, 183
Music Maker, 186
My Alana, 33; illus., 34
My Happiness, 45
Mystic Melody, 42
Nada, 100
Nana, 59, 86
Nashborough, 43
Native Daughter, 187
New Snow, 152, 161
No Mohr, 22, 80
Nylon Loveliness, 186
Oberon, 77
Ola Kala, 183
Olympic Torch, 37
One Desire, 38
On Parade, 43
Orange Crush, 39
Orange Frills, 39
Orange Parade, 39
Orchid Jewel, 40
Orchid Majesty, 90, 92
Orestes, 76
Oriflamme, 25
Pacific Panorama, 39, 40, 183, 184
Pacific Splendor, 112
Paganite, 72
Pagan Midget, 67, 69
Pagoda, 29
Paleface, 36
Palomino, 27
Paltec, 98, 100
Panamint, 119
Panay, 42
Patrician, 28
Patrician's Sweetheart, 36
Patterdale, 39, 160, 183
Pee Wee, 73; illus., 66
Persian Bronze, 77
Peshewar, 80
Picture Yellow, 67
Pillar of Fire, 91
Pinata, 29
Pink Cameo, 161
Pink Enchantment, 162
Pink Fancy, 71, 72
Pink Frost, 92
Pink Fulfillment, 39
Pink Opal, 38
Pink Reward, 71, 72
Pink Ruffles, 15, 29
Pink Satin, 38
Pinstripe, 22
Pin Up Girl, 42
Placid Waters, 87
Plickadee, 70
Poet's Dream, 33

Iris varieties (*continued*)
Polar Flame, 30
Polka Time, 40
Pomp and Circumstance, 22
Potawatomi, 30
Praiseworthy, 27, 162
Premier, 96
Pretender, 43
Pretty Carol, 39
Primrose Bonnet, 156
Primrose Drift, 183
Prince Albert, 120
Prince Henry, 119
Prince Indigo, 186
Prince of Wales, 120
Princess Aurora, 92
Princess Beatrice, 24, 119
Priscilla, 15, 29
Progenitor, 160
Promise, 22, 63, 76; illus., 64
Psyche, 76
Purissima, 155
Quaker Lady, 25
Queen's Grace, 100
Rainbow Gold, 36
Rainier Valley, 77
Ranger, 28
Real Gold, 80, 81
Red Amethyst, 61
Red Emperor, 84
Red Gem, 22, 63
Red Orchid, 72
Red Titan, 91
Rehobeth, 27
Renaissance, 31
Ribbon Round, 186
Rippling Waters, 45
Robby, 29, 30
Rococo, 41
Rosea, 104
Rose Flame, 39
Rose Garland, 44
Rose Hermosa, 39
Rose Tower, 92
Royal Blue, 115, 118
Royal Ensign, 87
Royal Sapphire, 91
Royal Thumbprint, 69
Royal Violet, 40
Ruby Glow, 70, 72
Rum Jungle, 44
Ruth Nies Cabeen, 96
Sable, 27, 160
Sable Night, 40, 160, 183; illus., 18
Saffron Charm, 77
Saffron Jewel, 187
Saugatuck, 96
Savage, 31

Iris varieties (*continued*)
Seafarer, 27
Seathwaite, 160, 183
Selma Sunlight, 112
September Sparkler. 31
Shelford Giant, 94
Shiloh, 43
Shimoyo, 92; illus., 18
Shine Boy, 69, 156
Shining Waters, 160
Sierra Skies, 22, 27; illus., 18
Silken Dalliance, 77
Silken Parasol, 92
Silver Tip, 87
Sindpers, 121
Sir Gordon, 187
Sky and Water, 92
Sky Caper, 63, 187
Sky Torch, 67, 70
Skywatch, 186
Small Cloud, 69
Small Sky, 69
Small Talk, 187
Small Wonder, 67, 69
Smoke Mist, 44
Snowcrest, 87; illus., 105, 169
Snow Flurry, 145, 152, 161
Snow Goddess, 28, 31, 33
Snow Maiden, 70
Snow Queen, 84
Snow Wheel, illus., 105
Snowy Hills, 89, 91
Soaring Kite, 36
Soft Answer, 42
Soledad, 70
Solid Gold, 28
Solid Mahogany, 28
Sorcerer's Triumph, 89, 92
Southland, 70
South Pacific, 27
Sparkling Waters, 22, 39, 40, 185
Speak Softly, 36
Speckled Sprite, 70
Spring Charm, 38, 39
Spring Festival, 161
Spring Joy, 61
Spring Mist, 70
Starshine, 28
Sterling Silver, 186
Stepping Out, 186
Storm King, 156
Striped Butterfly, 31, 80, 81
Suez, 80
Sulina, 19, 59, 61
Summer Blue, 30
Summer Red, 30
Summer Sunset, 28, 30; illus., 20
Summer Whitewings, 30

Iris varieties (*continued*)
Sunlit Sea, 96
Sunnydale, 37
Sunny Day, 22, 95; illus., 93
Swan Ballet, 162, 183
Sweet Allegro, 72
Sweetheart's Folly, 36; illus., 18
Sylphide, 77
Taholah, 41
Tall Chief, 38
Tarn Hows, 37, 160
Tea Apron, 41
Tealwood, 86, 87
Techny Chimes, 45
The Citadel, 33
The Kahn, 107
Thrush Song, 96
Tid-Bit, 73
Timmie Too, 30
Tinkerbell, 22, 67, 69
Toll Gate, 43
Tomeco, 38, 185
Tom Tit, 73
Tranquil Dale, 112
Tranquility, 28
Tricolor, 120
Trisha, 187
Trophy, 80, 81
Tropic Night, 87
True Charm, 25
Truly Yours, 161, 183
Tulare, 28, 29, 30
Tunkhannock, 87
Twilight Sky, 156
Two for Tea, 73
Two Opals, 96
Tycoon, 87
Ultrapoise, 185
Utah Cream, 36
Vandee, 61, 155; illus., 66
Velvet, 115
Velvet Caper, 69, 186
Velvet Night, 86
Velvet Robe, 38
Vera, 76
Verigay, 63
Violet Beauty, 115, 118
Violet Flare, 185
Violet Harmony, 22, 27, 183
Violet Hills, 40
Violet Ray, 107
Violet Virgo, 31
Vulcanus, 76
Wabash, 42
Wadi Zem Zem, 95, 96
Wake Robin, 96
Warbler, 73
Warlsind, 121

Iris varieties (*continued*)
Watermelon, 44
Waxing Moon, 36, 37, 45, 152; illus., 20
Wayward Wind, 36
Wedgwood, 119
Wenatchee Skies, 186
Wentworth, 115, 118
Wheelhorse, 107
White Excelsior, 119
White Heron, 95, 96
White Sprite, 28
White Swirl, 85, 87; illus., 20, 105, 169
Whole Cloth, 42, 160, 183, 184
Wide World, 42, 155
Widget, 73
Wild Ginger, 185
William Mohr, 80
Wind Shadows, 81
Wine and Roses, 186
Winter Olympics, 186
Witch Doctor, 80
Wonderful Sky, 162
Woodland Sprite, 36, 45
Woodmont Rose, 112
W. R. Dykes, 25
Yellow Dresden, 30
Zantha, 28, 161
Zimbrakeet, 187
Zing, 156
Zua, 30, 70
Italian Iris Society, 159, 188

Japanese irises, 10, 21, 84, 87-92, 98, 126, 128, 129, 139, 170, 173; illus., 3, 18
Junos, 6, 120-123, 126, 128, 129, 175; illus., 3, 4, 5, 116

Kitton, M. E., 85
Komarov Botanical Institute, 158

Labeling, 146, 150
Laevigatae (series), 6, 84, 87, 104
Lake iris, 101
Lawrence, Dr. G. H. M., 6
Lavender-flowered irises, 69, 72, 92, Appendix A
Leaf blight, 132, 133
Leaf spot, 54
L'Ecluse, Charles de, 1
Lenz, Dr. Lee W., 108, 110, 112, 158, 159
Lilac-flowered irises, 40, Appendix A
Linnaeus, Carolus, 101
Linnean Botanic Garden, 23
Longipetalae, 6, 112-113
Loomis, 162

Louisiana irises, 2, 6, 19, 104-107, 126, 127, 129, 157, 182; illus., 3, 105
Louisiana Iris Society, 107, 188
Luhrson, Richard, 112

McGarvey, Dr. William, 30
McGee, Flora, 187
McMillan, W. B., 106
Manure, 50, 51
Marhigo irises, 89, 90
Marx, Walter, 85, 89, 91
Median irises, 63-65
Median Iris Society, 65, 187
Melrose Gardens, 86
Milliken, Carl, 95
Miniature dwarf bearded irises, 6, 58, 59-61, 126, 127, 128, 172, 182, 187; illus., 18, 60
Miniature dwarf hybrids, 61-63; illus., 62
Miniature tall bearded irises, 6, 73, 127, 187
Mohr, William, 80
Moldovan, Steve, 186
Morgan award, 85, 86, 105, 182, 185
Mosaic, 134
Mourning iris, 78
Muhlestein, Tell, 95, 160, 162, 185
Mulching, 56

Naked-bulb irises, 114
Naturalized plantings, 15
Neel, Laurence, 123
Neglecta (color pattern), 43
Nepalensis (subgenus), 5, 6, 114, 123-124, 179; illus., 4
Netted-bulb irises, 114
New York Botanical Garden, 2, 104
New York State College of Agriculture, 159
New Zealand Iris Society, 188
Nies, Eric, 95; award, 96, 182; illus., 93
Noyd, Luella, 185, 186, 187

Oncobred irises, 71, 80
Oncocyclus irises (Oncos), 4, 6, 74, 78, 80, 129
Oncogelia hybrids, 76
Orange-flowered irises, 38
Orchid-flowered irises, 40
Orrisroot, 70
Ovary, 143; illus., 142
Ovules, 143; illus., 142

Pacific Coast irises, 6, 19, 108-112, 127, 128, 129, 157; illus., 109, 111

Palestine iris, 122
Pardanthopsis subsection, 83
Payne, W. A., 89, 90, 91
Peat moss, 53, 57
Perennial border, 10; illus., 9, 18
Perianth, 143
Perianth tube, definition of, 2; illus., 142
Persian iris, 122
Peterson, Adelaide (Mrs. R. E.), 67, 71, 187
Phenotype, 144
Pilgrim iris, 97
Pink-flowered irises, 27, 38, 72
Pistil, 143
Planting, 53-56; illus., 55
Planting times, Appendix A
Plicata (color pattern), 32, 41, 72
Plough, Gordon, 160, 186
Pollination, 141, 145, 154
Polychrome (color pattern), 44
Premio Firenze, 160, 162, 183
Presby Gardens, 25, 71
Prince, William, 23
Prismaticae (series), 104
Progression of bloom, 125-129
Pseudoregelias, 6, 74, 78
Purple-flowered irises, 69, 72, 87, 91, 96, 107, Appendix A

Rancho Santa Ana Botanic Garden, 158
Randall, Harry, 159, 160
Randolph, Dr. L. F., 6, 24, 152, 158
Reblooming irises, 23, 30-31, 126
Rechamp, Brother Charles, 160, 186
Record making and keeping, 146, 150
Red-flowered irises, 28, 38, 72, 87, 91, 107, 182
Regelia irises, 6, 74, 77, 127, 129; illus., 3, 4, 68
Regeliocyclus hybrids, 76
Replanting, 53
Reticulata irises, 5, 6, 114-118, 126, 128, 172; illus., 3, 4, 116
Rhizomatous irises, 4, 6, 114
Rhizome, definition of, 4, 47; illus., 48, 55
Rickett, Dr. H. W., 148
Roberts, Earl, 65, 69, 71, 187
Rodionenko, Dr. G. I., 158, 159
Roof iris, 19, 98
Roots, 47, illus., 4, 48
Rundlett, Edwin, 30, 31, 65, 69

Salsman, 71
Salter, John, 24
Sani, Dr. Gian Luigi, 159

Sass, Hans and Jacob, 70, 93; award, 71, 182, 185
Schortman, W. B., 160
Schreiner, Robert, 59, 65, 70, 160, 162
Schreiner's [iris gardens], 71, 80, 162, 185, 186, 187
Sclerotium rot, 131
Scorch, 135
Scorpiris (subgenus), 5, 6, 114, 120-123
Scott, W. F., 159
Seed harvesting and planting, 149
Seedlings, 59, 151, 153
Self (color pattern), 32, 33-41, 42
Selfing (self-pollination), 141
Sexton, Mrs. Neva, 160, 184, 186, 187
Siberian irises, 6, 10, 19, 21, 84-87, 108, 126, 127, 128, 129, 157, 170, 173, 182; illus., 3, 5, 18, 20, 105, 169
Sibiricae (series), 84
Simonet, Dr. Marc, 159
Small, Dr. John K., 2, 104, 106
Smaller bearded irises, 58-73; illus., 62, 64, 66
Smith, Dr. Raymond, 30
Società Italiana dell' Iris, 188
Societé Française des Amateurs d'Iris, 188
Society for Japanese Irises, 188
Society for Siberian Irises, 188
Soft rot, 132
Soil, 50, 52
Soils (U.S.D.A. Yearbook, 1957), 52
Southern blight, 131
Spanish irises, 6, 114, 118, 119, 120, 126, 127
Spathe, illus., 142
Spathula section, 83
Specht, Mrs. Flaminia, 159
Species Plantarum, 101
Spinster iris, 122
Spraying, 82, 131
Spuria irises, 6, 10, 19, 84, 92-96, 126, 127, 129, 170, 173, 182; illus., 3, 5, 88, 93
Spuria Iris Society, 96, 188
Stamen, 143; illus., 142
Standard (of iris), definition of, 2, 143; illus., 3, 142
Standard dwarf bearded irises, 6, 58, 65-70, 126, 173, 182, 186; illus., 18, 66, 68
Standard tall bearded irises, 7, 8, 23-28, 32-45, 46-47, 65, 80, 125,

126, 127, 129, 141, 148, 173, 186; illus., 3, 4, 5, 9, 14
Steiger, Max, 90, 159
Stem, illus., 142
Stevens, Mrs. Jean, 100, 159
Stigma (of iris), 143; illus., 142
Stinking iris, 83
Sturtevant, Grace, 25
Style (of iris), 143
Style-branches (-arms), 2, 143; illus., 142
Style-crest, 143; illus., 142
Swearengen Iris Gardens, 89
Synge, Patrick, 159

Table irises, 73, 127
Tall bearded irises: See Standard tall bearded irises
Tetraploid, 25, 42, 73, 155
Thrips, 139
Tompkins, Chet, 160, 186
Transplanting, 53, 151; illus., 55
Tripetalae (series), 103
Triploid, 155

Van Tubergen & Co., 76, 77, 115, 121
Variegata (color pattern), 42, 43
Verbena bud moth, 139
Vernae (series), 103
Vernal iris, 103
Vesper iris, 19
Vilmorin, 24
Violet-flowered irises, 27, 40, 69, 72, 87, 92, 96, Appendix A
Virus diseases, 134

Walker, Marion, 95, 184
Warburton, Mrs. S. W., 65, 67, 68, 69, 72, 186, 187
Waters, Don, 186
Welch, Walter, 59, 60, 67, 184
Werckmeister, Dr. Peter, 77, 158, 159
White, Clarence G., award, 80, 182, 184
White-flowered irises, 28, 33, 69, 72, 87, 91, 96, 107, 182
Williamsons' [iris gardens], 73
Wills, Jesse, 159
Winter rot, 131, 132
Wisley trial gardens, 161
Wister, John C., 25

Xiphium (subgenus), 5, 6, 114-120

Yellow-flowered irises, 28, 36, 70, 72, 96, 107, Appendix A